Critical Code Studies

Software Studies

Lev Manovich and Noah Wardrip-Fruin, editors

Critical Code Studies

Mark C. Marino

The MIT Press
Cambridge, Massachusetts
London, England

This book was set in ITC Stone Serif Std and by ITC Stone Serif Std and ITC Stone Sans Std by Toppan Best-set Premedia Limited. Printed and bound in the United States of America.

Library of Congress Cataloging-in-Publication Data

Names: Marino, Mark C., author.
Title: Critical code studies / Mark C. Marino.
Description: Cambridge, Massachusetts : The MIT Press, 2020. | Series:
    Software studies | Includes bibliographical references and index.
Identifiers: LCCN 2019024253 | ISBN 9780262043656 (hardcover)
Subjects: LCSH: Computer software--Social aspects. | Coding
    theory--Philosophy. | Programming languages (Electronic computers) |
    Rhetoric.
Classification: LCC QA76.9.C66 M628 2020 | DDC 005.3--dc23
LC record available at https://lccn.loc.gov/2019024253

10   9   8   7   6   5   4   3   2   1

for my family,

especially Barbara, Genevieve, & Dayveon

who give my life meaning

Contents

Series Foreword

Software is deeply woven into contemporary life—economically, culturally, creatively, politically—in manners both obvious and nearly invisible. Yet while much is written about how software is used and the activities that it supports and shapes, thinking about software itself has remained largely technical for much of its history. Increasingly, however, artists, scientists, engineers, hackers, designers, and scholars in the humanities and social sciences are finding that for the questions they face, and the things they need to build, an expanded understanding of software is necessary. For such understanding, they can call upon a strand of texts in the history of computing and new media; they can take part in the rich, implicit culture of software; and they also can take part in the development of an emerging, fundamentally transdisciplinary, computational literacy. These provide the foundation for software studies.

Software studies uses and develops cultural, theoretical, and practice-oriented approaches to make critical, historical, and experimental accounts of (and interventions via) the objects and processes of software. The field engages and contributes to the research of computer scientists, the work of software designers and engineers, and the creations of software artists. It tracks how software is substantially integrated into the processes of contemporary culture and society, reformulating processes, ideas, institutions, and cultural objects around their closeness to algorithmic and formal description and action. Software studies proposes histories of computational cultures and works with the intellectual resources of computing to develop reflexive thinking about its entanglements and possibilities. It does this both in the scholarly modes of the humanities and social sciences and in the software creation/research modes of computer science, the arts, and design.

The Software Studies book series, published by the MIT Press, aims to publish the best new work in a critical and experimental field that is at once culturally and technically literate, reflecting the reality of today's software culture.

Hacknowledgments

This book would not have been possible without the help, support, and encouragement of many people, so many that this list will likely omit more than I include. This list should begin with my close collaborators Jeremy Douglass and Jessica Pressman, who read draft after draft. I would also like to thank Tara McPherson, who supported my work on the Transborder Immigrant Tool, as well as the ASHSS sabbatical that gave me time to work on this manuscript. My thanks to Doug Sery, who always believed in this book despite various reviwer #2s. Thanks to Kathleen Caruso, Noah Springer, Michael Sims, copy editor extraordinaire Melinda Rankin, Noah Wardrip-Fruin, Lev Manovich, and the whole MIT Press team. This book would also not be here without Max Feinstein, whose interest in CCS gave rise to the working groups, the members of which continue to develop new methods and readings. Todd Millstein of UCLA and the computer science faculty of Loyola Marymount University gave considerable support, including Philip Dorin, Ray Toal, John David N. "Dondi" Dionisio, B. J. Johnson, Andrew Fourney, and especially Stephanie August, who delivered the first draft of the manifesto to a CS conference at UC Irvine.

The birth of a field requires tools and talent. For example, Craig Dietrich and Erik Loyer created the code annotation functionality for Scalar for the investigation of the Transborder Immigrant Tool. Thanks to all those who gave feedback on drafts, including, in addition to those already mentioned: Rochelle Gold, Jason Lewis, Jon Corbett, Stephanie Boluk, Sarah Lehne, Paul Feigelfeld, Brett Stalbaum, Susanne Holl, and Peter Berz. Thanks to my mentors, N. Katherine Hayles and Toby Miller. Thanks to those other scholars who have contributed to the development of the field: Evan Buswell, David M. Berry, Damon Loren Baker, Wendy Chun, Stephen Ramsay, Dennis Jerz, Judy Malloy, Mez, micha cárdenas, Chris Lindgren, Liz Losh, Federica Frabetti, Annette Vee, Kevin Brock, Kevin Driscoll, Matthew Kirschenbaum, Jessica Marie Johnson, Mark A. Neal, Arielle Schlessinger, Steve Anderson, Jacqueline Wernimont, Patsy

Baudoin, Nick Montfort, Ben Allen, Chandler McWilliams, Jim Brown Jr., Evan Gerst-
man, Stephanie Boluk, Patrick LeMieux, Ed Finn, Moritz Hiller, the Electronic Disturbance Theater, and Daniel Temkin, along with the many others who gave their time
to participate in the CCSWGs. Thanks to those who helped coordinate the CCSWGs,
including, Ali Rachel Pearl, Viola Lasmana, Catherine Griffiths, Jason Lipshin, and
Teddy Roland. Thanks to Ariane Hanrath and the Hammermann family for their help
translating German. Thanks to Rob Wittig for all his support and encouragement in all
matters related to writing. Thanks to all the members and affiliates of the Humanities
and Critical Code Studies (HaCCS) Lab at USC, as well as HASTAC, SLSA, MLA, and
ELO. Sections of this book were previously published in earlier versions in *Electronic
Book Review*, *American Book Review*, and *Digital Humanities Quarterly*, and I am grateful to
Joseph Tabbi, Steve Tomasula, and Jessica Pressman and Lisa Swanstrom who edited the
drafts for those publications, respectively. Thanks to Jentery Sayers, Lauren Klein, and
Matthew Gold who edited related CCS chapters. And lastly, I thank my family for their
love and support: my wife, Barbara, who has taught me about more than just assembly;
my parents, Arthur and Patricia, who offered boundless encouragement; and my uncle,
James Marino, who tirelessly proofread various drafts of the manuscript.

1   Introduction

Code Heard 'round the World

```
if n_elements(yrloc) ne n_elements(valadj) then message,'Oooops!'
```
—briffa_sep98_e.pro

Who reads computer source code, and what does it mean to them? Pundits and poets, hacktavists and humanities professors, lawyers and laypeople—far more than just programmers are reading code for a wide range of reasons. Whether finding Easter eggs or getting a whiff of code smells,[1] seeking aesthetic pleasure or searching for ways they have been manipulated, the curious have a sense that something awaits them in the code. If we are going to take up this communal practice of reading code, we must read it critically, for the way we read code is just as important as the fact that we are reading code. Consider the following example.[2]

In 2009, leaked emails from the Climate Research Unit (CRU) of England's University of East Anglia seemed to hand a smoking gun to climate change deniers, proof positive that climate change is a fabrication. These emails included code used to model climate change, and the comments in that code seemed to indicate a manipulation of the data. Soon the blogosphere was buzzing with quotations from the code, particularly from a file called Harry_Read_Me, named for its programmer, Ian Harris, who collaborated with Keith Briffa on the code.[3] As he attempts to document his progress, making sense of and reconciling the various data, Harris writes in the code comments, "What the hell is supposed to happen here? Oh yeah—there is no 'supposed,' I can make it up. So I have : -)."

Other comments throughout the leaked files express the frustrations of a programmer as he complains about the lengths to which he has to go to reconcile conflicting and at times contradictory data. Seizing on this code as raw meat, climate change contenders called the comments proof that the data used to demonstrate global warming was bunk, a conspiracy in the code. This source file purportedly provided a glimpse behind the curtain of a mass deception, and the staging ground for that charade was the computer source code itself.

The public criticism did not stop at the code's comments, either; conspiracy hunters also dove into the workings of the code, written in Interactive Data Language (IDL), discovering what Harris had labeled a *fudge factor*. Consider this excerpt (elided with [...]):

```
;****** APPLIES A VERY ARTIFICIAL CORRECTION FOR DECLINE*********
;
yrloc=[1400,findgen(19)*5.+1904]
valadj=[0.,0.,0.,0.,0.,-0.1,-0.25,-0.3,0.,-0.1,0.3,0.8,1.2,1.7,$
2.5,2.6,2.6,2.6,2.6,2.6]*0.75          ; fudge factor
if n_elements(yrloc) ne n_elements(valadj) then message,'Oooops!'
;
[...]
;
; APPLY ARTIFICIAL CORRECTION
;
yearlyadj=interpol(valadj,yrloc,x)
densall=densall+yearlyadj
```

In brief, the code takes a set of data, for years 1400–1994, and adjusts that data by adding, or subtracting in the case of the negative numbers, another set of numbers (listed as valadj, presumably for *value adjust*). The code makes these adjustments using what programmers call *magic numbers*, or unnamed constants, numbers introduced into the code with no explanation of their reference (Farrell 2008, 22). By adjusting the numbers in this way, the programmer created a data set that conforms better to his expectations. The *fudge factor* comment labels the numbers that adjust the data set.[4] Semicolons precede content that is not to be processed—in other words, comments in the code (and lines with only white space). The all-caps header comment stating that this is "a very artificial correction" seems to announce unambiguously that this code is pure manipulation. However, those labels lack a bit of context.

Rather than manufacturing some great deception, this code was written as an interim step in the process of consolidating several sources of data. Although it could be said that *all* code represents only one iteration of work in progress, this particular file was acknowledged to be provisional by its developers. Harris's other writings identify this adjustment in his code as a temporary placeholder measure; these markers in the code identify places where he had to temporarily correct a discrepancy. The leaked code was apparently written while Harris was preparing a paper with his team about the disparity between tree records and temperatures, entitled "Trees Tell of Past Climates: But Are They Speaking Less Clearly Today?" (Briffa, Schweingruber, Jones, Osborn, Harris, et al. 1998). In other words, this code was not written as the final word in climate change but to label and investigate a problem observed in the recorded data, in which latewood density (the measured density of tree rings) did not correlate to changes in temperature. The programmer wrote in this fudge factor temporarily while trying to account for the discrepancy, only to rewrite the code in the same year in a way that addresses the divergence more systematically.[5]

However, despite the meaning of the code to its programmer, the code came to signify something very different in the broader world. News reports and amateur bloggers seized upon the files, posting excerpts in their diatribes. Code was literally becoming the means of debate, used as evidence in arguments for and against the scientific validity of climate change. The damning comments were featured on major networks, such as the BBC and CBS, as well as in news magazines and newspapers. Bloggers seized upon the comments of the Harry_Read_Me.txt file and lambasted the coder for his fudge factor. The files were referred to as "the smoking gun" of climate change fabrication. As one blogger posted, "things like 'fudge factor' and 'APPLIES A VERY ARTIFICIAL CORRECTION FOR DECLINE' don't require programming expertise to understand" (Wheeler 2009). But apparently they do. Even that blogger recommends that readers consult someone who knows how to read code before exploring on their own. Regardless of the reader's training or comprehension, code had become a means of public debate.

In our digital moment, there is a growing sense of the significance of computer source code. It has moved beyond the realm of programmers and entered the realm of mainstream media and partisan political blogosphere. Those discussing code may not be programmers or have much fluency in the languages of the code they are quoting, but they are using it to make, refute, and start arguments. There is also a growing sense that the code we are not reading is working against our interests. Pundits and academics alike are challenging algorithms used for everything from police profiling to health insurance calculations. Scholars, such as Safiya Noble and Joy Buolamwini of the Algorithmic Justice League, have called public attention to evidence of bias in AI systems and other software. However, often these discussions are limited to assessing the algorithms based on their effects. As Noble writes, "Knowledge of the technical aspects of search and retrieval, in terms of critiquing the computer programming code that underlies the systems, is absolutely necessary to have a profound impact on these systems" (2018, 26). Although the code bases for many proprietary systems are inaccessible to us, an analysis of algorithms can go further through an analysis of the code.

Without access to the code, whether because it is proprietary or generated on the fly, as in the case of some machine-learning algorithms, analysts can only comment on the apparent operations of the code based on its effects. The operations of the code are left in the hands of those who can access it, usually those who have made or maintain it, and those who can read it. If code governs so much of our lives, then to understand its operations is to get some sense of the systems that operate on us. If we leave the hieroglyphs to the hierarchs, then we are all subjects of unknown and unseen processes. That anxiety drove online communities to pour through the leaked climate code—and led them to misread it. This example demonstrates that it is not enough to understand what code does without fully considering what it means.

Like other systems of signification, code does not signify in any transparent or reducible way. And because code has so many interoperating systems, human and machine-based, meaning proliferates in code. To the programmer, this fudge factor may have been a temporary patch in the larger pursuit of anomalies in the data, marking the code to bracket a question he wished to pursue later. However, read by a different audience and from a more suspicious perspective, that temporary solution becomes outright deception. An editorial in the magazine *Nature* claimed, "One lesson that must be taken from Climategate is that scientists do not get to define the terms by which others see them and their place in society" ("Closing the Climategate" 2010). The same can be said for code. Its meaning is determined not only by the programmer's intention or by the operations it triggers but also by how it is received and recirculated. The history of the misinterpretations of the Climategate code becomes part of its overall meaning.

That is not to argue that code can be removed from context (though portions of code are frequently recontextualized) or that code means whatever people say it means. Rather, the meaning of code is contingent upon and subject to the rhetorical triad of speaker, audience (both human and machine), and message. Although even that classic rhetorical triad is a bit poor when explaining a system of communication that is to varying degrees tied to hardware, other software, and state. In the process of its circulation, the meaning of code changes beyond its functional role to include connotations and implications, opening to interpretation and inference, as well as misinterpretation and reappropriation. The Climategate code is forever tied to these online debates, and that history gives it significance far beyond the designs of its creators. Code is a social text, the meaning of which develops and transforms as additional readers encounter it over time and as contexts change. That is the argument and provocation of this book.

It is time to develop methods of tracing the meaning of code. Computer source code has become part of our political, legal, aesthetic, and popular discourse. Code is being read by lawyers, corporate managers, artists, pundits, reporters, and even literary scholars. Code is being used in political debate, in artistic exhibitions, in popular entertainment, and in historical accounts. As code reaches more and more readers and as programming languages and methods continue to evolve, we need to develop methods to account for the way code accrues meaning and how readers and shifting contexts shape that meaning. We need to learn to understand not only the functioning of code but the way code signifies. We need to learn to read code critically.

But reading code requires a new set of methods that attend to its specific contexts, requirements, and relationships. As the next examples demonstrate, communication via code is hardly straightforward.

A Job Interview

Let us consider a question: What does code mean? First, it would be useful if I defined what I mean by *code*. For now, I will say, *computer source code*. Then I should probably say what I mean by *mean*. But such an approach is full of folly. So let me restate the question with another, expressed in relatively unambiguous words.[6]

The new phrasing of the problem could take the form of a job interview.[7] For the sake of this argument, let's imagine two programmers, a man and a woman, who are applying for the same job. Before they are interviewed in person, they are sequestered in a room and asked to solve a popular challenge, to write a program that computes an anagram of a string. An anagram contains all the same characters of the initial string or word in a different order (e.g., *critical code* becomes *circa dice lot*), although the code for this challenge does not have to produce recognizable words, just rearranged characters. At the end of their challenge, the programmers will submit their code electronically so the employers will not know who wrote which version.

One of the candidates submits the following JavaScript code:

```
function anagram(text) {
   var a = text.split("");
   for (var i = 0; i < a.length; i += 1) {
       var letter = a[i];
       var j = Math.floor(Math.random() * a.length);
       a[i] = a[j];
       a[j] = letter;
   }
   return a.join("");
}
```

Simply put, this code creates a function (anagram) that splits the string up into an array of individual characters and then repositions the items in that array (or the letters) in a random order before combining them.

However, the other candidate submits a very different solution:

```
function anagram(text) {
   return text.split("").sort(function () {return 0.5-Math.
random()}).join("");
}
```

This approach performs the same operation but accomplishes its task in one line of source code. This candidate splits any word into characters, reorders them randomly, and then joins the letters again. However, this code takes an unusual approach by passing to the sort function another function, which chooses a random value between 0.5 and 0.5. As a result, instead of comparing each item to the others—for example, which is greater or lesser—the sort function assigns that evaluation at random, performing a kind of end run around sorting. This code in effect replaces the sorting operation with coin tosses (plus the potential for a "0," in which case the two items are considered equal, as if the coin had landed on its edge).[8]

Which programmer will win the job? Certainly, the one who wrote the stronger code—but which one was that? The answer is clear: it depends on how the readers—in this case, the people doing the hiring—interpret the code.

On the one hand, the first version lays out its steps clearly. The process is easy to identify, and each step uses fairly basic, straightforward techniques. On the other hand, the second function may seem more clever for its concision. It uses the more sophisticated comparator function. This concept is typically not taught until more advanced courses because its operations are specific, even idiosyncratic, to this language. No doubt, programmers who read these code samples probably have already begun to form impressions of the two candidates in their minds: the one careful, organized, ordinary, perhaps fastidious; the other a wit with a tendency to show off. But every business is different.

Different companies, different programming cultures, different priorities, different work tasks require and desire different abilities. One set of employers might value most the code that is easy to read, modify, and sustain. Others might see the one-line solution as a sign of strong programming instincts, the ability to fully internalize the coding structures.[9] Interpreting further, each employer might have different assumptions about which code was written by the man and which by the woman. (Perhaps you have already made such assumptions.) Depending on their biases or hiring needs, they might favor one or the other, again depending on how they have read gender out of or into the presentation of the code. One need not look any further at the recent exposure of the gender divide in computer culture than the recent events at Google to see the crisis in gender equity in Silicon Valley and beyond.[10] This example and the use of such programming challenges in hiring suggests that code conveys more than mere ability: it expresses identity, even if these challenges are used primarily to make hiring decisions less dependent on other channels of identity, such as résumés or in-person interviews.

The programmers, aware of these possible interpretations, are choosing their strategies as well, realizing that they are representing themselves to the prospective employer. They cannot assume their code will be interpreted in a particular way. Employers may see the one-liner as a sign of a tendency to obfuscate or the multiline solution as a sign of a pedestrian approach to problems. The programmers may be torn between conflicting ideals and aesthetics taught in their programming classes or developed by interacting with other programmers professionally or otherwise online. They also may be influenced by their exposure to or immersion in various programming paradigms or languages that emphasize one virtue (say, reusability) over another (legibility or optimization).

Code in this example offers a medium for a *Turing test*, Alan Turing's thought experiment that challenges a computer to pass itself off as a human. However, rather than a computer and a human trying to prove who is more skilled at speaking human language, this scenario presents two programmers attempting to prove who can speak the language of computation more fluently, or at least most successfully in the dialect of the corporation from which they are seeking employment.[11] Only the surface challenge asks whether or not the human can speak in a way the computer understands.

The deeper challenge asks the programmers to communicate who they are to other humans, as coworkers and collaborators, through their use of code. Their code is not so much a litmus test, proving whether they can perform the task, as it is an essay exam, communicating character through process, values, and approaches to challenging questions. Simply put, code in this test proves again to be more than a functional tool: it is a means of expression between humans through communication with machines.

The many trade-offs in the minds of the programmers faced with this task and the wide variety of ways of reading these programs demonstrate just a portion of the complexity involved in the act of communicating through code. The meaning of the code goes beyond the functioning of the program because both programs perform the same task—a task which itself seems to have little significance for either party, though so much (i.e., employment) is at stake. Instead, the code itself is located within a broader communication exchange, one that is bound to time as marked by developments in programming paradigms, languages, hardware, and networks. Certainly, not everyone who reads code, as in this case with the employers, even shares the goal of realizing that particular software process. This is crucial because much writing about code, from textbooks to style guides, suggests that code is being written primarily to create a certain effect through software, which neglects the use of code in training exercises and artistic explorations, just to name two examples in which the computer program was not written to execute a solution to a problem. Here, the problem of the anagram was the sword in the stone, the evocative object.[12] This book will explore the ways source code becomes meaningful through its circulation in diverse contexts, how its tokens convey meaning beyond their functionality, and therefore how code serves as a communication medium including and beyond the realms of practical application on specific machines.

In this hiring example, source code is not merely the objective right answer to the straightforward mathematical question, not something that can be assessed as empirically better or worse. In fact, the notion of empirical truths or unquestionable values in computer programming proves to be even less stable than it is in the material world, the social constructions of which have been well articulated by theorists and philosophers. In either solution, the code is merely one version of how this process may be implemented. Its final form is the result not of mathematical certainty but of collected cultural knowledge and convention (cultures of code and coding languages), haste and insight, inspirations and observations, evolutions and adaptations, rhetoric and reason, paradigms of language, breakthroughs in approach, and failures to conceptualize.

Code is a meaningful measure of a job candidate's abilities and predilections because code communicates more than merely its functionality; as an interdependent object circulating through culture, it amasses even more meaning. The examples from the job interview situation were hypothetical but typical. Once we return our attention to code from the real world with a history of revision and correction, funding and fudging, functioning or failing, we have even more to discuss—or, as we say in the humanities, to unpack. As Alan J. Perlis writes in the foreword to Harold Abelson and Gerald Jay Sussman's foundational *Structure and Interpretation of Computer Programs*, "Every computer program is a model, hatched in the mind, of a real mental process. These processes, arising from human experience and thought, are huge in number, intricate in detail, and at any time only partially understood" (1996, xi). Unpacking the meaning of these programs locked in their technosocial context is the job of critical code studies (CCS).

Protesting in Code

Code holds a meaning beyond, and growing out of, what it does. That meaning does not necessarily depend on code authors intending to communicate something to an audience beyond themselves, as in the case of code comments. Consider two rather different examples.

In the summer of 2011, at a political protest in India, a young woman appearing in a photograph that was later shared on the online discussion board Reddit holds a sign (figure 1.1), which reads:

```
#include <india.h>
#include<jan lokpal bill.h>
#include <students.h>
void main( )
{
  do
    {
      no_of_indians ++;
      printf("Protest continues.");
    } while(lokpal bill not passed);
  printf("Corruption free India");
  getch();
}
```

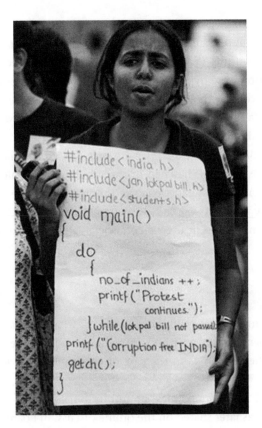

Figure 1.1
A woman holds a protest sign written in code.

The woman is protesting (mostly) in the programming language C. She is protesting by writing in code.

One interpretation of this sign is that the protester is calling for India, particularly the students primarily in engineering and computer science, to join in the support of the Jan Lokpal Bill. This code offers a little loop in which the number of Indians protesting should increase until the bill is passed, at which point, according to the program, India will be corruption free.[13]

Stepping through the functionality of this code, or pseudocode, helps to identify ways that it conveys its political message.[14] The code on her sign includes several libraries: india, jan lokpal bill, and students. In other words, it uses the preprocessing directive #include to load files with the names listed. The .h notation is the conventional way to name a header file, or files that are loaded first. In the context of the protest, the code seems to be playing on the pun to "include" the people of India (represent the wishes of the people), to "include" the bill (pass the measure), and to "include" students (invite into the process students, the main audience of this sign). Placing these three items as header files symbolically gives them priority because their contents are established as fundamental declarations for the rest of the code.

The `void main()` call begins the code of this particular function.[15] Next, the code begins the function with a loop (`do`) that increases the number of Indians (`no_of_indians`) and prints the message "Protest continues." while the bill is not passed (a condition).[16] Once the loop ends, the function prints "Corruption free India." The `getch()` function means that inputting any character will exit out of the program. In the analogy, the role of this last instruction, or waiting for any key to be pressed before terminating the program, is not obvious. Perhaps at some point the program, and by consequence the protest, will need to be interrupted. Pressing a character to stop the program could represent pressing for more character (integrity) or impressing upon the character of activated citizens, although there are not enough context clues for a definitive reading. But by placing the code on a sign and holding it up in a public event as political expression, the woman holding the sign is inviting open public interpretation by noncomputational systems.

The Reddit discussion of the photo is 169 comments long (over four hundred if you add the separate threads under the "India" and "pics" Reddit forums) as commentators (aka Redditors) weigh in on the elegance of her code (or perceived lack thereof), global outsourcing, crowdsourcing code, and criticism of the way programming is taught in universities, not to mention discussion of the subject of her protest, the Jan Lokpal anticorruption bill in India. That bill, also known as the Citizen's Ombusdsman Bill, was designed to establish a corruption oversight body called Jan Lokpal, which had first been proposed in 1968. The 2011 campaign, driven by political activist Anna Hazare's hunger strike, gained widespread attention due to a social media campaign largely run on Twitter, targeting India's media-savvy middle class (Stancati and Pokharel 2011). To create a protest sign in computer code during this particular campaign is to address directly India's influential body of professionals in the technology area. To express a political message in code-like text is to address a readership skilled in reading computer code, their professional language.

The debate over this code vacillates between thoughtful consideration of her point and (more often) the kinds of trolling common to message boards such as Reddit. A good deal of the commentary focused on perceived deficiencies of the code, which incites remarks about her sexual desirability and her perceived inferiority as an alleged outsourced programmer.[17] By protesting in code, this woman, presumably an Indian national, had triggered protectionist, elitist, and chauvinistic reactions from Redditors far beyond India, offering glimpses of *toxic geek masculinity*[18] or what I call *encoded chauvinism* (see chapter 5) that can overshadow programming cultures. Consequently, this code presents us with an opportunity to discuss not only its central topic, the Jan Lokpal Bill, but also the cultures of programming that emerge. To focus on the code of this sign, its competencies and whether it would compile, rather than its meaning in context, is to demonstrate the way the centrality of the machine, the need to make code utterances legible to the unambiguous processing of the compiler, takes precedence from and in turn deprecates other explorations of meaning. As one Redditor puts it in the top-voted comment, "I love that everyone in the comments immediately starts correcting errors in the code. Please never change internet" (account deleted, August 26, 2011, comment on "Protesting in C"), to which another replies, "Well if she's going to be making a sign that no one but programmers will understand, she might as well write it well" (m7600, ibid.). Style and technical validity clearly take priority in this coding community, at once identifying both the centrality of functionality in this unambiguous form of expression and the way that emphasis obscures other aspects of its communication. Critical code studies seeks to explore making these secondary meanings primary.

Admittedly, this protest sign hardly offers an everyday use of code. In fact, although the protestor is using code-like language, this sign has more in common with *codework*, a style of creative writing that uses code and code-like orthography to create poetic art, than it does with programming in the context of software development.[19] This code was written primarily to express a political position, not to produce a program. Nonetheles, this code speaks volumes in context. The fact that a woman in India holds up a sign written in C-like code, shows an expression of the intersection of gender, economics, and politics as women of the subcontinent face the gender divide in a growing and increasingly liberal middle class. Although there is much to discuss in this code extracted from a machine-centered programming context into a human-centered political forum, such as a march, I contend that even code written in an ordinary program to run on a computer can "speak," as Geoff Cox and Alex McLean (2012) put it in their book.

In contrast, consider a second example, selected for having as many parallels (e.g., perceived gender, nationality of the programmer, and aim for political expression) with the first as possible.[20] On the code repository GitHub, programmer Tapasweni Pathak has posted a project for a web app called Women on GitHub (Pathak et al. 2016).[21] This app, which makes use of a framework called Heroku, takes a list of names of female programmers "who inspired [the contributors] to code more." Two contributors,

Prabhanshu Attri and Fatima Rafiqui, have added code for displaying that list on a web page. The following is the PHP and HTML code that creates a grid of tables, each displaying a user in a profile box (figure 1.2), reminiscent of trading cards for baseball or soccer idols:

```
219 $count = 1;
220 while ($row = $result->fetch(PDO::FETCH_ASSOC)) {
221   echo '<div class="mdl-cell mdl-cell--3-col mdl-cell--4-col-
tablet mdl-cell--4-col-phone mdl-card mdl-shadow--3dp">
222     <div class="mdl-card__media user-img">
223       <img class="avatar" src="'.$row['avatar_url'].'"
alt="'.$row['name'].'">
224       <span class="id-element
mdl-typography--font-light">'.$row['id'].'</span>
225       <nav class="menu-'.$count.'">
              ... [ Navigation menu ] ...
234       echo '</nav>
235 </div>
236 <div class="mdl-card__supporting-text">
237 <span class="mdl-typography--font-light
mdl-typography--subhead">
238 <table>
239 <tr>
240   <td><i class="fa fa-user"></i>
241   <td><h4 class="android-header">'.$row['login'].'
</h4>
242</tr>';
243 if (strlen(trim($row['name'])) != 0 &&
!empty(trim($row['name'])))
244 echo '<tr>
245   <td>
246   <td>('.trim($row['name']).')
247 </tr>';
248 if ($row['company'])
249 echo '<tr>
250   <td><i class="fa fa-group"></i>
251       <td>'.$row['company'].'
252 </tr>';
```

```
253 if ($row['location'])
254 echo '<tr>
255     <td><i class="fa fa-location-arrow"></i>
256    <td>'.$row['location'].'
257 </tr>';
258 if ($row['created_at'])
259 echo '<tr>
260   <td><i class="fa fa-clock-o"></i>
261 <td>Joined on '.$row['created_at'].'
262 </tr>';
263 echo '</table>
264 </div>
```

This code produces the basic layout for the card. After setting the counter to one ($count
= 1;), it loops through all of the data using a while statement. The subsequent lines

tapasweni-
pathak
(Tapasweni Pathak)
SAP Labs
Bangalore, India
Joined on Apr 13, 2013

VIEW ON GITHUB

Figure 1.2
Sample image from Women on GitHub.

display aspects of user accounts using an echo statement (PHP for print or display).[22] Each element of the featured programmer's profile is surrounded by either `<div>` `</div>` or `<span></span>` tags for formatting or styling that item, whether through placement, size, or other design elements. The `<class>` specifications indicate which formatting to apply from a Cascading Style Sheets (CSS) file.

The second section (starting at line 236) creates the lower half of the card using conventional code that can be read by anyone who has tried to make a webpage using tables. The code includes a `<div>` or div tag, which creates the subsection; `<table>` organizes the space; and `<tr>` creates rows and `<td>` cells in columns, producing a growing procession of inspiring women programmers. Each row has two columns, one for an icon and one for the information. Several conditional statements check whether particular items (e.g., company and link) exist before displaying them, or inserting the HTML to display them, using echo statements. The initials *fa* in the class refer to Font Awesome, an open-source set of icons created by Dave Gandy,[23] which further links this project to the open-source community and its ethos of collaboration. Font Awesome gives the community icons for making professional-grade web apps, rendering artifacts and objects legible in the contemporary web design ecology. So too is the code awesome for presenting, as visual icons, the many women programmers in a profession currently skewed heavily toward men.

As the illustration shows, these programmer baseball cards (as in figure 1.2) are fairly straightforward, presenting an avatar, username, company, location, and join date. One item stands out, though: a white number on a black background superimposed onto the avatar. No Font Awesome icon identifies that number, nor are there other clues as to its meaning, yet its prominence on the image gives it significance. It was not until I looked into the code that I knew its denotation, the GitHub user number (`.$row['id'].`, line 224). As it turns out, this number is not obvious in GitHub either because it is not listed on a user's profile page or in the URL for a user.[24] By looking in the code, I could find the denotation of this number, and that exploration led me to consider its connotation.

On the face of it, that tally number is only significant to the program that generated it; however, on further consideration, the number conveys additional meaning by tying each contributor to when she joined GitHub, indicating how many other people had previously registered. A complete set of these numbers would offer the rate at which GitHub's user base expanded and, when combined with other profile information, could tell us how the proportion of users who are women changed over time.[25]

The Women on GitHub software gives this number further rhetorical significance through placement. Layered over the avatar image in such a prominent place, the

number offers a form of authentication and perhaps even validation of these programmers: here are their official numbers, the computer-generated signs of their member-
ship in this online community. The fact that the meaning of this number lies in the
code is appropriate to the software's audience; it is written, like the protest code, for
programmers who have the ability to interpret its meaning by inspecting the code. The
repository invites these readers who code to explore, to discover, to contribute, and
to join in, to be counted as another woman on GitHub or a confederate, extending,
revising, or forking this code. In this way, the code has made meaningful to its view-
ers a number that otherwise only has meaning in the software, mirroring the process
whereby we find a larger meaning of this number by exploring the computer source
code, code designed to present the significant number of women programmers contributing to this platform for open-source development.

Compared to the codework of the protest sign, this excerpt offers mere ordinary
code. Pathak says she does not even list the project on her resume (December 13, 2016,
comment on Kalbhor 2016). Neither do the two programmers who created the web
page. Nonetheless, code does not have to be extraordinary or difficult to read to be
remarkable. Arguably, this code does more computational work than the protest sign
because this code will produce effects on a web browser when it is run with the other
files. Rather than calling to increase the number of student protestors, this code is part
of a system that literally increases the number of women displayed on the Women
on GitHub webpage, growing as contributors add names and as GitHub assigns their
numbers. Unlike the sign that calls for inclusion, this code does the yeoman's work of
building signs of inclusion and involvement, one table cell at a time.

Context also makes this code meaningful. This code was contributed by a collaboration between women and men to celebrate female programmers. Not only does the
app display women who program, but the repository, too, speaks of women and men
collaborating on open-source software development. Furthermore, this code speaks
because it can function. Whereas the code on the sign would not compile, this web app
code does. Whereas the protest code is displayed on a poster, this code lives in a repository where it can continue to grow and develop. Whereas the code on the sign inspired
forum posts, this code has inspired collaboration, expanding, forking. The goal of this
comparison is not to call one coding act better than another but to demonstrate the
ways meaning in code arises from its context, not independent of its functionality but
growing out of its functionality.

Although it is important to note the difference between code and codework, I do
not want to call one of these examples a superior form of speaking through code or
even more worthy of explication. We have to be mindful of a kind of chauvinism

that creeps into discussions of programming, what I call encoded chauvinism (see chapter 5),[26] whereby we assert a hierarchy based on an arbitrary judgment of what is "real" or "good" or "right" code. Surely that chauvinism is driving much of the commentary on the Reddit boards mentioned earlier, and though it can grow out of rigor and critical integrity, it typically serves to suppress, to denigrate, and to diminish the work of others in a way that is poisonous to programming culture and its development. To write code that runs is not more important than the creative act of taking code out into the streets on a protest sign. In fact, I read the second program through the lens of the first. I juxtapose these examples to model one kind of code-reading practice (code read by comparison to other code) and to argue that speaking in code does not require programmers to make code behave like spoken language or to create puns with code. A person writing what to them is ordinary, functional code is making meaning already. Critically reading code does not depend on the discovery of hidden secrets or unexpected turns, but rather examining encoded structures, models, and formulations; explicating connotations and denotations of specific coding choices; and exploring traces of the code's development that are not apparent in the functioning of the software alone. As with all texts, the discovery and creation of meaning grow out of the act of reading and interpretation. As the product of creative processes carried out over time by human and machine collaborations, code offers details and foundations for those interpretations. Even very ordinary code designed to achieve some everyday purpose, some practical goal, to produce some output or process, carries with it meaning beyond what it does. I argue that computer source code since its inception has been a means of communication (and hence ideological), but that we are only beginning to discover the methods of explaining that ideology or, more broadly, that meaning.

When reading the examples of the protest sign and the Women on GitHub project code, I do not and cannot approach them in an ideologically neutral way. Instead, my reading is informed by feminist and postcolonial critical theories. Those theories attach valences to what might otherwise be framed as mere technology, a view which merely disguises its own ideological assumptions. My reading is influenced, for example, by the work of Roopika Risam, who in her book *New Digital Worlds* (2018) identifies a need for postcolonial digital archives structured on a more intersectional model. *Intersectional* here means drawing together multiple interconnecting aspects of identity. As Risam explains, "Within colonized and formerly colonized nations and for people outside of dominant cultures, access to the means of digital knowledge production is essential for reshaping the dynamics of cultural power and claiming the humanity that has been denied by the history of colonialism" (46). Risam and I are influenced by

Giyatri Spivak, whose seminal essay "Can the Subaltern Speak?" (1994) theorized how those without power, outside the cultural hegemony, cannot speak until they can represent themselves. Women programmers would not constitute a subaltern according to Spivak's definition because they have too much access to the tools of power. However, her theorizations of power and speech illuminate the dynamics at play in the significance of this code. In the global economy, female programmers born outside of first-world, Western countries, though part of a professional, educated class and though living elsewhere, such as Europe or the United States, have lower status and frequently lower pay than their male counterparts, especially those from more privileged economies, such as the United States. Arguably, by speaking in code, both the protest sign and the web page offer examples of women representing themselves. Although this is not the place for a full elaboration on Risam or Spivak's theories, this example offers one of the ways outside heuristics—in this case, postcolonial theory and intersectional approaches—can inform our code-reading practices.

I call the act of interpreting culture through computer source code *critical code studies*, and in this book I will attempt to characterize but not limit its methods primarily through a series of case studies. Critical code studies names a stance toward code as a unique semiotic form of discourse, the meaning of which requires specific techniques that are still being developed, even as the natures of code and programming are rapidly evolving. In other words, code is a unique expressive milieu that operates like, but is still distinct from, other forms of communication primarily due to its relation with hardware and other software systems.

Critical code studies names the methods and the scholarship of those involved in the analysis of the extrafunctional significance of source code, and this book offers a collection of case studies to demonstrate some of its potential.

The Origins of Critical Code Studies

Critical code studies grew out of a desire to read digital objects with more attention to their unique construction.

In 2004, when I was analyzing conversation agents, or chatbots, such as ELIZA, I was trying to find a way to perform what N. Katherine Hayles (Hayles and Burdick 2002) and Lev Manovich (2002) were calling *media-specific analysis*. What were the unique properties of conversation agents? What made analyzing them different from analyzing other digital or print objects? Soon it became obvious: the code. But how does one read code? In my search for answers, I found a few scholars who wrote about the ontology of computer source code. Kittler (1992) had written a bit. Lawrence Lessig (2006) had approached code in a broader sense, bringing ideas from the legal world. Code had also been taken up by a handful of other scholars, specifically Adrian MacKenzie (2005, 2006), Florian Cramer (2005), Loss Pequeño Glazier (2006), Alan Liu (2004), and Alexander Galloway (2004). Their gestures were powerful opening movements into the realm of code, but they did not include many examples of actually interpreting the code. If code is, as these critics were suggesting, a unique semiotic realm, what could one say about any one passage of code?

I had been trained in literary theory and cultural studies, as well as what we were then calling *new media*, so I sought tools there. Semiotics offered tools for analyzing any sign system, and deconstruction complemented that study by poking around in the cracks and fissures. Cultural studies offered a way to take the text off its pedestal, while also helping to change the object of study from "text" as a set of characters to "text" as any cultural artifact. The critical theories aimed at underlying structures of oppression and possibility, from feminism to Marxism, queer theories to postcolonialism and theories of race and racial formation, also provided frameworks for critiques.

Around the same time, Noah Wardrip-Fruin, Matthew Fuller, and Lev Manovich were beginning to theorize software studies, while Nick Montfort and Ian Bogost were launching platform studies. What all these studies had in common was their emphasis on analyzing the particularities of different categories of technology. However, platform studies focused primarily on hardware, at least in its first outing, on the Atari 2600 in *Racing the Beam* (Montfort and Bogost 2009), and in *Expressive Processing*, the first book in the Software Studies series, Wardrip-Fruin (2009) essentially bracketed the code. Focusing on code could supplement these, so simultaneous with the birth of these two branches of new media studies, I proposed critical code studies in an essay (updated in chapter 2), which I presented at the Modern Language Association meeting and which was published in *Electronic Book Review* (*ebr*).

The goal of that essay is to instigate scholarship on methods of interpreting code. I argued (and continue to argue) that rather than bracketing the code, we should read it, beginning with the tools of semiotic and cultural analysis and continuing by developing new methods particularly suited to code. We had to get past the understanding of code as meaningless math (also, as it turns out, a false conception) and instead approach it as a culturally situated sign system full of denotations and connotations, rendered meaningful by its many and diverse readers, both human and machinic. Daunting though it seemed, the time had come to take code out of the black box and explore the way its complex and unique sign systems make meaning as it circulates through varied contexts. I was discovering in the process a richness that computer scientists already knew, a sense of significance that grows out of and yet goes beyond the function of the code—only I had the additional benefit of heuristic tools developed in the humanities for interpretation and exegesis.

However, not everyone was so excited about this proposal. For example, some of the computer scientists who heard about the idea and read some of the early critical code studies writings (particularly my piece linking heteronormativity and malicious software worms) responded with derision and alarm (discussed in Marino 2016 and McPherson 2018). From its doubters' perspective, CCS marked another invasion of the humanists into what is known as "the science wars," a fierce contest between theoretical physicists and the humanists they felt were making much ado about insufficiently understood advances in science, specifically quantum physics. What would happen, they asked, when these literary scholars haphazardly applied their high theory to something so far outside their realm of expertise? The charges of imperialism and imperiousness were clear.

Not wanting to alienate the very community of experts whose works and whose realm I sought to explore, I spent the next few years in conversation with computer scientists. We convened online forums, five biannual Critical Code Studies Working Groups (CCSWGs), which included scholars of all levels and various backgrounds, especially computer scientists.[27] Out of those conversations came models for the interpretive practices demonstrated in this book, along with the basis of mutual respect born out of careful expressions and translations of our positions. As I say in the original essay, even the words *interpret* and *meaning* do not signify the same ideas in computer science as in the humanities. The group also included several scholars whose training bridged the gap between the humanities and computer science, further helping to cross the divide.

Born of those working groups were articles, conference presentations, and books, including the first CCS manuscript, the ten-authored *10 PRINT CHR$(205.5+RND(1)); : GOTO 10* (Montfort et al. 2013; aka *10 PRINT*), which analyzed the code of its title. Wendy Chun (Marino 2010a) presented what would be her first chapter of *Programmed Visions* (2011). Dennis Jerz (2011) offered the FORTRAN code of William Crowther's *Adventure* for collective annotation. Mark Sample's "Criminal Code: Procedural Logic and Rhetorical Excess in Videogames" (2013) offers a reading of C++ code in the video game *Micropolis*, the forerunner to *Sim City*.[28] Tara McPherson presented an early version of her analysis of the intersections of the civil rights movement and the development of Unix (2010; revised and extended in 2018). Federica Frabetti offered a take on a misread bug in the code of the first space probe, Mariner 1 (2010).

Subsequently, several books have expanded the cultural contexts for examination of code. David M. Berry's *The Philosophy of Software* (2011) takes up a formal consideration of the ontology and epistemology of code, as does Adrian Mackenzie's *Cutting Code* (2006). Bradley Dilger and Jeff Rice have collected reflections that center on HTML tokens in *A to <A>* (2010). As I've mentioned, *Speaking Code* (2012) by Geoff Cox and Alex McLean offers an exploration of the way code acts as speech in the form of a duet, with text by Cox intertwined with code passages by McLean. D. Fox Harrell's *Phantasmal Media* (2013) offers programming as a potentially disruptive culturally situated practice. James Brown Jr. applies rhetorical theory to code in *Ethical Programs: Hospitality and the Rhetorics of Software* (2015). In *Coding Literacy: How Computer Programming Is Changing Writing* (2017), Annette Vee analyzes code from a legal perspective and examines what the framework of literacy brings to larger conversations about teaching code in cultures. Finally, the most recent work, Kevin Brock's *Rhetorical Code Studies* (2019), offers a specific application of critical code studies that reads code as a means of rhetorical discourse.

A lot of the early work has been spent trying to understand what is possible to read and code and even what code itself is. Several scholars have found it useful to speak of code as *performative language*, drawing upon the speech act theories of J. L. Austin. Hayles, Cox and McLean (2013), and numerous others have found this framing to be productive because code seems to do what it says. However, it is clear that speech act theory is only partially applicable. Others, such as Daniel Punday (2015), have cast programming as writing. Still others, such as Roger Whitson (in the 2012 CCSWG), have suggested that actor-network theory might be usefully applied. In this formulation, code becomes an entity (an actor) as it networks together other bodies of code, machines, and humans. Certainly, such a theorization speaks better to Kirschenbaum's sense of the critical importance of context to interpreting code (see chapter 2).[29] If the study of natural language and semiotics is any indication, these initial theoretical frameworks are merely the beginning.

There are quite a few texts that take up the ontology of code. Chun's *Programmed Visions* (2011) and Hayles's *My Mother Was a Computer* (2005) offer important interventions that situate computation and our fascination with it. Gabriella Coleman's *Coding Freedom* (2012) takes up the ethos of the culture of open-source programming. Jussi Parikka's *Digital Contagions* (2007), although containing very little code, offers a robust media archaeology of viruses and worms. Because of their philosophical interventions into the study of technoculture, these works provide a foundation for readings of code.

Critical code studies has also had an effect on the production of code-based art projects. Artists, such as Nick Montfort and Stephanie Strickland (2013), have begun to publish their source code (or even essays embedded in their source code) with an awareness that critical code studies scholars will be perusing their code later. Similarly, artists such as J. R. Carpenter (2011) and Brendan Howell (Griffiths et al. 2010) have published book versions of procedurally generated literary texts that have included their source code. The creators of the Transborder Immigrant Tool, discussed in chapter 3, have likewise published their code along with excerpts of the verbal poetry of the piece. As these artists foreground the code in the publication of their works, they invite readers to include an exploration of their code in the interpretation of the larger work.

This brief overview does not even begin to count the many books published in the field of computer science that are discussing code beyond functionality. One notable collection is *Beautiful Code* (Oram and Wilson 2007), which asked influential programmers to share essays on examples of code that were beautiful in their eyes. Opening the discussion about aesthetics, including multiple perspectives, and acknowledging the subjectivity of aesthetic claims is the starting point for recognizing code as a realm of discourse that deserves deep discussions that go beyond functionality and efficiency.

Over ten years after it began, the movement to develop critical code studies is well on its way as a field. Much of the initial pushback has dissipated because scholars have become more aware of the pitfalls and possibilities of this field. The idea of literary scholars or what we call *digital humanists* interpreting code is no longer novel but is now accepted and so can do what I hoped it would do—supplement other projects of cultural and media analysis. Take, for example, Anastasia Salter and John Murray's platform studies book on Flash (2014), which includes analysis of code from a representative piece of ActionScript. Software studies, platform studies, and media archaeology having dug their foundations can now work to strengthen one another rather than existing in unnecessary, balkanized fiefdoms.

As the field of critical code studies has expanded, so has the range of approaches. In a recent working group, Jessica Marie Johnson and Mark Anthony Neal, editors of and writers of the introduction to a special issue of *The Black Scholar* entitled "Black Code" (2017), led an exploration through the Afro-Louisiana History and Genealogy Database and the Trans-Atlantic Slave Trade Database, asking how the encoding of slave trade in manifests and in scholarly projects can either dehumanize or offer a means to reemphasize the humanity of victims of enslavement. By exploring databases and spreadsheets, this study also brought into focus one of the most widespread and yet understudied environs for programming, a reminder that the work of programming and coding is happening in places that may look nothing like what we expect as well as noting that contemporary programming activities often have predigital origins that also need to be interrogated.

And yet the work is far from done. In fact, it is still very much in the early stages, which is why I am writing this book: not to offer a complete compendium of all CCS practices, but to share some of the initial reading approaches that I have found useful. I hope this collection of case studies will inspire others to create and discover what they can make of code.

E-Voting Software

To read and interpret code does not necessarily mean to discover secret content or to uncover its unconscious bias or even to reveal unusual functioning. Instead, to read code critically is to explore the significance of the specific symbolic structures of the code and their effects over time if and when they are executed (after being compiled, if necessary), within the cultural moment of their development and deployment. To read code in this way, one must establish its context and its functioning and then examine its symbols, structures, and processes, particularly the changes in state over the time of its execution. Reading these elements requires a philosophical heuristic, also referred to as *critical theory*, although that can be a contentious term. Suffice to say, all interpretation relies on a stated or unstated philosophical disposition, at the very least. For the third example, then, let us take code from an open-source voting system, specifically the free and open-source software (FOSS) Votebox system.[30] It is worth noting that when reading any new piece of code, even for a programmer who is not trying to perform an interpretation, it can be difficult to get a handhold. I offer this example not to give a definitive reading but to model some strategies for approaching any piece of code, and specifically code that constitutes software.

The first thing I look for when analyzing a piece of code is the context. Who wrote the code and why? In this case, its purpose is electronic voting. Electronic voting, or *e-voting*, has been a divisive topic of debate for the past two decades, dating back to problems with punch cards: the infamous "hanging chads" in the 2000 US presidential election (Conrad et al. 2009). E-voting at once offers a potential solution to ballot box stuffing and election rigging and an unprecedented opportunity for election hacking in times when the electronic distribution of our information seems increasingly vulnerable. In the decades after the panic over paper ballots, e-voting machines also became a source of fear. For example, in the 2016 US presidential election, the threat of international tampering loomed over these vulnerable systems. How do these historical contexts frame the software?

Next, I examine the general class of software. Voting software, like many types of software, for a time was mostly constituted of proprietary systems unavailable to the public. However, as questions mounted about the security of voting software and as the code of some software was leaked, this practice began to change. Some groups began to argue for the need for open-source voting software that could be readily examined by the public voting on these machines. Their release of free and open-source software led to the subsequent release of the code for proprietary software by companies in the commercial market. With that context briefly presented, I turn my attention to this specific piece of software: who created it, when, where, and why. This begins the historical, archaeological, and sociological research that will ground the reading. If the authors of the code are still alive, I may try to interview them.[31] Otherwise, their documentation is extremely valuable in this process.

Votebox presents one free and open-source, digital-recording electronic (DRE) voting software developed by researchers at Rice University. That the code was created for research purposes rather than other goals, such as hactivism, artistic reflection, or commerce, informs the way I read this code. Votebox is written in Java, although it originated in C#, in what the authors hope is a "clear, modern, object-oriented style" (Sandler, Derr, and Wallach 2007, 360). This emphasis on clarity may reflect the scholarly goals for creating this software or the desire for the code to be legible to a broader public for auditing purposes. In any event, the confines and affordances of the chosen language and the software design paradigm are key to interpreting any piece of code, and these programmers note that their choice of Java added length due to its sheer verbosity in comparison to Python (ibid., 360).

The comments of the code, particularly well-documented code, offer a guide to its functionality but often convey more. In his book *The Philosophy of Software*, Berry (2011) notices that the comments in the Votebox code always refer to the voter by using the male pronoun:

```
/**
 * This is the event that happens when the voter requests
 * to challenge his vote.
 *
 *    format: (challenge [nonce] [list-of-race-random pairs])
 *
 * * @author sgm2
 *
 * */
```

Berry reflects on the implications of these pronouns in the code (2011, 116). A quick search of the current release code turns up over seventy instances of *his* in the code and its documentation. Some have argued that comments are not a part of the code, but others see comments as situating and contextualizing code (Douglass 2010). Just as Berry reads these comments as implying a gender of the voter, another might argue that the code outside the comments does not offer any signs of gender. Later, Berry considers the affordances of the voting interface in contrast with a traditional ballot and the ways the systems bound or constrain certain aspects of the voting process.

How else might we approach this code? We could explore its cryptographic security in relation to contemporary conversations of voting insecurity. We could consider the readability of the code in a project built on increasing the transparency of the voting process. We could place its approach against other varieties of voting software that have since been released. What vision of democratic participation of voting does this code implement?

Consider the following passage from the VoteBox.java file (excerpts from lines 195–221):

```
currentDriver.getView().registerForChallenge(new Observer() {
    /**
     * Makes sure that the booth is in a correct state to cast a
 ballot,
     * then announce the cast-ballot message (also increment
counters)
     */
    public void update(Observable arg0, Object arg1) {
        if (!connected)
            throw new RuntimeException(
                "Attempted to cast ballot when not connected to any
machines");
        if (!voting || currentDriver == null)
            throw new RuntimeException(
                "VoteBox attempted to cast ballot, but was not
currently voting");
        if (finishedVoting)
                throw new RuntimeException(
                "This machine has already finished voting, but
attempted to vote again");
```

```
        finishedVoting = true;


        auditorium.announce(new ChallengeEvent(mySerial,
                        StringExpression.makeString(nonce),
                        BallotEncrypter.SINGLETON.
getRecentRandom()));


            BallotEncrypter.SINGLETON.clear();
      }
    });
```

As the comments that accompany this code indicate, this section will "listen for challenges [sic] ui events. When received, discard the ballot (as the vote is no longer countable)/ ... and reply with the random key needed to decrypt this particular vote." If the three conditions are met (i.e., the machine is connected, voting was underway, and a vote had not already been cast), the program will note that voting is finished, then announce the challenge event to the auditorium before clearing the ballot. A challenge ballot will not be counted in the final election. If any of the three conditions are not met, which would indicate another problem with the voting software's processes, run-time exceptions are thrown in the form of error messages.

Within this passage of code, key constructs of the software appear. For example, Votebox uses a model of a persistent auditorium, a closed network separated from the internet by an "air gap," with which each device or instance of Votebox is constantly communicating to create transparency and redundancy of records of the voting (Sandler and Wallach 2007). Also, because any voter can challenge any vote, the software is always listening for a challenge event ("Votebox" 2008). We might consider how those constructs and their implementation attempt to intervene in contemporary concerns about paper balloting. How does the auditorium object implement the concept of transparency while providing redundancy in registered vote counts?

There are many further technical considerations to explore as well. How does the choice of Java impact the implementation? How does an object-oriented approach serve or confound the programmers' goals? How does this passage of code interact with the larger Votebox system and Votebox interact with the software and hardware on which it will run? How do the constructs in Votebox, such as the auditorium, supervisor console, and challenge event, instantiate a vision of elections in democracy?

In further media archaeology, we could also dig further into the context in which this code was created. How do the goals of the academic researchers who built the code manifest themselves in the code itself—for example, the carefulness of the documentation? How do these goals differ from those of the creators of commercial voting software?

It is not my intention to limit these readings or even perform them here but instead to demonstrate how much more fruitful a reading can be when performed on real-world code, not merely hypothetical code or pseudocode. These questions offer models of ways to begin to interrogate and explore the code as a text.

Certainly, for every line of flight from one reading of the code, one could present an alternative reading or response. For example, consider Berry's remark about gender in the code. If code comments are essentially distinct from operational code, does the use of the male pronoun in the documentation have any real implications on the code itself? Are there other ways in which the voter/user has been gendered? Such ambiguity, such indeterminacy, such uncertainty may produce unease in more empirically minded positivists. However, uncertainty is fundamental to the search for meaning. Code may have unambiguous effects on software and the state of the machine, but the implications of those effects are anything but. Exploring and making meaning from symbols requires a letting go of the need for right answers, for that which is empirically verifiable.

From this example, a few general techniques suggest themselves. To explore code, a scholar should first read the code and its documentation to determine what the code does. If the scholar is not very familiar with the programming language or architecture, a guide with more fluency may assist. In rare occasions (including some in this book), a scholar can discuss the code with its authors, keeping an eye out for an intentional fallacy or the sense that the program's author can definitively say what the code means. Regardless of the scholar's experience with code, I recommend reading code with one or more others to discover a variety of perspectives. The meaning of symbols in communication is never an individual affair. Code's meaning is communal, subjective, opened through discussion and mutual inquiry, to be contested and questioned, requiring creativity and interdisciplinarity, enriched through the variety of its readers and their backgrounds, intellectually and culturally.

Code can be difficult to navigate even for its own author. To aid in this process, I find it useful to scan the overall architecture while reading comments if available. Guide and commentary texts (articles by the creators or critics of the code) can be priceless here. If possible, the scholar should see the code in action, executing it (once compiled, if needed), even using additional software to monitor state changes. It is also useful to explore the genre of the code to better identify typical techniques versus innovations, aberrations, anomalies, or other notable variations, guided by the question, What's worth noting?

However, reading code does not mean staring at monochromatic character strings. Douglass (2011) early in the evolution of CCS suggested using a syntax highlighter or even an integrated development environment (IDE) to see the code the way developers do. IDEs also include advanced features for tracing variable states, arguments, and functions while providing a nonlinear means for exploring code. There are several freely available IDEs, such as Eclipse or Netbeans, which was used to develop the Transborder Immigrant Tool (chapter 3). Alternatively, code readers could use web applications such as Jupyter Notebooks, R Markdown, Apache Zeppelin, or Spark Notebook, which enable the creation of documents with running code in them so that code readers can more readily see the effects of code. Reading code is not like examining other texts because software contains assemblages of processes with changing states (Vee 2017). Nonetheless, this emphasis on reading more complex software does not exclude the reading of code-like artifacts through CCS.

Throughout my readings, I have found some basic questions to be useful: How does the implementation of the code (inside) reflect or contrast the functioning of the software (outside) or vice versa? How typical is this code within its more general class of software or algorithms? Where do its core ideas lie? What is anomalous about this code (for so much code is reused from similar code found elsewhere)? What methods or other sections of the code seem to capture the central idea of the software, its key contributions? (See the final chapter of this book for more of these initial questions.)

But the code is not enough in itself. It is crucial to explore context. Who wrote the code? When and why? In what language was the code written? What programming paradigm was used? Was it written for a particular platform (hardware or software)? How did the code change over time? What material or social constraints impacted the creation of this code? How does this code respond to the context in which it was created? How was the code received by others? Although many of these questions address the technical aspects of the code, I do not want to limit context to the material condition of the code itself. Other paratexts (what Mackenzie calls *non-code-like entities*) also impact the meaning of the code.[32] The *critical* in critical code studies encourages also exploring the social context through the entry point of code.

Asking these questions is not enough. Critical reading requires critical lenses. Examining the code from a critical perspective requires a system of analysis or critical hermeneutics as reading practices. To this point, most of the techniques and questions I have listed are not much different from those any programmer or technical analyst might use when analyzing a piece of code. However, critical code studies apply additional lenses drawn from philosophy, cultural studies, media theory, and literary theory. Some of these lenses focus on aspects of identity, others on issues of power, and still others on ontology and signification. They are largely drawn from, but are not limited to, philosophy and semiotic analysis, then adapted to the specific attributes of source code. Theories that seem to apply mostly to social environs, such as queer theory and post-colonial theory, offer considerable insights into the technosocial realm. Critics may (and perhaps cannot help but) choose their hermeneutic before choosing the code that it helps interpret, or, more productively, they can follow a more emergent approach, seeing which hermeneutic the particular code and contexts warrant.

Although every piece of code has its own context, these foundational techniques have proved useful in my interpretations. I have applied them to even a single line of code (with nine other authors in Montfort et al. 2013) and found them useful tools in opening an exploration. To the observant, the universe can be seen in the line of code.

What Does It Mean to Interpret Code?

When I approach programmers about interpreting their code, a wry smile arises on their lips. After a bit of discussion, it becomes clear that they suspect I want to read their code as an English major would read a poem by Nikki Giovanni or a sonnet by Shakespeare. Will I treat their methods as stanzas? Their routines as rhymes about roses? Am I elevating their just-in-time or labored code to the status of art? Their smiles reflect their ambivalence about their own code. On the one hand, they tend to dislike their code and feel a certain degree of shame. Perhaps it can be said of code what da Vinci said of art: It is never finished, merely abandoned, meaning that code as a unit of mechanisms is always partial and potential. It can always be improved, developed, reworked, reimagined, and repurposed. On the other hand, programmers seem to feel a degree of bemusement that I would try to understand them through their code, treat them as I would an author, seek their fingerprints or their signature style. Will I celebrate them or use their code against them? But critical code studies is not some grand game of gotcha, nor some return to the harsh critiques programmers received at school, online, or at work. Nor does critical code studies primarily seek to understand and map the mind of the inspired computer programmer as artist. Some may pursue that tack, but the search for the genius of the programmer is not at the core of this project any more than it is the primary focus of archaeology or cultural studies. In fact, this misapprehension of the goals of critical code studies marks an instructive moment of miscommunication between humanities scholars and computer scientists about what we do.

Even in literary studies, at the start of the twenty-first century, interpretation is not that search for what the author secretly meant, that subjective hunt that computer programmers probably recall with dread from their English literature classes. Instead, interpretation is the systematic exploration of semiotic objects for understanding culture and systems of meaning. The subtle difference is that though many scholars still focus their attention on specific sets of authors, authorial intent and absolute meaning are not the ends of interpretation. Rather, more like the artifact examined in archaeology, the cultural object acts as an opening to a discussion of its significance within the culture that formed it. What aspect of culture and what realm of meaning (or *hermeneutic*) depends on the disposition of the scholar? The shift from the quest for the hidden meaning of the romantic (capital A) Author to the exploration of the object as a cultural text for exploring systems of meaning and culture is largely the result of the influence of semiotics and cultural studies, the field linked to the Birmingham school and Stuart Hall (see Hall 1992). Additionally, *semiotics*, the study of signs and signification, opens the interpretive process to all systems of information and meaning—what some might call *communication*, though that term is perhaps too strongly associated with another discipline. Cultural studies examines every object, every artifact, as a text for study. The distance between the haiku and the can of Coca-Cola as "texts" marks the shift from the study of artistry, on the one hand, to the broader study of signification and the manner in which objects acquire meaning on the other. Cultural studies scholars do not ask what the Coca-Cola Company intended by choosing red for the color of its cans and logo or what meaning it is hiding in the signature style of the words on the can. Instead, they perform a semiotic analysis on the possible meanings conveyed by those details of the can (the color red, the cursive script) and discuss what the can and, by extension, the company have come to represent.

In some ways, this type of analysis reverses the process by which this object came to be, as it was designed by artisans quite likely with feedback from other corporate executives in consultation with focus groups and consultants. At this point, one might note that the can is an object of commercial exchange. That too becomes part of the cultural analysis. Would the critic have any less to say about a cultural artifact that had a less purposeful marketing purpose, like a user's manual or a recipe in a cooking magazine? Probably not. Nonetheless, a reading of that text, an interpretation of that text, would require putting it in the context in which it is communicating: manuals, recipes, cooking culture. The cola can, in this case, is a text.

This is a useful moment to pause on this word, *text*. Because I am primarily a literary scholar with a background in analyzing poetry, prose, and plays, one might think that

I am implying that we read code the way we read poetry. But I am using that word not in the literary sense but in the much broader sense of cultural studies, situating the code as a cultural object of inquiry. Stuart Hall and others, for example, have written a book analyzing the Sony Walkman as a cultural text, examining its origins and impact on culture (Du Gay et al. 2013). Add to this works of semiotic analysis, such as Fredric Jameson's (1991) "reading" of the Biltmore Hotel as a text, and a more robust notion of *text* emerges, one that has subsequently influenced and expanded what is studied by literary scholars as well. The source code is a text, and to read it as a cultural object would be to consider it in all its history, uses, and interconnections and dependencies with other code, hardware, and cultures (Hall 1992).

However, to say that code is a cultural text is not to deny that it is the text of the code that specifically interests me. Most of the code examples I will be discussing here are also made of text—and by that, I mean written characters, numbers, letters, and symbols.[33] Although critical code studies examines code as it operates—whether compiled or not—in its executable form, CCS seeks to address a specific omission in contemporary scholarship on technology and technoculture. The text of code offers an opportunity for close analysis that often is too quickly abandoned by scholars in order to move into looser discussions of what software does or seems to do. Code should be read, and read with the kind of care and attention to detail that a programmer must use when debugging it, further augmented by the many reading strategies and heuristics that scholars have been developing for the interpretation of other kinds of texts and supplemented by new kinds of reading practices that speak more directly to the nature of code in its contexts.

So what is culture? Recently, I had a discussion with a computer scientist about critical code studies, and I raised this notion of coding culture. He mentioned the high number of Indian programmers working in this particular part of the country and suggested I speak with them about the way their cultural background appears in code. Although that inquiry would no doubt lead to some interesting exchanges, this suggestion revealed something to me: for him, *culture* largely signified *ethnic culture*. When humanities scholars evoke culture, they are typically referring to any social sphere, from particular workplaces to activities (e.g., skater culture, knitting culture), from regions of the world to virtual worlds (e.g., *World of Warcraft*), from realms of production and commerce to realms of scientific and academic inquiry. In programming, these cultures emerge around coding paradigms, languages, roles, and specializations, but also from an ethos or ideology, such as the FOSS community (see Coleman 2012). All these cultures, or subcultures, possess rituals, discourse conventions, meeting grounds (virtual or in real life), et cetera. They have shared texts, shared values and norms, shared vocabularies, and shared tools. As a result, any artifact, object, or text offers a glimpse of the cultures in which it was produced and circulated.

CCS emerges as a close-reading practice at the very time when other scholars are advocating "distant" and "surface" reading. At this early stage in the interpretation of code, we still need to develop methods that make sense for and of code. Thus, though some are using software to perform computational analyses on large corpuses of texts, these early code readings look closely at smaller portions of code, closer to the readings of individual poems. However, this interpretation of code as a cultural text grows out of a very different analysis than the close examination of a lyric poem that seeks the answer to some riddle the reader believes to be hidden in the text (unless, as in chapter 7, that code was written to be poetry). The cultural text is not the work of art whose every aspect is admiringly explored but instead an object that is read with the archaeologist's attention to detail and meaning in context. That does not mean that this interpretive practice is somehow objective or that the practitioner is only the documentarian of the technology industry. Interpreting code requires the search for and creation of meaning tied to but not restricted to the intended purpose of the source code. Meaning is something on top of materiality, and its pursuit is deeply subjective, but that makes it no less valuable to the pursuit of understanding our world.

Meaning is not a straightforward process, and interpretation in the early twenty-first century has been radically altered by the advent of what Paul Ricoeur (2008; originally published in 1965) calls "the hermeneutics of suspicion" embodied in contemporary critical theory, specifically deconstruction and poststructuralism (356).[34] Although it is well beyond the scope of this book to detail the influence of these two enormous approaches to knowledge, it would be disingenuous for me to represent interpretation free from critical and creative interventions. This suspicion grows from the understanding that the arbitrary nature of language and symbolic representation and the difference (or *différance*) between the signifier and signified open the process of communication to a host of social and ideological influences.

Deconstruction and its network of critical theories, stretching from feminism to critical race studies to queer studies, to name just a few, open texts to understanding beyond their surface meaning, seeking out gaps and remainders. They read, if you will, between the lines. I am advocating for reading practices that explore exactly the very human levels of ambiguity and social contest of which computational machines are assumed to be but never have been free. In other words, with studies of technology and innovation, analyzing culture through code will include discussions of race and ethnicity, gender, sexuality, socioeconomic status, political representation, ideology, et cetera—all those messy human topics that complicate our social relations because the walls of a computer do not remove code from the world but encode the world and human biases.[35] These skeptical and suspicious reading practices in concert with more traditional ones combine to make these critical approaches to code more than a documentation of its place in the world and instead a means of discussing that world. I call these approaches *critical code studies*. Critical code studies names the applications of hermeneutics to the interpretation of the extrafunctional significance of computer source code.

This book offers an introduction to critical code studies through demonstrations of some of its approaches, methods, and gestures. Chapter 2 contains an updated version of that original argument, although the manifesto spirit remains intact as a document meant to incite scholarly inquiry and debate. Over a decade has passed since the publication of the manifesto, and many of its ideas have been pursued by scholars, whether under the name of CCS or not. Others of its ideas continue to be contentious. The subsequent chapters offer case studies, readings of specific passages of code in their cultural contexts, to demonstrate some initial reading methods and explore what and how code means.

Chapter Overviews

Reading code is not like reading other objects. It has its own unique characteristics, specifically unambiguous consequences on other software and hardware. Because of the specific functional nature of code, that it is a symbolic construction in an artificial language embedded in a processing system, any reading depends on a precise and accurate understanding of the exact operations of that code. That is not to say that reading poetry or history requires less rigor, but instead that at least one part of this process is unambiguous, even if its meaning is open for debate. Also, due to its complexity, code can be difficult for human readers, even to those familiar with programming, to parse. Moreover, often it is part of software that can be more than a million lines long, interoperating with systems of similar length. Not to mention the fact that code also can run differently on different hardware and in different operating environs.

For these reasons, this book is written around a series of case studies of readings of relatively small and self-contained passages of code. Scholars of print or even digital texts typically can rely on the reader's familiarity with their object of study and merely excerpt as needed. A scholar of history can depend on familiarity with the general events in history. However, because I do not have that luxury, in order to make these readings as clear as possible I have chosen to explain how the code works through summaries and detailed annotations before giving my interpretation. Also, rather than excerpting individual lines of code, I include a large portion of the code so that the reader can see some context and hopefully to encourage alternative readings of the same code. In at least one reading, my analysis of Kittler's code in chapter 6, I will remark on code beyond the passage excerpted at the start of the chapter. Not every code study requires this approach, but because code can be very difficult to follow and because this book is written for a range of readers, from experienced programmers to those with little experience programming, I want to make sure that everyone can access my readings to evaluate my interpretations and hopefully develop their own.

Thus, the first part of each case study chapter presents a code excerpt, explaining its context and its functioning in detail. The second part presents an exploration of the meaning of the code beyond and yet growing out of what that code does—the *extra-functional significance*, as I call it. Because of this book's wide target audience, to the extent possible, I will attempt to define terms, to explain programming structures, and to render the code legible for the uninitiated programmer. That said, this book cannot offer a comprehensive introduction to computer programming. Rather, it is my hope that the book will be intriguing enough to nonprogrammers to draw them deeper into the study of computers and programming languages, for programming is one of the key literacies of our age.[36]

Before embarking on those case studies, I offer in chapter 2 a revised version of the *Electronic Book Review* essay that launched this endeavor. Although I have reworked various parts of this essay, I have left large portions in their original state because this manifesto now plays a historical role in the emergence of this field. Therefore, some of the gestures and ideas in the case studies that follow go beyond what was envisioned in this initial call. Nonetheless, it contains both the spark and seed of what grew from it.

Chapter 3 offers an example of code written for a hacktavist art project, the constructs and comments of which inform, extend, and complicate the meaning of the larger work. This chapter examines code from the Transborder Immigrant Tool (TBT), a mobile phone application designed to help sustain travelers in the last mile of their journeys, migrating across a border between two nation-states by giving them directions to water and playing recorded poems full of survival advice. This code was written in Java (J2ME) by an artist collective with an eye toward those who would encounter the code as an art project. TBT also was brought to a secondary audience of politicians and political pundits, who reacted to their own imagined executions of the code. Following the collective's categorization of TBT as Mayan technology, I situate this code as a form of ritualized knowledge, prescriptions and provocations, written as procedures. The reader who traverses the code encounters an experiential passage through dramatic potential scenarios. Reading TBT demonstrates the ways code can contain world simulations that present ideologies and counterideologies and how named methods and variables can inform the broader reading of the code. This chapter offers an example of code embedded with metaphors that extend its meaning.

Chapter 4 turns from meaning embedded into the code to meaning that is misread during the public circulation of code. In this chapter, I explore climate modeling software, which when leaked caused the public uproar known as the *Climategate scandal*. In that whirlwind of online outcry, an overheated internet of climate change deniers and others thought they had found the smoking gun, the code that proved climate scientists were manipulating data to deceive the public. As it turns out, the smoking gun was more like the discarded cigarette butt of a programmer creating a momentary patch in a visualization. This code is notable not for how it functioned on the computer but for its role in the larger debate about climate change. It is a clear example of the way the debate over the meaning of code is already a realm of public discourse. This chapter will examine the way code becomes a tool of political discourse when recontextualized in public conversations and how code taken out of context can lead to misunderstandings that can influence public debate.

Chapter 5 examines the role English plays in higher-level programming languages and its colonizing effect on programmers subject to learning and using it. For this examination, the chapter presents FLOW-MATIC, a predecessor of COBOL, which presents an English-like syntax. A team led by Grace Hopper created FLOW-MATIC to offer business managers a programming language less intimidating than some of the contemporary alternatives. This chapter discusses the dream of natural-language programming and how natural language enables and muddles critical readings of code. On the one hand, FLOW-MATIC demonstrates the way legibility and writability in programming adhere to different criteria than natural spoken and written languages. On the other hand, FLOW-MATIC offers a clear sign of how the linguistic culture of what some have called *global English/es* were built into programming languages. This chapter shows how code readings rely on more than recognizably "readable" elements because the function of language is fundamentally different in programming environs. In looking back on the work of a pioneering woman, this chapter also reflects on the way the gender divide has expanded over the ensuing years in professional programming cultures. At the end of the chapter, I offer several recent projects in which artists have developed alternatives to English-based languages in order to contest the colonizing effects of global English embedded in code.

Chapter 6 situates making code as a theoretical practice: it brings together the approaches of code, software, and platform studies, along with media archaeology, in its consideration of the work of one of that field's most eminent theorists, Friedrich Kittler. This chapter explores the code of a computer graphics program called a *raytracer* written by Friedrich Kittler, the media theorist who provocatively wrote "There Is No Software" (1992).[37] Rather than a chapter-long gotcha, this case study examines the ways in which Kittler used the code to develop a mastery of C and assembly language, while tracing out the algorithms of the physical and mathematical formulas he would theorize. In this chapter, I argue that Kittler's work in programming languages illuminates, informs, and extends his theories.

Chapter 7 examines code written to generate poetry that its author also situates as poetry. This chapter examines Nick Montfort's Taroko Gorge and its progeny in the context of Montfort's desire to create code objects that inspire others to play with and revise them. Prior to making Taroko Gorge, Montfort had, with Andrew Stern, given a presentation in which he framed Joseph Weizenbaum's ELIZA as just such an inspirational program and a model for code-centered electronic literature. In this chapter, I analyze Taroko Gorge and its variants in light of ELIZA and its legacy to examine the ways these adapters reimagine and remix the poem. Although most code is not written to be poetry, Taroko Gorge invites its exploration as a literary object and thus offers an opportunity to read code as a literary text.

Finally, chapter 8 offers some thoughts about the future application of critical code studies, particularly in the academy, and outlines steps for commencing a critical code studies reading.

To those who look to critical code studies to make better programmers, I say that I hope these readings make programming better by enriching our understanding of what it means to communicate through code. This is not the first book of critical code studies (*10 PRINT* gets that distinction), nor will it be the last. Let the case studies that follow exemplify some initial methods of this approach to inspire deeper and richer explications of source code in the larger exploration of culture through digital artifacts.

2 Critical Code Studies: A Manifesto

Hello, World

"Hello, World" is one of the first programs that students customarily write in a programming language they are attempting to learn. The program, usually only a few lines of code, causes the computer to output a greeting, as if it were speaking. The LISP (list-processing language) version of such a program, for example, looks like this:

```
(DEFUN HELLO-WORLD ()
       (PRINT (LIST 'HELLO 'WORLD)))
```

DEFUN defines the function HELLO-WORLD (with no set arguments). As a result, the computer will speak its greeting to the world in our natural language. What could be a more appropriate language for this activity than LISP, a family of algebraic list-processing languages developed for artificial intelligence (McCarthy 1978)? In this simple program, the computer comes to life in natural language, speaking to us.

But of course, the computer does not understand what it says. Literally speaking, the computer does not even interpret that code. When the function is called, the computer will print (output) the list of the two *atoms* (as symbolic units are called in LISP) Hello and World. The single quotation marks tell the computer not to interpret the words *Hello* and *World* (much like the italics do in this sentence). With this distinction, language becomes divided between the operational code and data. The computer here merely shuffles the words as so many strings of data, unconcerned about the contents. It does not interpret but only uses those strings. However, those words in quotation marks are significant to us, the humans who read the code. *Hello* and *World* have significance, just as the function name *PRINT* has a significance that goes far beyond its instructions to the computer and gestures toward a material culture of ink and writing surfaces. More importantly, because the word *PRINT*, that special construct, could have been any set of characters in the programming language, the choice of the language designers in choosing *PRINT* reveals a central notion: code exists not for machines but for humans who need to communicate with the machine and with other humans.

Nonetheless, it is as if to this point in the study of computer programming, all of computer code lies before us with single quotation marks preceding its lines. While we examine programming architecture and admire modularity and efficiency, the study of computer code does not currently emphasize interpretation, the search for and production of meaning. That is the realm of the humanities, the liberal arts, not computer science. Even when aesthetics intervenes, it comes in the form of calls for stylistic clarity for more efficient modification and development, though the subjective notions of "beauty" and "elegance" in code offer an opportunity for future conversations across the disciplines. However, there is so much more to be interpreted. Beyond the aesthetics of the code, there are questions of discourse (connotations, implications, resonance), social and material history, and ideology, just to name a few of the realms of inquiry that interpretation attempts to answer. By contrast, this emphasis on functionality neglects the meaning that code bears for its human audiences. For code, especially mid- to high-level languages, exists not solely for computers, which could operate on machine language (essentially, representations of electronic signals) or electronic signals alone, but for programmers as well. Therefore, the computer may be one recipient of the code, but there is also the programmer, other programmers, managers, and at times even users who have access to its text. In fact, the audiences for code have expanded as judges and lawyers, politicians and pundits, and even poets bring code into their discourse.

Thus, to critique code merely for its functionality or aesthetics is to approach code with only a small portion of our analytic tools. In *Life on the Screen*, Sherry Turkle describes the *Julia effect* by which interactors ascribe intentionality and sentience to the computer that might display "Hello, World" (Turkle 1997, 101). This is to project humanity onto the computer, but is it possible that with regard to coding we do just the opposite and strip the code of its human significance, imagining that it is a sign system within which the extensive analyses of semiotic systems and signification, connotations that lead to denotations, do not apply? Is "Hello, World," a rite of passage into many computer languages, the beginning of a literacy constrained by restricted interpretation? What would happen if we began to interpret the meaning of the code?

Consider again the example of the LISP "Hello, World." I have already discussed the relationship of the programming language to the code, but that is just the beginning.

As it turns out, programmers learning to program in LISP tend to begin with code to produce the Fibonacci sequence rather than Hello, World.[1] Printing or displaying "Hello, World" does not always directly provide an introduction to the affordances of a language. Consider Ralph Westfall's (2001) alternative "Hello, World" model that stresses the strict typing and object-oriented features of Java, an approach that in turn draws other alternatives. In fact, the debate over the use of "Hello, World" as an introductory exercise offers a glimpse into the ways that the how and the why of even simple programs can become the object of discourse and analysis in the social life of source code.[2]

As a new media scholar trained in literary theory, I would like to propose that we no longer speak of the code as a text in metaphorical terms, but that we begin to analyze and explicate code as a text, as a sign system with its own rhetoric, as semiotic communication that possesses significance in excess of its functional utility. Computer scientists can theorize on the most useful approaches to code, whereas humanities scholars can help by conjecturing on the meaning of code to all those who encounter it—both directly by reading it and indirectly by encountering the effects of the programs it creates. In effect, I am proposing that we can read and explicate code the way we might explicate a work of literature or other texts in a new field of inquiry that I call *critical code studies* (CCS).

Critical code studies is an approach to code studies that applies critical hermeneutics to the interpretation of computer code, program architecture, and documentation within a sociohistorical context. CCS holds that the lines of code of a program are not value-neutral and can be analyzed using the theoretical approaches applied to other semiotic systems, in addition to particular interpretive methods developed specifically for the discussions of programs. Critical code studies follows the work of other critical studies, such as critical legal studies (Fitzpatrick and Hunt 1987; Tushnet 1991) and critical race studies (Delgado and Stefancic 2001; West 1995), in that it applies critical theory to a functional document (legal document or computer program) to explicate meaning in excess of its functionality and claims that this meaning warrants analysis on more than an aesthetic of efficiency. Meaning grows out of the functioning of the code but is not limited to the literal processes the code enacts. Through CCS, practitioners may critique the larger human and computer systems, from the level of the computer to the level of the society in which these code objects circulate and exert influence.

Rather than creating a language separate from the work of programmers, critical code studies will build on preexisting terminology and analysis used within the programming community. Much of the current examination of code seems to revolve around efficiency of code, reusability, and modularity. This new critical approach will stress meaning, implication, and connotation, though not in terms of a self-contained system of meaning but with respect to the broader social contexts. Whereas a computer scientist might argue for or against various pragmatic approaches, scholars of CCS will interrogate the contexts and implications of a programmer's choices. Whereas a computer scientist or programmer will focus primarily on how code functions or how it makes use of limited resources, critical code studies analyzes the extrafunctional significance of the code. *Extra* here means not *outside of* or *in addition to* but instead *growing out of*. The meaning of code is ambiguous because it is social, even while it is unambiguous because it is technological. The programmers' expertise derives not solely from scientific knowledge but also from experience in the culture of programming.

Although some in the area of CCS may have an in-depth knowledge of programming, many analyses will benefit from the collaboration of critical theorists and programmers. Just as developing new media technologies requires the collaboration of artists and programmers, the scholarship will require the artful combination of knowledge of programming languages and programming methods and knowledge of interpretive theories and approaches. These analytic projects will require programmers to help open up the contents and workings of programs, acting as theorists along with other scholars as they reflect on the relationships of the code itself, the coding architecture, the functioning of the code, and specific programming choices, or expressions, with that which the code acts upon, outputs, processes, and represents.

Like literary analysis, CCS is an interpretive process rather than an instrumentally proscriptive or solely descriptive process. Other branches (lines of flight) of code studies may be concerned with pragmatics, but CCS focuses on meaning, read from the often collaborative and certainly iterative performance that is coding. Specific coding ideologies, such as open-source programming, also will be important, though CCS holds that language, as Gunther Kress and Robert Hodge (1979) have asserted, is already ideology. If "software is ideology," as Wendy Hui Kyong Chun (1999, 207) has announced, then we might also say computer code is also ideology, but an ideology that is doubly hidden by our illiteracy and by the very screens on which its output delights and distracts (ibid., 207). Whereas open source embodies a particular ideology that makes code accessible for analysis, CCS will analyze more than open-source programs, though access may be more limited. CCS will look broadly at choices in paradigms (such as object-oriented approaches) and closely at specific lines of code, their constraints, and their effects. Only through close attention to the specific details of the code will CCS be able to articulate what we might call the *connotation* of the code.

Critical code studies draws upon the work of other scholars who have begun to interpret code, particularly Matthew Fuller's *Software Studies: A Lexicon* (2008). Fuller's collection, discussed in more detail ahead, offers a lexicon for the interpretation of software and its role in society. If *Software Studies* offers "a handbook of supplements to some of the key standard objects of computer science, programming and software culture" (2), critical code studies names a set of approaches, or an interpretive attitude, to code. Indeed, Fuller's sense of software relates well to perspectives of CCS as he argues that "software can be seen as an object of study and an area of practice for kinds of thinking and areas of work that have not historically 'owned' software, or indeed often had much of use to say about it" (2). *Software Studies* opens the door for a formalized practice of (and quite a few tools for engaging in) critical code studies.

The mention of literature can be misleading here: I do not want to limit critical code studies to the study of code written as literature (as in Perl poetry), although this interpretation is certainly related. The focus of CCS is not on making code that has aesthetic value and additional meaning but on a view of code as already having meaning beyond its functionality because it is a form of symbolic expression and interaction. Nonetheless, analyses of Perl poetry, and codework in general, perform CCS and model methods for interpreting specific lines of code that can be applied to other kinds of source code.

I also do not want to confuse CCS with literate programming, as outlined by Donald Knuth, author of *The Art of Computer Programming* (1973). In "Literate Programming" (1984), Knuth wrote, "Instead of imagining that our main task is to instruct a computer what to do, let us concentrate rather on explaining to human beings what we want a computer to do." Knuth continues, "The practitioner of literate programming can be regarded as an essayist, whose main concern is with exposition and excellence of style" (97). By identifying code as a means of communicating not just with machines but also with other humans, Knuth contextualizes code as a mode of discourse, emphasizing the roles of clarity and style in its legibility, in its ability to communicate its purpose. However, the goal of critical code studies is not to aid programmers to write more readable code, though that may be an indirect effect, but instead to develop rich methods of reading that code. Drawing upon Knuth's work, we can add style and clarity to the many aspects of code we analyze, but we must not end there.

Fundamental to CCS is the assumption that code is a social, semiotic system employing grammar and rhetoric. As Rita Raley (2006) argues, "Code may in a general sense be opaque and legible only to specialists, much like a cave painting's sign system, but it has been inscribed, programmed, written. It is conditioned and concretely historical." Adrian MacKenzie (2003, 19) writes, "Code is written and run within situated practices, with reference to particular domains, and within particular orderings and disorderings of collective life. Its forms and abstractions are attached to lives." It is in the way this sign system circulates within actor-networks of computers and machines that it develops connotations worthy of interpretation.

In his entry in *Software Studies*, "Code (or, How You Can Write Something Differently)," Friedrich Kittler (2008) warns against diluting, and thereby mystifying and universalizing, the term *code*. (Kittler's own code is the subject of chapter 6.) Kittler warns, "Codes—by name and by matter—are what determine us today, and what we must articulate if only to avoid disappearing below them completely. ... The notion of code is as over-used as it is questionable" (40–45). Resistant to loose, associative interpretation, Kittler traces the derivation of the word back to *codex* and farther to *codicilla*, "the small tablets of stripped wood coated with wax in which letters could be inscribed." In its later form, *codex*, the word signifies "simply the name of the bound book of law" (41). Code thus becomes the means and medium of long-distance control. Kittler follows the term from classical empires to nation-states to the moment when it becomes synonymous with *cipher* (42).

But interpreting code critically is not deciphering. Indeed, the very notion of "interpretation" can present an obstacle on the bridge between computer science and the humanities. A more mathematical mind might prefer the use of isomorphisms to this inexact relationship. In Douglas Hofstadter's *Gödel, Escher, Bach: An Eternal Braid* (1979), he presents "interpretation" as meaningful isomorphisms, relationships drawn between one system and another. By Hofstadter's formulation, an isomorphism, or interpretation, is meaningful only when the truths in one system produce truths in another system. To create an isomorphism, the two systems have to be completely interchangeable, such that each sign in one system can be equated to a sign in another system, essentially deciphering or decoding (51). This form of interpretation looks much more like transliterating or even compiling from a high-level language to a low-level one than it does interpretation in the humanities sense. By contrast, interpretation in a humanities context is less about mapping a one-to-one correspondence and more about identifying connections and resonances between signs and referents, as well as identifying disconnections and slippages along with the forces that shape or distort meaning.

For example, PRINT from our "Hello, World" program is a token that causes that data to display on the screen. As we discuss in *10 PRINT*, the command PRINT has its origins as a command to put ink on paper. An isomorphism can be made between the command PRINT as a command to display text on the screen and the teletype putting a word on paper, or between PRINT and a similar token in another programming language, such as WriteLine in C#. However, the command PRINT can be interpreted in many ways that are more associative. *Print* evokes a system of inscription, the history of print, the way the computer screen remediates text printed on paper.[3] Although the isomorphism offers a parallel, interpretation can indicate more extensive realms of meaning.

Interpretation is not limited to compiling or porting. Interpretation in the humanities sense is more akin to porting a program from one language to another, where a programmer has to make conscious choices about how to represent one system in another and the porting requires a subjective assessment of what is the essence of the program. Yet interpretation in the humanities goes beyond compiling and porting because it asks, "If x represents y, what is being communicated about both systems?" It asks, "How does one realm of meaning inform or affect another?" In other words, interpretation in the humanities sense is neither deciphering nor translating, but instead uses those techniques (and other hermeneutics) to get at meaning beyond the isomorphic systems. Interpretation then is not merely decoding but the production of another kind of knowledge: insight. Those insights may appear quite arbitrary when someone is approaching the code with a systematic point of view, when one is attending the logic of the systems rather than potentially challenging it.

Kittler offers this more robust model of interpretation as he explores the origins and context of computer code. In this historical narrative, codes prove to be central to subjugation as the military motto changes from "Command, Control, Communication, Intelligence" to "Command, Control, Communication, Computers" (C^4). He writes, "Today, technology puts the code into practice of realities, that is to say: encodes the world" (2008, 45). Central to control is the ability to make "code" a ubiquitous, universal operator. Moreover, he adds, "But perhaps code means nothing more than codex did at one time: the law of precisely that empire which holds us in subjection and forbids us even to articulate this sentence. At all events, the major research institutions which stand to profit most from such announcements proclaim with triumphant certainty that there is nothing in the universe, from the virus to the Big Bang, which is not code" (45).

Here, the military-industrial complex employs the codes for control, and by making "code" the essence of all life, a few elite, literate researchers establish themselves as the only mediators. To regain command and control of the term, Kittler sets out to restrain it within a technical definition. He announces, "Only alphabets in the literal sense of modern mathematics should be known as codes, namely one-to-one, finite sequences of symbols, kept as short as possible but gifted, thanks to a grammar, with the incredible ability to infinitely reproduce themselves" (2008, 45). Kittler is circumscribing the notion of code here, but to what end? Critical code studies may observe some of Kittler's suggested restraint, keeping code from becoming a controlling, transcendental imaginary. However, these one-to-one unambiguous systems develop ambiguous meanings the moment they enter the social sphere—in other words, the moment they are uttered or even the moment they are thought, come into existence in the context of human consciousness, in meaning-making machines. In examining code in context, CCS will look toward and beyond characters to interpret gestures, performances, and possibilities.

What Can Be Interpreted?

Everything. The code, the documentation, the comments, the structures, the compiled versions—all will be open to interpretation. Greater understanding of (and access to) these elements will help critics build complex readings. In his essay "The Code is Not the Text (Unless It Is the Text)," John Cayley (2002) argues that much of the code that was being analyzed in works of electronic art was not code per say, but gestures toward code. At the time, Cayley argued that code was not really the text unless it was executable code.[4] In "A Box, Darkly," Michael Mateas and Nick Montfort (2005) counter Cayley's claim of the necessity for executability by acknowledging that code can be written for programs that will never be executed. Within CCS, if it is part of the program or a paratext (understood broadly), it contributes to meaning. In the case of codework, if the artifact is code-like, it can shape how we read code. I would also include interpretations of markup languages and scripts as extensions of code. Within the code, critics will examine the actual symbols but also, more broadly, procedures, structures, and gestures. There will be paradigmatic choices made in the construction of the program, methods chosen over others, and connotations.

In addition to symbols and characters in the program files themselves, these paratextual features also will be important for informed readers. The history of the program, the author, the programming language, the genre, the funding source for the research and development (be it military, industrial, entertainment, or other), all shape meaning, although any one reading might emphasize just a few of these aspects. The goal need not be code analysis for code's sake, but analyzing code to better understand programs and the networks of other programs and humans they interact with, organize, represent, manipulate, transform, and otherwise engage. Reading code functions as an entry point to reading culture.

There are multiple audiences for code. At first glance, the only audience appears to be the machine itself, but, as mentioned, humans are the ones who require symbolic representation. First, assuming it is created by a human and not other software, the programmer reads the code even while compositing it. Second, other programmers may read the code. Third, nonprogrammers, such as project managers or audiences of interdisciplinary conferences, may read the code. The code also may end up in the hands of hackers. Even the machine on which the computer runs may prove to be multiple audiences, as parts of the code are passed to other processes and other parts of the machine. Furthermore, there already are many sites of conversation about code. Jeremy Douglass (2011) notes several of these in his call to find code discussions "in the wild," noting discussions in business meetings, in the courts, and even in the mainstream news.

To return to the example that started this chapter, we might note that the LISP "Hello, World" program did not appear out of nowhere. It was written by Mark Singletary, a programming architect, variously employed by NASA and software firms. His apparent specialty is usability, or the development of easily read human-computer interfaces, the facilitation of interaction between human and machine realms. The relationship between code and coder, the program that makes computers speak to a "world" and the programmer who works (for a government-funded, space-exploration, C^4 institution) to make computers speak more clearly, creates meaning. Moreover, Singletary submitted this "beginner" code to the Association for Computing Machinery (ACM) "Hello World" Project (Singletary 2005), a project that in its very being suggests additional audiences for practice code. What does it mean for ACM to collect samples of "first exposure to a new language" (Singletary 2005)? What does it mean when an exercise, a rite of passage, is anthologized?

Suddenly this practice code has a showcase.[5] Thus, the "world" the program greets has expanded to include other programmers at computers with internet access (qualifiers that constrain the world to an absurdly tiny portion of the Earth's population). This particular code joins a conversation of comparative study rather than merely demonstrating incipient ability in a language. Moreover, it is hardly the only way to write a "Hello, World" program in LISP. So, like all semiotic utterances, it offers a glimpse into what Saussure calls the paradigm of possible formulations (Saussure and Riedlinger 1983, 121–124). Certainly, this program is not just a piece of code processed by the computer. It is an artifact circulating in a broader exchange. Although I will not offer definitive readings of the material, sociohistorical factors of this code object, risking the unnecessary circumscription of CCS at its outset, I merely wish to demonstrate how all these contextualizing aspects potentially affect the way "Hello, World" means.

Key to critical code studies will be programming literacy. Just as a student of literature might learn a foreign language or sign language or dance, a student of CCS only will be able to access code by learning (and preferably mastering) the language.[6] Rita Raley (2002) has speculated about the possibility of computer languages counting for language requirements in undergraduate and graduate programs in the humanities. Alternatively, an interpreter could collaborate with someone who is literate in the language, building networks of literacy, coalitions of meaning-building. We might consider such fluency *cyborg literacy*. Computer scientists already write translations through their ports of programs. Perhaps computer scientists one day even will write exegetical guides. In textbooks on programming, no doubt they do.

Although it may seem that a literary critic can only interpret the natural language elements, critical code studies cannot narrow its scope to only the natural language or arbitrary features of the code. For example, a program that calculates automobile insurance rates might have a variable called *victim*. However, variable and method names are relatively easy targets for interpretation and themselves fall victim to the accusation that they are arbitrary elements of the code, comparatively meaningless to the functioning of the machine. *Victim* could just as easily be *f2s989*. On the one hand, the relationship between most signifiers and signifieds is, in semiotic terms, arbitrary, and yet is still quite meaningful. On the other hand, the names of built-in methods, the syntax and logic of a computer language, seem to have a more notable operational significance to the computer system. Therefore, a critical code studies that only speaks of variable names and never of language tokens and fundamentals would be relatively shallow. Former professional programmer and scholar of technoculture Evan Buswell (ebuswell, comment on Feinstein et al. 2011) has made this point eloquently. Imagining the consequences of such an approach, Buswell sees a future in which a group of programmers worry about making things work, while the code critics discuss variable and method names in some room off to the side.

Critical code studies is not limited to any one type of programming schema, whether imperative, object-oriented, functional, or other. Nor should it be limited to programming languages that use textual symbols. CCS is built on semiotic analysis, so its methods can be applied to any representational system, be it text-based, visual, or even gestural. In fact, for CCS to be fully robust, its methods also should be applicable to direct programming through hardware—for example, in the building of microcircuits. Although some may argue that analysis may seem to encroach upon platform studies, policing those boundaries will only obscure the complex interrelations between software and hardware. In other words, CCS should not stop its analysis merely when it crosses out of some limited jurisdiction but must instead collaborate with the interrelated fields of study that are making rich understandings of contemporary technoculture possible.

Computer code is not some undiscovered continent. Nor is it some magical sign system. It is a realm of creativity and production that has been around for more than half a century. It would be a terrible mistake to enter discussions about code by offering to interpret it for the very programmers who have been slogging away in it for so long. To do so would be to commit the offense of techno-Orientalism. Numerous definitions have been offered for such an act, but they all trace back to Eduard Said's term for the way scholars in the West create a sense of the inscrutable East, Asian culture and language, and then proceed to interpret it devoid of an understanding of the contexts or even of those who have already established a conversation of interpretation. It is the epitome of the hubris of cultural imperialism to offer to explain someone else's culture to them. Critical code studies must therefore work in collaboration and in conversation with those who have already laid the groundwork for this analytical endeavor.

The Code as Means, Not Ends

At this point, someone might ask, Shouldn't we be interpreting machine language? Perhaps. But that would not bring us closer to the truth of the code. That is not what we're after. Such interpretations might find models in critiques of numerals, such as Brian Rotman's *Signifying Nothing* (1993), which suggests that much can be made of nothingness. Equations have lives of their own, as texts such as David Bodanis's $E = mc^2$ (2000) demonstrate. Perhaps one of the most powerful texts that illustrates the move between modes of representation and systems of expression is Hofstadter's *Gödel, Escher, Bach* (1979), which draws correspondences between natural languages, math, programming, music, and drawing. Where the line between mathematics and CCS is, I do not wish to declare. I would merely suggest that there are qualities of computer languages that give a program more footholds for interpretation.

However, it is important not to think that reading assembly or machine language or binary code is reading a truer code. Wendy Chun has expressed concerns about the tendency to treat source code as something essential, as the heart of the program, even conflating it with the executable code that the source code is compiled into. Such a search risks engaging in what she calls a kind of "sourcery" (Chun 2011). The question is not whether it is better to read a higher- or lower-level language, but what someone wishes to explore. For example, Patrick LeMieux (2015) has read the assembly language of Cory Arcangel's *Super Mario Clouds* to study the mechanisms of that work. To be sure, machine language code offers access to a level that is more directly tied to hardware. However, just as Chun's critique helps remind us that source code is an intermediate representation of machinic commands, her intervention also suggests that no level of the code need be privileged. I would add that meaning is produced when the code is interpreted by human readers. Therefore, though no one level of the code is more meaningful than any other, every level of the code and hardware is a potential source of meaning.

Although critics do not need to dive down to some deeper level of code for more meaning, they must also be careful not to read the code as sufficient unto itself. Matthew Kirschenbaum (2011) has raised concerns on several occasions about the hazards of reading code separated from its context. He warns that to stop at the code is to lose sight of the many other systems with which code interacts and on which it operates. Instead, he argues a critic should explore the way the code interacts with other systems and hardware. High-level code is portable across multiple platforms, but it is no less situated. Although those situations may be too numerous to count, the software and hardware circumstances of the code are crucial to its interpretation.

With both these cautions in mind, we who are setting out to explore and develop critical code studies have developed a few practices. The first practice is the acknowledgement that code is an entry point to an investigation rather than an end in itself. Perhaps the clearest example of that method was the eponymous study of a one-line basic program: `10 PRINT CHR$ (205.5 + RND (1)); : GOTO 10` (Montfort et al. 2013). The ten-authored exploration used this simple yet influential program as the starting point for a discussion of the BASIC programming language, the Commodore 64 computer, procedural art, and even mazes. Although each token of the program (`10`, `PRINT`, `CHR$`, etc.) was analyzed, so too were concepts of randomness and regularity, hardware and specifications, and design principles that made the program possible. Material aspects were analyzed, such as the configuration of the Commodore 64's monitor, but so too were social aspects, such as the zeitgeist of "home computing." Rather than a beach ball bouncing in undirected free association, the program acted as the hub of a spoked wheel, with lines of inquiry running outward from yet always linked back to it. And apropos of such a recursive program, the process led back to its center, to that one line and its seemingly unending potential energy. Thus, even the analysis of a program one line long could not be discussed in isolation.

Another development from this intervention has been the recognition of the need for tools to discuss code without having to strip it from its setting. Offering a solution to the challenges of contextualizing code, Kirschenbaum proposed reading code within its version control setting. We have begun experimenting with such a possibility in projects built on ANVC Scalar and a specific adaptation of it called ACLS Workbench.[7] In both contexts, the Scalar software platform allows users to import code as text from source code repositories, maintaining its connection to its fuller context. For example, in my reading of the Transborder Immigrant Tool (chapter 2), I have used Scalar to import specific files from the repository of the code so that the files are still connected to their context in the much larger piece of software. Using this technique of importing situated files, critics can comment on code in situ rather than excerpting it and removing it from its development environment. This approach still involves an abstraction because the code is being read through a browser separated from the platform (or even an emulator of that platform) on which it is intended to run. Nonetheless, these examples mark merely the early efforts in the development of platforms for the scholarly analysis of code. The lesson is clear: every piece of source code is only ever partial.

Code Is Not Poetry (or at Least, Most of It Isn't)

Loss Pequeño Glazier's (2006) article in *Leonardo Electronic Almanac*, "Code as Language," argues that "if language is defined as written symbols organized into combinations and patterns to express and communicate thoughts and feelings—language that executes—then coding is language." Glazier is establishing code as a creative, even literary, act, a kind of inscription or "thinking through thought." In his essay, Glazier offers additional objects for CCS analysis, including the amount of processor speed a particular operation requires. His example points to the double nature of code as a record and a piece of a real-time process. More than utilitarian commands, code presents signs of "humor, innovation, irony, double meanings, and a concentration on the play of language. It is the making of marks with a sense of marksmanship." Again, key to CCS is an understanding that the challenges of programming and encoding are not finding one correct command out of a codex of commands, but of choosing (and at times creating) a particular combination of lines to build a structure that resonates and operates aesthetically, functionally, and even conceptually with the other discourse of encoded objects, as well as mathematical and natural language discourse.

If code is language, does that make programs poetry? In "The Aesthetics of Generative Code," Geoff Cox, Alex McLean, and Adrian Ward (2000) compare code to poetry as they develop some techniques for interpreting it. In their words, "Evidently, code works like poetry in that it plays with structures of language itself, as well as our corresponding perceptions." Like Cayley and others, they argue that code's meaning is bound up with its execution. However, their reading is not limited to the performance of the code, as they also "stress more purposeful arrangements of code by the programmer." For example, they note that even the visual presentation of code is designed for human readers because "the same code could be expressed in any shape or arrangement and would run the same output." Nonetheless, in an exemplary move of CCS, they examine the play of language from a Perl poem in which the author uses "=" ("a string comparison operator") instead of "eq" ("a numeric one"). Here through an act of close reading, they articulate the significance of a paradigmatic choice to the larger meaning of the piece. To further argue that code is a linguistic form for human audiences, they present their paper as a "conditional statement" of code (if, then), wherein an "if" is followed by their abstract as the {condition} and the essay body is marked as the {statement}. Although they make a strong case for a human poetics in the construction of code, to suggest that all code adheres to an aesthetics or works toward readability is to overstate the case. Nonetheless, code communicats through symbols and whitespace.

Excluding the few art objects written as poetry, most code is worlds away from literature, film, and visual art and more similar to legal code, inasmuch as the text is functional and primarily designed to do rather than to be, to perform rather than reflect. Unlike legal code, however, computer code typically is presumed to be unseen by human eyes. Nonetheless, except in cases in which the computer generates code that its programmers and users never see, computer code is often seen by other programmers who must rework it. Further, even if the code is only seen by its programmer, like a diary locked away or letters never sent, it is still a semiotic expression. (Of course, computer-generated code presents the author as cyborg, with the human author at least one step removed from the produced code. Surely, humans will need to enlist machines as collaborators for the interpretation of such code.) More importantly, and I hope this is not too vague, there are implications in the way code tries to perform a function that bear the imprint of epistemologies, cultural assumptions about gender, race, and sexuality; economic philosophies; and political paradigms. This list, however, does not begin to get at the more computer-specific issues.

Authorship is a much more complex issue in interpreting code than in traditional writing. Code frequently has multiple authors, mostly uncited, and large portions of code are adapted from previous code or code found online. Moreover, some of it is little more than boilerplate, at times autogenerated by an IDE. To use a common algorithm could be thought of as using a screw. Mechanics do not cite the inventor of the screw every time they use one, although programmers at times attribute code to particular sources. Nonetheless, literary analysis has found other means of dealing with questions of authorship, including the Foucauldian notions that the authors themselves are assemblages of influences. Simply put, it is not necessary to determine the author of a particular line to interpret the larger work of code. Meaning does not require

[handwritten margin note: Code as a semiotic expression]

fingerprints. That said, if the writers publish their commentary, as in Terry Winograd's SHRDLU, to name just one example, that commentary becomes a paratext that shapes the meaning of the code.

Code Is More than a Static Text

One of the problems with analyzing code is that its written expression represents only its static form before it has been processed. Code is at once what it is and what it does. That is not necessarily the same as saying that code is performative language in Austin's sense, but rather to say that the static code represents a form of its existence before it is processed by the machine, whether it is compiled or not. As Wendy Chun (2011) has pointed out, the source code is not the same as the executable file. That said, the study of code requires not only reading the symbols but understanding that those symbols cause changes in state to software and hardware over a duration of time in dynamic engagement with other systems, including humans.

Evan Buswell has been developing tools for annotating the state of a software system when it occurs, which gives the critic/reader/operator the ability to comment on the code in action, which we can also call the *software*. From a software studies point of view, such tools allow the reader the chance to identify states of the software in action. However, I consider this a principal aspect to reading the code because this state has been caused by the interaction of the encoded symbols with the system. Such readings of code in action are necessary due to the complexity of the interaction between the running code and the system (or other systems)—a complexity that often leads to states that cannot easily be predicted.

Consider, by contrast, film. The individual frames of a film (on celluloid) interact with any given projector in predictable ways. Certainly there are variations in projectors (bulb brightness, motor speed due to wear); however, those variations are comparatively minimal. The action of the machine on the medium, shining a light through the celluloid, does not vary. Except when seeded by some unpredictable outside element, code also produces a predictable set of effects when processed. Nevertheless, the sheer complexity of the system makes the effects of code difficult to predict—one reason debugging is such a key part of programming. The operation of the machine upon the medium is not a straightforward activity, like the projection of film, but instead a set of interoperating processes enacted through and upon hardware. For this reason, analyzing code includes interpretation in the Saussurian sense of the signs and signifiers, but also analysis of this constantly shifting understanding of state.

For perhaps a nearer analogy to code and executed software, consider blueprints. Although they may spell out the ingredients, a blueprint does not specify how the finished product will perform. True, any given platform will process the code in discrete and repeatable ways. However, the performance of the constructed object can be unpredictable, especially when human factors, such as users and operators, or real-world forces, such as heat or wind, are introduced. Because of that consistency and because that consistency is the necessary condition for software production and distribution, making and reading code relies on an ability to predict, produce, and test the states of the systems over the duration of the implementation (compiling, processing, and execution). Because of the complexity of these systems, full understanding of the code requires an understanding of the code in action.

// Cautionary Comments

One of my early experiences with CCS may serve as a cautionary tale. When I proposed an incipient version of CCS to a group of programmers, one of them asked if I could prove CCS by applying these methodologies to a program with low natural language content, even in terms of input and output. The reviewer suggested Quicksort, an algorithm used for quickly ordering groups of numbers through a divide and conquer approach. In my early attempts at what Wardrip-Fruin would equate to interpreting a stop sign, I suggested Quicksort as a metaphor for social organization in communities, drawing out an analogy for the way a neighborhood street or even highway may serve to divide and conquer a demographic, for example through redlining. However, though my analysis said something about neighborhood hierarchies, it offered little insight on Quicksort itself, nor did it draw from Quicksort a lesson about the society from which it came. Here Hofstadter's appeal to isomorphic analogies returns. My main error was analyzing Quicksort aside from its historical, material, and social context. For an algorithm such as Quicksort, the code meets the social realm at the site of its implementation and in the context of the application in which it is used. I was not engaging the cultural origins of Quicksort within the history of computation or even a particular incarnation of Quicksort in a language (I was using pseudocode). Without discussing the human context of the Quicksort code in terms of authorship, use, development, circulation, or operations, I was left with little more than an abstract process.

Interpretation requires reading an object in its (post)human context through a particular critical lens. This context involves human machines operating in actor-networks.[8] Thus, a simple looping subroutine, say, might remind one of the eternal return of the repressed, but unless that metaphor has significance with respect to the particular, material context of the script itself, the interpretation will seem more of an imposition, a projection. That does not decrease its value but does signal less engagement with the production of code and its significance. However, if one found a recursive loop in a program designed to psychoanalyze its users, perhaps a connection could be drawn between recursion and the psychoanalytic view of the return of the repressed. Thus, though these computer programs are quite meaningful, like any cultural text, they yield meaning to the extent to which we interrogate their material and socio-historical context, both immediate and more broad, and read their signs and systems against this backdrop.

Throughout this proposal, I have tried to highlight the moments in other critical writings when they have read specific coding elements because this is the kind of interpretation that is most lacking in analyses of codework and code. Cultural critics often speak abstractly of coding practices or the processes of code without getting to the code itself. My emphasis, however, should not understate the need for interpreting these structures with an eye toward fundamental human concerns, concerning race, ethnicity, gender, and sexuality; concerning the military-industrial-entertainment-academic complexes; concerning surveillance and control over electronic systems—to name but a few. Such readings will prove critical in the analysis of systems that do everything from facial recognition to tactical simulation of political systems to modeling human reasoning about peoples and places.

Since I first proposed this idea, some scholars have balked at the idea of reading code. There is simply too much code, they say. I cannot access the code of the object I want to study, they say. To the former complaint, I point back toward critical legal studies, which does not attempt to analyze every word of legal code but focuses its energies on particular moments and texts. To the latter, I point to literary history, in which so many texts have been lost to history, yet scholars continue to read and interpret what we have. Not everyone who studies digital objects will study the code, but to those who can, much meaningful communication and engagement awaits you.

The Moment Is Critical

Many developments have transpired to make this the moment for critical code studies. First, higher-level programming languages are becoming readable to a wider population. The interactive fiction language Inform 7 is just one example.[9] Second, a growing number of critical theorists (and artists) are becoming literate in programming languages. Third, the programming community is beginning to consider aesthetics in a new way, which will no doubt lead to new styles of programming artistry. Fourth, colleges and universities are continuing to develop more programs in the humanistic analysis of science and scientific culture. Not least, works of code in art, art in code, codeworks, and electronic literature are proliferating, offering more moments of connection between represented signs and programmatic signs, as in the objects Cayley described earlier in *ebr*. Code increasingly shapes, transforms, and limits our lives, our relationships, our art, our cultures, and our civic institutions. It is time to take code out from behind quotation marks, to move beyond execution to comment, to document, and to interpret. Let us make the code the text.

3   The Transborder Immigrant Tool

File: TBMIDlet.java

Programming Language: Java (J2ME)

Developed: 2007–2010

Principal Authors: Brett Stalbaum and Jason Najarro, as part of Electronic Disturbance Theater (EDT) 2.0

Platform: Motorola i455 ($40 at time of the project)

Libraries Used: edu.ucsd.calit2.TransBorderTool.international, javax.microedition.midlet, javax. microedition.lcdui, javax.microedition.location, java.io, java.util.*, javax.microedition. media.*, net.walkingtools.javame.util.AudioArrayPlayer

Source File: SourceForge (2010): https://sourceforge.net/p/walkingtoolsgpx/code/HEAD/tree/ tbtool/src/edu/ucsd/calit2/TransBorderTool/

Interoperating Files: DowsingCompass, DowsingCompassListener, TBCoordinates, TBGpxParser

Code

```
1. /* WalkingtoolsGpx: XML, APIs, and Apps for Walking Artists
2. Copyright (C) 2007-2012 Walkingtoools project/B.A.N.G Lab UCSD
3.
4. This program is free software: you can redistribute it and/or
modify
5. it under the terms of the GNU Affero General Public License as
6. published by the Free Software Foundation, either version 3 of
the
7. License, or (at your option) any later version.
8.
9. This program is distributed in the hope that it will be useful,
10. but WITHOUT ANY WARRANTY; without even the implied warranty of
11. MERCHANTABILITY or FITNESS FOR A PARTICULAR PURPOSE. See the
```

```
12. GNU Affero General Public License for more details.
13.
14. You should have received a copy of the GNU Affero General
Public License
15. along with this program. If not, see <http://www.gnu.org/
licenses/>.
16. */
17.
18.
19. // note: good idea to extend the dowsing interface to also
include (or redirect users)
20. // to sites that are within 500 meters.
21.
22. package edu.ucsd.calit2.TransBorderTool;
23.
24. import edu.ucsd.calit2.TransBorderTool.international.*;
25. import javax.microedition.midlet.*;
26. import javax.microedition.lcdui.*;
27. import javax.microedition.location.*;
28. import java.io.*;
29. import java.util.*;
30. import javax.microedition.media.*;
31. import net.walkingtools.javame.util.AudioArrayPlayer;
32.
33. /**
34. * @author Brett Stalbaum and Jason Najarro
35. * @version 0.5.5
36. */
37. public class TBMIDlet extends MIDlet implements
DowsingCompassListener, CommandListener {
38.
39. private Display display = null;
40. // current displayable will normally be the tbDowsingCompass,
but if expired, an alert.
41. private DowsingCompass tbDowsingCompass = null;
42. private Vector nearbyWPList = null;
43. private static final int SEARCH_DISTANCE = 10000; // 10K
```

```
44. private List targetList = null;
45. private Alert arrivedAlert = null;
46. private Alert waypointAheadAlert = null;
47. private Alert expired = null;
48. private boolean isExpired = false;
49. private Alert expirationWarning = null;
50. private boolean expireWarning = false;
51. private Alert startUpDisplay = null;
52. private boolean startUpAlert = false;
53. private Alert noNearbyWaypoints = null;
54. private Alert minimalistInfoAlert = null;
55. private Command exit = null;
56. private Command ignore = null;
57. private Command cancel = null;
58. private Command listNearbyWPs = null;
59. private Command setTargetManual = null;
60. private Command setTargetAuto = null;
61. private AudioTimer audioTimer = null;
62. // private String URL = "http://internetjunkee.com/transborder/
GPScourseFinal.gpx";
63. private LocationProvider lp = null;
64. private TBCoordinates aheadCoords = null;
65. // using only one audio player for two kinds of sound. The
first is the
66. // poems, the second is the Audio UI elements
67. private static final String[] audioStrings = {
68. "1-GAIN_04-02.wav", "2-GAIN_02-03.wav", "2-GAIN_03-01.wav",
69. "3-GAIN_01.wav", "3-GAIN_02-02.wav", "5-GAIN_02-07.wav",// 6
poems
70. "arriving.wav", "expiration.wav", "expired.wav", "found.wav",
// AudioUI
71. "lowgps.wav", "move.wav", "nosites.wav", "pointing.wav", //
AudioUI
72. "read.wav", "searching.wav", "startup.wav", "beep.wav" //
AudioUI
73. };
74. private static final int NUMBER_OF_POEMS = 6;
```

```
75. private boolean running = false;
76. private boolean navigating = false;
77. // if the MIDlet is getting an update
78. // interval which is adequate for
79. // dymanic navigation, dynamicNavigation should be true
80. private boolean dynamicNavigation = false;
81. private Ticker minimalistTicker = null;
82. private net.walkingtools.international.Translation translation
= null;
83. private AudioArrayPlayer audioPlayer = null;
84. private byte moveWarningEnervator = 1;
85.
86. /**
87. * Constructor for a TransBorderMIDlet
88. */
89. public TBMIDlet() {
90. // load the translation
91. translation = Translation.loadTranslation(getAppProperty("lang
uage"));
92.
93. // get the display
94. if (display == null) {
95. display = Display.getDisplay(this);
96. }
97.
98. // test value for jad file ... can delete
99. //System.out.println(System.
currentTimeMillis()+1000*60*60*24*8);
100.
101. // set up the test alert first (for debugging on phone)
102. exit = new Command(translation.translate("Exit"), Command.
EXIT, 0);
103. // get the gpx file
104. String gpxFile = this.getAppProperty("GPXFile");
105.
106. tbDowsingCompass = new DowsingCompass(gpxFile);
107.
```

```
108. int width = tbDowsingCompass.getWidth();
109. Image errorImage = null;
110. Image tbImage = null;
111. if (width < 150) {
112. errorImage = loadImage("error_sm.png");
113. tbImage = loadImage("tb_sm.png");
114. } else {
115. errorImage = loadImage("error.png");
116. tbImage = loadImage("tb.png");
117. }
118.
119. // first, validate the expiration value
120. ignore = new Command(translation.translate("Ignore"),
Command.CANCEL, 0);
121. String expirationDate = this.
getAppProperty("Expiration-Date");
122. long exp = Long.parseLong(expirationDate);
123.
124. if (exp <= System.currentTimeMillis()) {
125. expired = new Alert(translation.translate("Data expired"),
126. translation.translate("The data is expired, TBTool is not
safe to use."),
127. errorImage,
128. AlertType.ERROR);
129. expired.setTimeout(Alert.FOREVER);
130. expired.addCommand(exit);
131. expired.addCommand(ignore);
132. expired.setCommandListener(this);
133. isExpired = true;
134. } else if (exp <= System.currentTimeMillis() + (1000 * 60 *
60 * 24 * 7) ) { // 7 day warning
135. Date date = new Date(exp);
136. expirationWarning = new Alert(translation.
translate("Expiration Warning"),
137. translation.translate("\nThe data will expire on:\n") + date.
toString() +
```

```
138. translation.translate("\nTrans Border Immigrant Saftey Tool\
nEDT/BANGLAB/CRCA/CALIT2/VISARTS/UCSD\n\n"),
139. errorImage,
140. AlertType.WARNING);
141. expirationWarning.addCommand(ignore);
142. expirationWarning.setTimeout(15000);
143. expirationWarning.setCommandListener(this);
144. expireWarning = true;
145. } else {
146. Date date = new Date(exp);
147. startUpDisplay = new Alert(translation.translate("Trans
Border Immigrant Tool"),
148. translation.translate("\nExpires: ") + date.toString() +
149. translation.translate("\nTrans Border Immigrant Saftey Tool\
nEDT/BANGLAB/CRCA/CALIT2/VISARTS/UCSD\n\n"),
150. tbImage,
151. AlertType.INFO);
152. startUpDisplay.addCommand(ignore);
153. startUpDisplay.setTimeout(10000);
154. startUpDisplay.setCommandListener(this);
155. startUpAlert = true;
156. }
157.
158. noNearbyWaypoints = new Alert(translation.translate("No
Nearby Points"),
159. translation.translate("There are no sites within ") +
160. (int)((SEARCH_DISTANCE / 1000.0) + .5)
161. + translation.translate(" Kilometers."),
162. tbImage,
163. AlertType.WARNING);
164.
165. noNearbyWaypoints.addCommand(ignore);
166. noNearbyWaypoints.setTimeout(10000);
167. noNearbyWaypoints.setCommandListener(this);
168.
169. minimalistInfoAlert = new Alert(translation.translate("Minimal
Mode"),
```

```
170. "",
171. tbImage,
172. AlertType.WARNING);
173.
174. minimalistInfoAlert.addCommand(ignore);
175. minimalistInfoAlert.setTimeout(Alert.FOREVER);
176. minimalistInfoAlert.setCommandListener(this);
177.
178. nearbyWPList = new Vector();
179. cancel = new Command(translation.translate("Cancel"),
Command.CANCEL, 0);
180. listNearbyWPs = new Command(translation.translate("Find"),
Command.SCREEN, 1);
181. setTargetManual = new Command(translation.translate("Select"),
Command.SCREEN, 1);
182. setTargetAuto = new Command(translation.translate("Set
Target"), Command.SCREEN, 1);
183.
184. /* through a lot of tedious testing, I discovered that these
185. constructors of the TextFields were throwing an
IllegalArgumentException
186. when using TextField.DECIMAL or TextField.NUMERIC constraints.
The
187. following is from the javadoc. It seems not to contradict the
188. use of TextField.DECIMAL or NUMERIC given that I was setting
189. the forms to a decimal/numeric value ... hmmmmm ... this must
be an
190. issue in in iden implementation.
191.
192. "Some constraints, such as DECIMAL, require the implementation
to
193. perform syntactic validation of the contents of the text
object.
194. The syntax checking is performed on the actual contents of
the text
195. object, which may differ from the displayed contents as
described
```

196. above. Syntax checking is performed on the initial contents
passed
197. to the constructors, and it is also enforced for all method
calls
198. that affect the contents of the text object. The methods and
199. constructors throw IllegalArgumentException if they would
result
200. in the contents of the text object not conforming to the
required
201. syntax."
202. */
203. tbDowsingCompass.addCommand(exit);
204. tbDowsingCompass.addCommand(listNearbyWPs);
205. tbDowsingCompass.setCommandListener(this);
206. tbDowsingCompass.addNavigatorListener(this);
207.
208. targetList = new List(translation.translate("Select a
Target"), List.IMPLICIT);
209. targetList.addCommand(cancel);
210. targetList.addCommand(setTargetManual);
211. targetList.setCommandListener(this);
212.
213. waypointAheadAlert = new Alert(translation.translate("Site
Ahead!"),
214. translation.translate("Site Ahead!"),
215. tbImage, AlertType.INFO);
216. waypointAheadAlert.setTimeout(Alert.FOREVER);
217. waypointAheadAlert.addCommand(ignore);
218. waypointAheadAlert.addCommand(setTargetAuto);
219. waypointAheadAlert.setCommandListener(this);
220.
221. arrivedAlert = new Alert(translation.translate("Arrived at
Site"),
222. translation.translate("Arrived at Site"),
223. tbImage, AlertType.INFO);
224. arrivedAlert.setTimeout(Alert.FOREVER);
225. arrivedAlert.addCommand(ignore);

```
226. arrivedAlert.setCommandListener(this);
227. minimalistTicker = new Ticker(
228. translation.translate("Minimal or no GPS signal. Alert will
give direction and distance information if possible.")
229. );
230. dynamicNavigation = true; // assume active navigation at
startup of gps to give it a chance to fix
231.
232. // set up location provider
233. // Set criteria for selecting a location provider:
234. // accurate to 50 meters horizontally
235. try {
236. Criteria cr = new Criteria();
237. cr.setHorizontalAccuracy(50);
238. // we can set other criteria that we require
239. cr.setSpeedAndCourseRequired(true);
240. cr.setPreferredResponseTime(2000);
241. cr.setAltitudeRequired(true);
242. try {
243. // Get an instance of the provider
244. lp = LocationProvider.getInstance(cr);
245. } catch (LocationException e) { // if this happens, lp could
not get a location
246. display.setCurrent(new Alert(translation.translate("Exception
on getting location provider"),
247. translation.translate("Exception on getting location
provider") + ':' + e.toString(),
248. null,
249. AlertType.INFO));
250. }
251. // register this with the location listener
252. // the second argument is the interval. -1 is a flag that
says, "whatever works best for you"
253. // the third arg is the timeout, or, how many seconds past
the interval defined in arg 2
254. // the provider should wait before it returns and invalid
Location
```

```
255. // the fourth is the maxAge of a valid location. The provider
may provide a valid location
256. // in lieu of a current location as long as it is not older
than this.
257. lp.setLocationListener(tbDowsingCompass, 2, 2, 2);
258. } catch (SecurityException se) {
259. Alert noLocationService = new Alert(translation.
translate("TBtool requires location"),
260. translation.translate("The Transborder Immigrant Tool needs
access to location services.") +
261. translation.translate("Try answering \"Yes\" on startup to
grant TBtoool access."),
262. errorImage,
263. AlertType.INFO);
264. noLocationService.setTimeout(Alert.FOREVER);
265. noLocationService.addCommand(exit);
266. noLocationService.setCommandListener(this);
267. display.setCurrent(noLocationService);
268. }
269. }
270.
271. protected void startApp() throws MIDletStateChangeException {
272. // get the display
273. if (display == null) {
274. display = Display.getDisplay(this);
275. }
276.
277. // this thread to randomly play audio file
278. try {
279. audioPlayer = new AudioArrayPlayer("audio", audioStrings,
true); // true, in audio cueing mode
280. //InputStream in = getClass().getResourceAsStream("/audio/
beep.wav");
281. audioTimer = new AudioTimer();
282. running = true;
283. audioTimer.start(); // start audio thread
284. } catch (IOException e) {
```

```
285. Alert bailOnAudioException = new Alert(translation.
translate("Could not load audio"),
286. translation.translate("Could not load audio"),
287. loadImage("error_sm.png"),
288. AlertType.INFO);
289. bailOnAudioException.setTimeout(Alert.FOREVER);
290. bailOnAudioException.addCommand(exit);
291. display.setCurrent(bailOnAudioException);
292. } catch (MediaException e) {
293. Alert bailOnAudioException = new Alert(translation.
translate("Could not play audio"),
294. translation.translate("Could not play audio"),
295. loadImage("error_sm.png"),
296. AlertType.INFO);
297. bailOnAudioException.setTimeout(Alert.FOREVER);
298. bailOnAudioException.addCommand(exit);
299. display.setCurrent(bailOnAudioException);
300. }
301.
302. // make sure the data is not expired
303. if (isExpired) {
304. display.setCurrent(expired);
305. display.vibrate(1000);
306. playAudioFile("expired.wav", true);
307. } else if (expireWarning) {
308. display.setCurrent(expirationWarning, tbDowsingCompass);
309. display.vibrate(1000);
310. playAudioFile("expiration.wav", true);
311. } else if (startUpAlert) { //first time only
312. startUpAlert = false;
313. display.setCurrent(startUpDisplay, tbDowsingCompass);
314. display.vibrate(1000);
315. playAudioFile("startup.wav", true);
316. } else { // we are good to go
317. display.setCurrent(tbDowsingCompass);
318. }
319. }
```

```
320.
321. /**
322.  * edu.ucsd.calit2.TransBorderTool.CompassListener interface
method
323.  * Called when user is facing a waypoint
324.  * Displays waypointAheadAlert pertaining to type of waypoint
325.  */
326. public void witchingEvent(TBCoordinates mc) {
327. aheadCoords = mc;
328. if (display.getCurrent().equals(tbDowsingCompass)) {
329. waypointAheadAlert.setString(tbDowsingCompass.getInfo(mc));
330. waypointAheadAlert.setImage(aheadCoords.getIcon());
331. double distance = tbDowsingCompass.distanceTo(mc);
332. if (distance > SEARCH_DISTANCE) {
333. display.vibrate(100);
334. } else if (distance > 1000) {
335. display.vibrate(300);
336. } else if (distance > 500) {
337. display.vibrate(500);
338. } else if (distance > 100) {
339. display.vibrate(800);
340. }
341. display.setCurrent(waypointAheadAlert);
342. display.vibrate(1000);
343. playAudioFile("found.wav", false);
344. }
345. }
346.
347. /**
348.  * NavigatorListener interface method
349.  * Displays alert when user arrives within range of target
350.  */
351. public void arrivedAtTarget(int distance) {
352. navigating = false;
353. // stop the compass from navigating
354. tbDowsingCompass.stopNavigation();
355. display.setCurrent(arrivedAlert);
```

```
356. display.vibrate(1000);
357. playAudioFile("arriving.wav", false);
358. }
359.
360. // all of the UI audio files are played through this method
361. // the poems are not played through this method,
362. // see second arg in playFileName below
363. private void playAudioFile(String name, boolean interrupt) {
364. try {
365. audioPlayer.playFileName(name, interrupt); // true will
interrupt a poem if playing
366. } catch (MediaException e) {
367. try {
368. audioPlayer.playFileName("beep.wav", true);
369. } catch (MediaException ex) {
370. return;
371. } catch (Exception eb) {
372. eb.printStackTrace();
373. }
374. }
375. }
376.
377. /**
378. * NavigatorListener interface method
379. * Called to populate nearby waypoint vector
380. * once the CompassCanvas detects a valid location
381. * so user may begin "dowsing" for waypoints
382. * @param ready true for ready to navigate
383. */
384. public void navigationReady(boolean ready) {
385. if (ready) {
386. nearbyWPList = tbDowsingCompass.
getNearbyWaypoints(SEARCH_DISTANCE);
387. if (navigating) {
388. tbDowsingCompass.removeCommand(listNearbyWPs);
389. tbDowsingCompass.addCommand(cancel);
390. } else {
```

```
391. tbDowsingCompass.addCommand(listNearbyWPs);
392. tbDowsingCompass.removeCommand(cancel);
393. }
394. } else {
395. if (!navigating) {
396. tbDowsingCompass.removeCommand(listNearbyWPs); // can't use
397. }
398. }
399. }
400.
401. /**
402. * NavigatorListener interface method tells the midlet the GPS
refresh rate
403. * of the Navigator (DowsingCompass...) If the MIDlet is
getting an update
404. * interval which is adequate for dymanic navigation then
dynamic
405. * (compass based) navigation should be on.
406. * Otherwise the phone enters into a minimalist mode that can
still provide
407. * an occaisional alert, useful with less capable phones or in
place where
408. * GPS coverage is poor. In these cases the user may still be
able to navigate
409. * with a magnetic compass.
410. * @param milliseconds reported milliseconds since last update
411. */
412. public void updateInterval(long milliseconds) {
413. // if the device is without update for 10 minutes, enter
minimal mode
414. if (milliseconds > 1000*60*10) { // signal is not good
415. if (dynamicNavigation) { // entering non dynamic mode from
dynamic
416. tbDowsingCompass.setTicker(minimalistTicker);
417. if (!navigating) {
418. tbDowsingCompass.removeCommand(listNearbyWPs); // can't use
419. }
```

```
420. display.vibrate(1000);
421. playAudioFile("lowgps.wav", true);
422. }
423. dynamicNavigation = false;
424. } else { // we have a good signal
425. if (!dynamicNavigation) { // we are now returning from a bad
signal
426. // because dN is set to true in the constructor
427. // we must be returning from non-dynamic to dynamic, not just
starting
428. // restore interface to last state
429. tbDowsingCompass.setTicker(null);
430. // Offer any available help to user
431. // get closest point data into alert string if available
432. nearbyWPList = tbDowsingCompass.
getNearbyWaypoints(SEARCH_DISTANCE);
433. if (nearbyWPList != null && !nearbyWPList.isEmpty()) {
434. TBCoordinates target = (TBCoordinates)nearbyWPList.
elementAt(0);
435. Coordinates current = tbDowsingCompass.getCurrentCoords();
436. float distance = current.distance(target);
437. String distanceStr = null;
438. if (distance >= 1000) {
439. distanceStr = (int)(distance/1000) + translation.translate("
Kilometers");
440. } else {
441. distanceStr = distance + translation.translate(" Meters");
442. }
443. // create minimalist info alert (if it is just an itermittant
single report
444. // then at least this info will be left on screen as the
system goes
445. // back into non dynamic navigation mode.
446. minimalistInfoAlert.setString(
447. translation.translate("Nearest Site: Distance ") + distanceStr
+ ", " +
```

```
448. translation.translate("Azimuth ") + (int)current.
azimuthTo(target)
449. + translation.translate(" degrees, General Direction ") +
450. tbDowsingCompass.directionTo(target)
451. );
452. display.setCurrent(minimalistInfoAlert, tbDowsingCompass);
453. display.vibrate(1000);
454. playAudioFile("read.wav", false);
455. } else {
456. display.setCurrent(noNearbyWaypoints);
457. display.vibrate(1000);
458. playAudioFile("nosites.wav", false);
459. }
460. }
461. dynamicNavigation = true;
462. }
463. }
464.
465. /** (non-Javadoc)
466. * @param arg0
467. * @throws MIDletStateChangeException
468. * @see javax.microedition.midlet.MIDlet#destroyApp(boolean)
469. */
470. protected void destroyApp(boolean arg0) throws
MIDletStateChangeException {
471. // TODO Auto-generated method stub
472. }
473.
474. /**
475. *
476. */
477. protected void pauseApp() {
478. // TODO Auto-generated method stub
479. }
480.
481. private Image loadImage(String str) {
482. Image image = null;
```

```
483. try {
484. image = Image.createImage("/img/" + str);
485. } catch (IOException e) {
486.
487. image = null;
488. }
489. //System.out.println(image);
490.
491. return image;
492. }
493.
494. public void commandAction(Command c, Displayable d) {
495. if (c == exit) { // exit
496. running = false;
497. notifyDestroyed();
498. } else if (c == cancel) { // stop navigation and reset
softkey commands
499. navigating = false;
500. tbDowsingCompass.stopNavigation();
501. tbDowsingCompass.removeCommand(cancel);
502. if (dynamicNavigation) {
503. tbDowsingCompass.addCommand(listNearbyWPs);
504. }
505. display.setCurrent(tbDowsingCompass);
506. } else if (c == ignore) { // Returns to compass interface if
user chooses not to
507. // set a dowsingEvent as a target
508. if (navigating) {
509. tbDowsingCompass.removeCommand(listNearbyWPs);
510. tbDowsingCompass.addCommand(cancel);
511. } else {
512. tbDowsingCompass.removeCommand(cancel);
513. if (dynamicNavigation) {
514. tbDowsingCompass.addCommand(listNearbyWPs);
515. }
516. }
517. display.setCurrent(tbDowsingCompass);
```

```
518. } else if (c == listNearbyWPs) { // Display a List of
waypoints within range
519. // from which user can manually choose a target
520. // Update nearby waypoint vector
521. nearbyWPList = tbDowsingCompass.
getNearbyWaypoints(SEARCH_DISTANCE);
522. if (nearbyWPList != null && !nearbyWPList.isEmpty()) {
523. targetList.deleteAll();
524. // Loop through waypoint vector adding waypoint
525. // image and information to list
526. for (int i = 0; i < nearbyWPList.size(); i++) {
527. TBCoordinates mc = (TBCoordinates) nearbyWPList.elementAt(i);
528. targetList.append(tbDowsingCompass.getInfo(mc), mc.getIcon());
529. }
530. display.setCurrent(targetList);
531. } else {
532. display.setCurrent(noNearbyWaypoints);
533. playAudioFile("nosites.wav", true);
534. }
535. } else if (c == setTargetAuto) { // Set a waypoint detected
by a dowsingEvent as the target
536. navigating = true;
537. tbDowsingCompass.setTarget(aheadCoords);
538. // Change commands on tbDowsingCanvas
539. tbDowsingCompass.removeCommand(listNearbyWPs);
540. tbDowsingCompass.addCommand(cancel);
541. display.setCurrent(tbDowsingCompass);
542. // Set a waypoint selected from nearby waypoint List as the
target
543. } else if (c == setTargetManual) {
544. navigating = true;
545. int index = targetList.getSelectedIndex();
546. tbDowsingCompass.setTarget((TBCoordinates) nearbyWPList.
elementAt(index));
547. //Change Commands on tbDowsingCanvas
548. tbDowsingCompass.removeCommand(listNearbyWPs);
549. tbDowsingCompass.addCommand(cancel);
```

```
550. display.setCurrent(tbDowsingCompass);
551. }
552. }
553.
554. public void motionStatusUpdate(boolean isMoving) {
555. if (isMoving) { // updated to moving
556. nearbyWPList = tbDowsingCompass.getNearbyWaypoints(SEARCH_
DISTANCE); // so update nearby points
557. } else { // updated not moving
558. display.vibrate(200);
559. if (moveWarningEnervator % 5 == 0) { // only play this file ~
every 5th time
560. playAudioFile("move.wav", false); // the "move for compass"
message can be too frequent
561. }
562. moveWarningEnervator++;
563. }
564. }
565.
566. // inner class to control audio
567. class AudioTimer extends Thread {
568.
569. Random rand = new Random();
570.
571. public void run() {
572. while (running) {
573. try {
574. Thread.sleep(1000 * 60 * (rand.nextInt(19) + 1)); // sleep
random minutes
575. //Thread.sleep(1000 * 60); // sleep one min (test)
576. } catch (InterruptedException e) {
577. running = false;
578. }
579. try {
580. int randIndex = rand.nextInt(NUMBER_OF_POEMS); // poems at
the top of the audio array
```

```
581. audioPlayer.play(randIndex, false); // false means to cue the
audio if something else is playing
582. } catch (MediaException ex) {
583. Alert bailOnAudioException = new Alert(translation.
translate("media exception"),
584. ex.getMessage(),
585. null,
586. AlertType.INFO);
587. bailOnAudioException.setTimeout(Alert.FOREVER);
588. display.setCurrent(bailOnAudioException);
589. }
590. }
591. }
592.
593. public void finalize() {
594. running = false;
595. }
596. }
597. }
```

Notes

TBMIDlet contains many of the core functions that operate the Transborder Immigrant Tool. They handle everything from updating the coordinates to establishing whether or not the traveler is moving.

1–2: Free and open source software exists through copyright. The copyright dates on Walking Tools are a reminder of the protections that keep the software from being treated as public domain.

4–15: Comments presenting licensing information and programmer comments. This is a GNU Affero General Public License. See, for example, https://www.gnu.org/licenses/agpl-3.0.en.html.

/* indicates comments.

9–12: Although it is boilerplate of the standard license, on a piece of software that purports to help save lives, the phrases "WITHOUT ANY WARRANTY" and "without even the implied warranty of ... FITNESS FOR A PARTICULAR PURPOSE" stand out, and not merely because they are in uppercase. This app might be a lifeline, but there are no guarantees. Though EDT did not write these specific lines, because they appear in this potentially life-saving code, their meaning changes.

19–20: First comment from authors to themselves or perhaps to future coders. This comment reacts to an aspect of the code already implemented because line 334 checks if the water cache is more than one thousand meters away.

22–31: Packages and imports, libraries of code also being included with this code. The class being imported includes `international`, `midlet`, `lcdui`, `location`, `io`, `util`, `media`, and `Audio-ArrayPlayer`, which will be used to play the poems.

Because of such package and import statements, the visible code does not reveal all. More importantly, these imports point to one of the many ways visible code is always partial. I am reminded here of Roland Barthes's distinction of the work and text (1979). The *work* is an individual, discrete object assigned to an author. The *text* is an unlimited continuum of discourse of which discrete objects (like this file of code and this manuscript) are only ever partial excerpts.

24–30: Although much of the code of the app is imported from other sources, this passage offers authorship credits and a version number, reminding us that authorship (and the author function) still maintains significance even in free and open-source software.

37–597: From line 37, everything that follows line 37 "extends MIDlet" or extends the class of `MIDlet`, the app class, by defining what `TBMIDlet` adds to and modifies in that class.[1]

39–84: Variable declarations. The `SEARCH_DISTANCE`, 10K, represents meters.

62: The test app was designed to download coordinates of water caches (which changed frequently) as opposed to placing them on the phone as was the plan for release among border crossers.

66–69: Although there are many published poems for this project, this version of the code only loads six, including 1-GAIN_04-02.wav and five others.

86–269: Constructor for `TransborderMidlet` (or `TBMIDlet`): defines the class `TBMIDlet`. In this file, the core functionality and design of the app are defined.

98–99: This "commented out" line tests the output by displaying the current time. The // before `System` means this line of code is not processed by the code. *JAD* stands for Java Application Descriptor, a file format for java files.

108–117: Checks the display with the app to determine which size of graphics to display.

124–137: These lines use various freshness tests on the data, seeing if it is expired or will expire in seven days because the water caches were moved frequently to avoid vandalism. These lines show some of the pressing real-world concerns that appear in the code.

147–156: Declares `startupDisplay`, the methods used at startup, including one that displays the title. Notice that the `translate` method is used on all displayed messages to keep the app from being tied to one language. However, the poem audio files would have to be individually translated to other languages before being uploaded.

158–167: These lines establish `callback`, a method to call back to when no nearby waypoints are detected, one of the more alarming states of the software for one trying to survive the desert.

178–183: The code that establishes the basic interface options.

184–202: Comment: An extensive commentary on an error and workaround, including an extensive citation from the documentation of the code. This comment, as a survival guide to this knotty problem, mirrors the structure of the poems that lead the traveler through the desert.

233: `Criteria` is a javax.microedition class that helps prioritize a selected location provider.

279: Creates the audioplayer that will play the poems.

285: `bailOnAudioException`: The use of the word *bail* meaning *to leave* or *depart*, or in this case *to terminate*, though not a singular usage,[2] has a particularly colloquial ring, as in "gotta bail." This alert named by the programmers (in other words, not a reserved word) offers an example of the way a variety of registers of diction enters code.

302–317: Checks to see if the location data is still fresh.

322–345: `CompassListener` declares the `witchingEvent` method (water detected).

351–358: `NavigatorListener` signals when arrived within range of target.

360–375: Code for handling user interface audio.

377–399: `navigationReady` to "populate nearby waypoint vector."

401–463: `NavigationListener` checks the refresh rate or provides minimal information if GPS is out of range (and location not being dynamically updated). Note that lines 406–409 describe the "minimalist mode" for scenarios of "less capable phones" or "where GPS coverage is poor." This code caters to and creates the scenario in which a "magnetic compass" may be the only resort. This mode is specified starting on line 446 in `minimalistInfoAlert`.

465–471: Autogenerated method to terminate the app and enter the "Destroyed state" ("Class Midlet").

477–479: Autogenerated method to pause app.

481–494: Method for loading images.

494–552: Code managing the actions.

554–564: `motionStatusUpdate` marks the potentially life-or-death moment, when the traveler is either moving or needs to be encouraged to keep moving.

567–596: This next block of code plays the randomly selected poems and runs several checks for exceptions, or parts of the code that would terminate the program. These include the phone being asleep and some other audio currently playing. Both exceptions are followed by "catch" code that addresses how to respond to these exceptions.

Functionality

TBMIDlet, or Transborder midlet, presents the core code for the Transborder Immigrant Tool (TBT; figure 3.1). The primary function of this code is to extend the MIDlet class, or the basic object for MIDlet applications, with the methods and other attributes of the TBT, creating, of course, TBMIDlet. The `Main` call in another file will start this applet by creating an instance of this class. The code uses, among other libraries, the WalkingTools library, also created by Brett Stalbaum with Brazilian media scholar and artist Cicero I. da Silva, for a Global Positioning System (GPS). Because this project was begun before the advent of contemporary smartphones, Stalbaum had to create extensions to the GPX standard for associating media information (audio in this case) with GPS information. The TBT uses the GPS information to establish the walker's proximity to various waypoints, either a city or a water cache left in the desert by a volunteer organization. As the person gets closer to the water cache, the system vibrates more frequently. In the meantime, the app will play randomly selected audio files of recitations of poems, which contain information on how to survive in the desert. The traveler using the app has the opportunity to choose a target or destination. If the app detects that the traveler has stopped for too long, it will emit vibrations and audio alerts to try to motivate the traveler to move. The code also is designed to translate all messages into whatever languages are added to the system.

Figure 3.1
Demo image of the Transborder Immigrant Tool. Image by Brett Stalbaum. CC-BY-SA 4.0.

Origins of a Tool

One way of reading code involves simulating its operations in one's mind, tracing the effects of changing conditions on the state of the software as it executes. This means that reading code can involve a simulated execution of the software. As a result, code can present to its reader imaginary scenarios, which carry rhetorical and discursive meaning because they represent real-world scenarios and modeled worldviews. In this chapter, I offer a reading of some of the code of the Transborder Immigrant Tool, a hactivist art project, the code of which resituates the contemporary geopolitical border debate in potential scenarios of life-or-death survival. For readers of the code, as opposed to users who are engaging in these imaginary scenes, the code conveys its perspective the way a ritual does, offering passages of narrative movement to convey understanding.

The Transborder Immigrant Tool, or TBT, as it is known,[3] presents itself as a last-chance rescue application to sustain imperiled travelers, border crossers, by leading them to water and sustaining them with poetry. *Transborder* could (and does) refer to any border: political or otherwise. Yet the use of *border* and *immigrant* in a project emanating from San Diego, just north of the US-Mexico border, unmistakably engages with incendiary border politics that demonize the undocumented as "illegals" and "aliens," as an incursion of dangerous, job-stealing invaders, a threat to the nation-state. This artwork inverts that narrative by marshaling empathy for the border crosser who has already passed into the United States but who is about to die of thirst. Its tactic: drawing the audience into a ritualistic enactment of that perilous journey.[4] The work does not aestheticize the undocumented as avatars for first-world observers; instead, by reframing the journey in life-or-death terms, it helps to deny the rhetorical construction of transgressing "illegals" by recasting the travelers as immigrants with the most human of needs: water for their bodies and poetry for their souls.

The Transborder Immigrant Tool is a mobile phone application under development by the Electronic Disturbance Theater (figure 3.2), in residence at UC San Diego as the b.a.n.g. (bits, atoms, neurons, genes) lab.[5] When deployed, the app will help a traveler crossing the desert to the north of the US-Mexico border, presumably on foot, to find water by means of a simple compass navigation device and aural and haptic cues.[6] Once the device finds a water cache nearby, the tool begins its wayfinding process, leading the traveler, likely dehydrated and disoriented, to the nearby cache. These caches have been placed in the desert by volunteer organizations—specifically Water Stations, Inc., a humanitarian organization that works to fill brightly painted barrels labeled *agua* with gallon jugs of water (Marino 2011a).

Figure 3.2
The members of Electronic Disturbance Theater 2.0 (from left): Brett Stalbaum, Amy Sara Carroll, Ricardo Dominguez, Elle Mehrmand, and micha cárdenas.

The app uses GPS information from an inexpensive Motorola phone to find the traveler's location. Although this tool will not provide sustenance for an entire trip across the border, it does attempt to aid the traveler in what its developers refer to as the "last mile" of the journey.[7] The traveler activates the phone in their moment of extreme dehydration because the phone has only approximately an hour's worth of battery charge. After locating its own position, the phone searches for nearby water caches. It is important to note that as of the writing of this essay, TBT has not been used by undocumented immigrants dying in the desert but instead has been tested by EDT team and has been implemented rhetorically by fans and foes alike, for whom the mere mention of the tool stirs strong emotions.

However, the code does not exist merely for the functioning of the software. Released at the 2010 Critical Code Studies Conference at the University of Southern California, four years after the birth of critical code studies, the source code of the Transborder Immigrant Tool represents an example of code written to be interpreted by CCS scholars, or at least written by programmers who were aware of a potential critical and interpreting readership. In publications about the project, including a print book, the creators include the code side by side with the recited poems. In other words, this code was designed to be traversed as an instantiation or even execution of the project. Although fully functional, the code becomes meaningful in its potential implementation, existing as what Jessica Pressman (pers. comm., June 14, 2007) has suggested could be called *conceptual code*. Unlike other code examples in this book, this code was written not only to be read by humans but also to be analyzed and interpreted.

Just as the poems help the traveler navigate the unforgiving climate of the desert, the complex terrain of the code requires a guide to navigate the dangerous landscape of the man-made methods and the interoperating systems of both hardware and software on which the code must operate. However, rather than merely draw an analogy between the comments and Carroll's survival poems, I would like to examine the code itself as another channel of poetry and poetic intervention—not because it resembles the structures of traditional verse, as is often the case in Perl poetry or many instances of codework, or poetry that plays upon the semantic structures and conventions of code, but rather because the code represents a text of semantic signs that when performed (either through human or machine reading) intervene in culture by creating a poetic disruption.

The project's poems in many ways teach readers the aesthetic conditions under which the code can also be poetry. Both poetry and code present scripts of performed instructions that act as channels of artful communication, intervening in overdetermined narratives of undocumented immigrants. Electronic Disturbance Theater presents its interventions as a kind of guerrilla theatre, including all who interact with the piece, even in protest, as part of the performance (Marino 2011b). However, rather than situating this poetry and code as theatrical scripts, I read this project through a metaphor embedded in its code: ritual. A *ritual* is a process that when enacted conveys valued cultural knowledge through participation. The human readers of the code experience the process, or participate, through their imagination, following a meaningfully contextualized procedure. Whether in code or poetry, these instructions for an imagined journey are embedded with cultural imagery, resonant with customs of affiliated cultures, and address a set of possible stories, or use cases, about a traveler who is about to perish while crossing the desert. To read the code, to trace its functioning as an imaginary border crosser is either sustained by water and poetry or perishes, is to engage with a counternarrative of the border that disrupts the popular rhetoric of pundits and politicians.

Poems Becoming Code

The TBT project grew out of the unique ensemble that makes Electronic Disturbance Theater. It began in 2007 as an application of EDT member Brett Stalbaum's

WalkingToolsGpx API, a library of tools for use in art projects involving GPS-navigated walks, often in rural or even dangerous areas. University of California, San Diego professor Ricardo Dominguez proposed to his EDT collaborator that they consider applying these tools to the US-Mexico border, and Transborder Tools for Immigrants (as the project was originally called) was born, though not before EDT applied for funding both to purchase phones and to develop a poetry component of the project to be written by EDT member Amy Sara Carroll.[8] As the project progressed, the collective developed all elements, including the poetry and code, in conversation with one another, according to Carroll (pers. interview, Skype, March 12, 2012). The group began the development in earnest, together with the other members of EDT: Elle Mehrmand and micha cárdenas, and a UCSD undergraduate, Jason Najarro, who over the summer of 2008 wrote the core code for the tool together with Stalbaum. Even while in development, the tool they have created has caused quite a disturbance.

TBT emerged at a time of heated and divisive debate about the US-Mexico border, a debate which long precedes this episode and which persists today. These were the days of Arizona's Senate Bill 1070, the Support Our Law Enforcement and Safe Neighborhoods Act, which gave law enforcement the authority to make "reasonable attempts to determine the immigration status" of any person they encountered, essentially authorizing the legal profiling of the undocumented. In that incendiary climate, within a few months of the publication of articles about TBT in 2009 in *Vice* magazine (Dunbar 2009) and then the geek culture link site Boing Boing, the University of California received a letter from Congressman Duncan Hunter and two others. Hunter "found the project to be a poor use of taxpayer money, particularly during a recession" (Miller 2010). As Fox News gave the story national coverage, the University of California began an audit of the project, while several other investigations began to pursue Dominguez. Between op-ed pieces and a featured spot on the *Glenn Beck Program*, the project grew in infamy, even as the production of the project was delayed, provoking violent emotions even before the app had ever been used (Morlan 2010).

The Transborder Immigrant Tool exemplifies Rita Raley's (2009) concept of "tactical media," the "critical rationale" of which is "disturbance" (19). She explains, "In its most expansive articulation, tactical media signifies the intervention and disruption of a dominant semiotic regime, the temporary creation of a situation in which signs, messages, and narratives are set into play and critical thinking becomes possible" (19). Raley posits tactical media as a response to "a shift in the nature of power, which has removed itself from the streets and become nomadic" (1), a notion inspired by the Critical Art Ensemble, one of the major creative influences of EDT of which Dominguez was a member.

Again, disruption is at the heart of these tactics. For example, by focusing the application not on the overcoded moment when the illegal immigrant crosses the border but on the moment the border crosser is dying in the desert, the project disrupts contemporary neoliberal narratives about the border. As Raley explains about another EDT project: "The aim is not to theorize liminality but to force a rupture in the binaries of interiority and exteriority, here and there, native and alien, friend and enemy. The radical dichotomies integral to the war on terror—'you're either with us or against us'—find their counterpart in art practices that themselves depend on the solidarity of the 'we' against the 'them.' A fence has been built, binaries constructed, and these artists intend to overturn them" (2009, 50).

This project overturns the border binary by rephrasing the question, What should be done about those national subjects who cross illegally? as, What should be done about those humans who have already crossed but are now about to die in the desert? In this way, the Transborder Immigrant Tool essentially leaps over the border fence and thus escapes the pageant that plays politics with the poor as it resettles in the realm of life and death and humanitarian aid. However, the app not only can lead a person to water, it also can deliver aid in the form of poetry. Here is another disruptive tactic of the Transborder Immigrant Tool, breaking the categorization of the app as a mere tool of physical survival just as it disrupts an image of the border crosser as a laborer for whom poetry would be at best a distraction. EDT's message is clear: this tool is an aesthetic object, resonating through artistic interventions even while providing for fundamental physical needs.

The poetry for the app was written by Carroll, though other members of Electronic Disturbance Theater have been contributing to the larger corpus of poetry that has been shared in other contexts, such as museum installations. Carroll (pers. interview, Skype, January 4, 2011) describes the poetry as very different from her other work but suited to the occasion, describing her process of developing it after reading piles of survival guides and the migration account of Luís Alberto Urrea in *The Devil's Highway* (ibid.): "I wrote pared-down prose poems, ideologically neutral (Is any writing 'ideologically neutral'?), procedural, if you will—a poem about locating the North Star, a poem about what to do if you are bitten by a rattlesnake or tarantula, poems that contained details about how to weather a sandstorm or a flash flood" (Electronic Disturbance Theater 2014, 4).

With the term *procedural*, Carroll begins to cue the reader on how to read the poems as instructions, or more specifically as code. Transgressing more borders, Carroll writes, "At base, I worked from two assumptions. A desert is not just a desert. And, poetry-becoming-code/code-becoming poetry could transubstantiate, translate into a lifesaving technology, sounding off" (Electronic Disturbance Theater 2014, 4). In this work, poetry becomes code when it becomes instructions for procedures; code becomes poetry when it disrupts and resituates overdetermined signifiers, when it creates use cases of human suffering and assistance. The poetic and the procedural are inextricably connected at the border of instructions and reflections, between operations and meditations, between possibility and reality. Language becomes operational; functional code becomes rhetorical.

Carroll also situates these poems within the larger context of "conceptual writing," as laid out by Craig Dworkin, Vanessa Place, and Robert Fitterman. Dworkin identifies this genre, drawing upon the works of Kenneth Goldsmith, as *nonexpressive poetry*, akin to conceptual art, "in which the idea cannot be separated from the writing itself: in which the instance of writing is inextricably intertwined with the idea of Writing: the material practice of écriture" (Dworkin 2003). However, Carroll notes that this piece moves away from the aesthetic and formal focus of North American conceptual writing, toward the Latin American tradition, which embraces a more explicitly political mission. A full review of conceptual writing is beyond the scope of this book. By gesturing toward conceptual writing, Carroll situates the poetic in a realm that moves beyond surface characteristics, in which formal conceits and formalized procedures become central to how the writing is read—a genre in which the writing process and computational algorithm become much more compatible bedfellows.

This is not to say that Carroll has written code poems or codework. Following the subversive approach of the larger project, Carroll's poetry engages with the aesthetics of instructions, of survival knowledge, derived from folk wisdom more than the episteme of scientific knowledge epitomized by the mobile phone that delivers the app. Like the rest of the work, the strategy is to transgress all manner of borders, walls, and boundaries and the hierarchies and divisions they create and maintain. The poems themselves are individual meditations on some aspect of the desert, particularly the Anza-Borrego Desert in San Diego County, as each poem combines imagery of the desert with tips on survival in that trying terrain. Consider the following poem as an example: "The desert is an ecosystem with a logic of sustainability, of orientation, unique unto itself. For example, if the barrel cactus—known otherwise as the compass cactus—stockpiles moisture; it also affords direction. As clear as an arrow or a constellation, it leans south. Orient yourself by this mainstay or by flowering desert plants that, growing toward the sun, face south in the Northern Hemisphere." In the poem, the reader, or more properly the listener, will encounter information about the barrel cactus, which suggests how it can be used both for physical sustenance and direction. Other poems offer advice on how to cope with and manage exposure to the sun, dehydration, and desert snakes while conserving energy in the extreme heat. The nature of these poems reframes the tool within a larger tradition of sharing knowledge of survival through folklore and rituals, knowledge in the form of instructions for procedures.

The first characteristic the poems share with folk wisdom is their instructions. Though situated as poetry, these passages appear as practical instructions, survival guides, embellished with poetic flourish. Folklorist Tok Thompson (pers. interview, September 12, 2011) offers the parallel of "leaves of three, let it be" as a sign of the poetry of folk wisdom. I am using *folklore* here to designate communal, shared knowledge, as opposed to the kind of formalized knowledge taught in schools or patented and commodified by corporate or private entities, though folklore has also been commodified by corporate entities. Communicating folklore, these poems convey knowledge of the land, its dangers, its hopeful sustenance, and knowledge derived from the land, delivered in a deceptively plain-spoken style. These instructional poems thus evoke forms of artistry that transmit communal knowledge, like folktales or aphorisms, memorable for their images and formulations yet crucial for their practical information. They deliver poetic imagery with the rhetorical and aesthetic formulation of instruction.

Reading the poetry as instructions with deep communal ties, or instructions that lead into the folk, situates the poems as the mirror image of the code, a set of instructions that also bears the deep imprint of cultural practice. Or rather, if poetry seemed an unlikely place to find practical instruction, code strikes many as an odd place to find culture. However, as the poetry takes up these practical formulations, it outlines the nature of a kind of folklore, how the practical instructions bear the communal practice and wisdom. The program is literally the codification of the folk knowledge as procedure and objects, threads and events.

Second, the poems are performed. They are read aloud (in multiple languages) through recordings on the phone.[9] Although the text I quote in this paper has been copied from a digital text file shared with me by Carroll, those travelers who encounter the poems will hear them played through the phone at a random moment while using the tool. Context, even an imagined or speculative context, is critical. The poems have been recorded by cárdenas, Merhmand, and others and stored as WAV files to be played on the mobile phones as part of a portion of a set of use cases. The poems that play are not part of a collection, an anthology, to be perused or thumbed through, but part of this specific process. However, the poetry is never disconnected from that potential process. That process is not merely accessible to the person who is dying in the desert but is also accessible to anyone who traces her way through the code (or code repository), either using the machinery of the phone (or the software equivalent) or by reading through the code. The poetry then offers knowledge situated in a performance that is part of a process.

But the poetry itself also suggests folk ritual, as it offers knowledge or advice that has been embroidered with rich semantic inflections. Consider again the poem about the barrel cactus. The simplest version of its contents is "the barrel compass stores water and points south." However, Carroll frames this information within the metaphor of "an ecosystem with a logic of sustainability, of orientation." Of course, the phrase "logic ... of orientation" speaks both to the poetry and to the tool itself, which now by extension is grounded in the deeper nature of the desert. Evoking the basic compass wheel interface of the tool itself, Carroll refers to the barrel cactus by its alternate name, *compass cactus*. Abruptly, the sentence switches its frame with the metaphor of *stockpiles*, an industrial term more often used not in survival but in accumulations of destructive materials. And again, she shifts registers with *affords*, a term with deep resonance in the realms of tool design and programming. The end of the poem entangles or emplaces the tips for survival knowledge into the larger realm of geography and contested borders, as the piece encourages the traveler to orient himself or herself by facing "south in the Northern Hemisphere," which at once evokes a sense of human divisions of the land in the context of a worldview into which nation-states and what Dominguez calls "the aesthetic fiction of the border" dissolve (UCSBLitCultureMedia 2010b). Carroll's seemingly plain-spoken directions call forth the conflicts of worldviews, pulling on metaphors from production, war, and design while reorientating the reader toward land and country.

It is perhaps only in the realm of science that we entertain a notion of cultural knowledge devoid of cultural dispositions. Without rehearsing the entire epistemes of Foucault, it is worth noting that scientific knowledge is culturally situated and constructed and that the long shadow of worldviews colors or frames all descriptions of empirical phenomena. The genre of "directions" or "instructions" becomes emblematic of knowledge that has been systematized, seemingly stripped of unnecessary verbal trappings, especially when what is being described is a naturally occurring process. It is easy to conceive of computer source code in this context: a series of instructions (although not everything is an instruction) devoid of cultural inflection: pure process.

Carroll's poetic instruction in the Transborder Immigrant Tool, however, suggests ways in which instructions become more than mere directions. Her poems draw to the forefront the extent to which knowledge, even knowledge of survival, when communicated is by necessity situated in other kinds of cultural frames of reference—that knowledge is always cultural knowledge and instructions are always something more. Her work calls to mind other forms of practice that more obviously mix instruction with story, with song, with art.

She evokes these other forms through allusions, direct and indirect, to these other stores of knowledge, as the poems meditate on the landscape of the desert, reading it for its evocations and its indications of how to survive. Consider Poem 15, Arborescent monocot:

> Arborescent monocot. "Mothers of the Disappeared." "I Still Haven't Found What I'm Look-
> ing For." "Bullet the Blue Sky": "Put El Salvador through an amplifier." Seldom free-standing
> (Mexican as the Irish in the United States), the Joshua tree sends out yellow-green flowers—
> like flares—in the spring. Mormons referred to the trees—actually shrubs—as "praying plants."
> Anthropomorphizing each's branches, they compared the largest of the yucca evergreens to
> the Old Testament prophet Joshua as he pointed toward the promised land. Use the Joshua
> tree's lightweight wood to splint broken limbs. Chew the plant's roots for the steroid-like com-
> pound released (in cases of allergic reaction or swelling).

Carroll's poem on the Joshua tree quickly moves into song titles from the Irish rock band U2, whose album *The Joshua Tree* broke sales records in the late 1980s and delivered soulful ballads and anthems to that generation. In fact, after the scientific name of the Joshua tree, Carroll includes other voices in the form of their song titles uninterrupted: "Mothers of the Disappeared," "I Still Haven't Found What I'm Looking For," and "Bullet the Blue Sky." The final quotation, "Put El Salvador through an amplifier," is Bono's instructions to guitarist the Edge (Wharton 1998) that no doubt leads to the Latino-Irish connection, "Mexican as the Irish in the United States." By linking this poetic project with the Irish rock band's iconic album, Carroll aligns the project with its brand of social and political commentary. The commentary that follows seems to mix the scientific description with the historical commentary, tying the plant to the Biblical prophet. A final voice, however, delivers practical advice on how to use the plant to survive ("Chew the plant's root"), a necessary and common strain throughout the poems.

Yet Carroll claims that the code of the tool is the poetry of the project. To some, such a claim might be more disturbing than anything else called forth by the project, and yet given the context of conceptual writing, the code, as a manifestation of the logic and loglines of the art project, becomes poetry not just through that very framing but also by the very instructional nature of the poems it delivers.

Code Becoming Poetry

To read the poetry of TBT is to imagine a traveler in an hour of need receiving just-in-time guidance and sustenance. To read through the code of the Transborder Immigrant Tool is to stage a ritual in which mythical travelers cross the desert through the software. On the surface of the comparison, these traversals seem inconsonant: one involves physical movement and the other an act of the imagination of execution. I would argue that because the act of reading code requires models of materially tied processes—models, even black-boxed models, of the effects of the executed translation of the code on software and hardware—it is not necessary for someone to be physically moving to be enacting this journey.

The code of the Transborder Immigrant Tool is set to function in a particular set of use cases of a traveler lost in the desert in desperate straits. To read the code is to implement the code, to imagine the realization of that code, the software produced by it, and consequently the desert and the desert traveler, as well as the water to which the software leads. To read the code is to enact the ritual of the code, which carries with it communal knowledge and a communal history. Such an enactment is not meant to trivialize or aestheticize the real lives of those who could benefit from using the tool but instead to meditate not on their political representations but rather on their (potential) lived conditions by tracing through a procedure designed to rescue them.

Code is routinely conceptualized as *abstracted procedure*. However, I am setting that conventional term aside for a more culturally situated formulation. *Procedure* calls to mind a series of steps aimed at a goal; *ritual* is a performance aimed at cultural connectivity, at instilling community, of signifying allegiance, of remembering. The code, like the text of the oral performance, is more of a transcript of a performance to be realized in the mind, either by the mind of the reader or by the processes of the computer. It bears signs of its performance, as well as its history. Which is not to say that code does not have an end in mind. The Transborder Immigrant Tool does produce the app and govern the interactive experience of the app. I am focusing rather on the human reading of the code. Thus, I would argue that to engage with the Transborder Immigrant Tool through the code is to engage in a ritualistic imaginary performance of the software, a speculative deployment, an engagement that has many parallels with folk practice of ritual, song, and tale.

The act of reading code then involves a willful attempt to process like the computer, to emulate the system that will be operated on by the performative, automatic triggers of the code. The notion of literacy, therefore, in the sense of reading literacy, is insufficient for the act of reading code. As in processing textual symbols, reading code does require an understanding of the connotations of the instructions. However, connotation and electrical effects are not the same. Andrea diSessa (2001), in her book *Changing Minds: Computers, Learning, and Literacy*, offers the notion of *material intelligence* to substitute for literacy, meaning "intelligence achieved cooperatively with external materials" (5). Because of the specifications of hardware and software, including operating systems, it is not enough to say that reading code requires the same kinds of knowledge of the interdependent corollaries and theorems as in the case of mathematics—though, as diSessa notes, these both require similar skills. Annette Vee offers the term *proceduracy* for "the literacy associated with computer programming," which she defines as "the ability to break down complex processes into smaller procedures and express them explicitly enough to be read by a computer" (Hunter 2009). Reading code requires establishing an adequate representation of the state of the software (and at times the hardware) at any given time in the program. As I have mentioned elsewhere, this work often can function as a threshold paradigm that conflicts with the act of interpretation, which looks to connotation rather than this highly material form of denotation. Nonetheless, establishing the precise effects of code must precede interpretation.

The Transborder Immigrant Tool was written by then undergraduate Jason Najarro and UC San Diego instructor Brett Stalbaum in Java—specifically, Java 2 Micro Edition (J2ME) for the iDEN platform on the Motorola i455, a comparatively inexpensive mobile phone. Java, originally developed by Sun Microsystems, has been an opensource programming language since 2007, undergoing development from a worldwide community of programmers. Like Java, the tool itself is offered with a GNU Affero General Public License, which makes it available for others to continue or modify. Java often is considered a verbose language for enterprise or corporate production of software (Flanagan 1999). From a more favorable perspective, the Java language syntax requires some redundancy, which can increase legibility and facilitate longterm production of software by programming teams. The use of this language in this code, which is so carefully documented, places the software in the company of other team-built projects, rather than more lightweight personal projects. In other words, in this piece that is about wayfinding and sustenance, the code is crafted with an eye toward sustainability and navigability, helping readers to find their way though it.

The choice of Java also relates to another theme of this project: security. Compared to the languages that preceded it, Java also is a more secure language, one of the reasons that it is used in apps and widgets. In a project that deals with transgressing borders,

Java is by contrast relatively strong at maintaining borders. As a "managed language," it prevents something called *buffer overflow*, a vulnerability that can be exploited in malware attacks by which a program can place data into a location beyond an array's limits and thereby access another storage location.[10] Java, as one of the first so-called memory-safe languages, prevents this exploit and keeps these borders firm. Although this hacktavist project problematizes rhetoric around the border security of nation-states, the language the programmers have chosen for constructing the app could be said to maintain borders. However, though the choice of a memory-safe language protects users from these exploits, the choice to make this code open source reflects a broader ethos of openness. Furthermore, what is being protected through this choice of language is the device being used by a traveler, the immigrant, whose survival the app makes its primary function.

Although I will read a file from this program, only a portion of the code is visible in the repository. The tool makes use of preexisting libraries, namely those of Java and J2ME and WalkingTools, developed by Stalbaum and da Silva. Stalbaum has described these tools as an open platform he has been developing for use in art and education projects (Marino 2011a). This code builds upon and literally extends those code libraries, while it adopts walking as a central trope. In another presentation of the TBT project, a "play"[11] entitled "Sustenance," EDT offers Gloria Anzaldúa's framing of this northward migration: "We have a tradition of long walks. Today we are witnessing *la migracion de los pueblos mexicanos*, the return odyssey to the historical/mythological Aztlan" (Electronic Disturbance Theater 2010). With this quote and with the Walking-Tools code, EDT casts the act of the border crosser not as transgression but as an odyssey. If a program can be said to have an ethos, this program could be said to inherit the ethos of the libraries on which it builds, to use a metaphor from the object-oriented programming paradigm that this code employs.

As in the cases of most software, not all this code is novel or even "handwritten." Online resources and books about J2ME Midlet development offer basic frameworks and examples similar to the code used in this file. In fact, at least some of the code was likely created by the IDE. For example, the NetBeans IDE, which the developers were using, adds the following code when a J2ME Midlet file is created:

```
import javax.microedition.midlet.*;
public class MidletHelloWorld extends MIDlet {
    public void startApp() {
    }
```

```
    public void pauseApp() {
    }

    public void destroyApp(boolean unconditional) {
    }
}
    ("J2ME Tutorial")
```

This same code can be found in the TBTMidlet file. Note that when included in the code, each of these lines is followed by `// TODO Auto-generated method stub`, indicating that the code was created by the IDE. I point this out as a cautionary note about attributing too much intentionality to elements of the code, especially those required by and/or produced by other systems. For example, Najarro and Stalbaum did not choose destruction as a central metaphor of their piece. Rather, `destroyApp` is a method inherited from the `MIDlet` class. Nonetheless, meaning is not dependent on authorial intent, which has been largely downplayed even in fields such as literary studies.[12] Along with the names of the authors, this code is full of affiliations and attributions, and those markings link code to context.

Attribution and Affiliation in Code

A flag salute, a kiss on a cheek, a communal dance—these ritualistic conventions create a sense of connection even as they serve as sorting methods, as shibboleths, as barriers to entry, as borders between inside and outside the community of knowledge. In this way, ritualized forms signal affiliation.

Code is similarly marked by such affiliation, and the Transborder Immigrant Tool establishes its community with the open-source code movement through its choice of programming language, its licensing agreements, and, of course, by releasing the code on the SourceForge site (archived at this book's website). Bruce Perens, who developed an early definition of *open source*, wrote in 1999 that it is a specification for licenses that ensures "the right to make copies of the program, ... the right to have access to the software's source code, ... [and] the right to make improvements to the program." In that seminal article and his definition, he promoted a new model for software development. The Transborder Immigrant Tool is a piece of folklore that circulates in affiliation with the open-source folk and all the attendant ethos of collaborative development and sharing of resources.

The header code in the DowsingCompass file holds many such signifiers of connection: The comments at the top of the code begin the file by locating this code within the larger WalkingTools project, a platform for developing apps such as TBT. The second line announces a copyright even as it precedes the explanation that the software is free and can be redistributed freely. The text of that copyright, like many portions of the code, serves a performative function that signals and establishes the project's links with the open-source movement by applying the GNU Affero General Public License. Consider the part of the code that mentions the license:

```
/* WalkingtoolsGpx: XML, APIs, and Apps for Walking Artists
Copyright (C) 2010 Walkingtoools project/B.A.N.G Lab UCSD
    This program is free software: you can redistribute it and/or
modify
it under the terms of the GNU Affero General Public License as
published by the Free Software Foundation, either version 3 of the
License, or (at your option) any later version.
    This program is distributed in the hope that it will be useful,
but WITHOUT ANY WARRANTY; without even the implied warranty of
MERCHANTABILITY or FITNESS FOR A PARTICULAR PURPOSE. See the
GNU Affero General Public License for more details.
    You should have received a copy of the GNU Affero
General Public License along with this program. If not, see
<http://www.gnu.org/licenses/>.
*/
```

This license text presents another instance in which language is operating as functional, performative utterance even as it signals affiliation. However, this license text is not a unique expression of the programmers. Instead it is *boilerplate*, or rather a scripted part of the ritual, used by many across the community. The inclusion of the license in the code fulfills the strict sense of Austin's performative utterances. Like Austin's classic example, the pronouncement in a marriage ceremony, "I now pronounce you man and wife," these words place the code under the license described therein. At the same time, the use of the GNU Afffero License affiliates this code with a vibrant FOSS community. Yet even as the project reaches for the freedom of FOSS, it acknowledges a legal regime under which it would fall victim if it even "implied" a warranty of "FITNESS FOR A PARTICULAR PURPOSE." Here is the paradox of freely available code for a survival tool that cannot legally warranty its fitness to help with survival. With this ominous reminder in all caps, we see how the code places itself under two realms of affiliation, one free and open and one defensive and protective.

The open-source community becomes a folk through its licenses, which have become a precedent for the Creative Commons licenses that have so shaped creative symbolic production and circulation on the internet. At the turn of the millennium, Rick Borovoy et al. (2001) described a process they called *folk computing*, "an approach for using technology to support co-present community building inspired by the concept of folklore" (1). This notion, born of the MIT Media Lab, becomes *folk programming*. In a presentation titled "Forking Encouraged: Folk Programming, Open Source, and Social Software Development," Kirrily Robert, Yoz Grahame, and Jason Douglas (2009) use *folk programming* as name for contemporary open-source software development. In both cases, the open-source programming community becomes the site of a folk because the emphasis is on collective development.

Of course, that is not the only form of affiliation. The choice of a programming language represents a choice of affiliation, linking this project to its ethos, as well as its paradigms and its users. Also, the application affiliates itself by making use of pre-existing libraries—in this case, various Java and J2ME libraries, and more particularly WalkingTools. These libraries serve as a necessary groundwork for the application while situating the tool itself in a clan or network of software applications. The code calls these libraries through import statements:

```
Import edu.ucsd.calit2.TransborderTool.international.*
```

The name bears the affiliation of the code to its source, as a file name and as an institution, calit2 at UC San Diego. The naming reflects a file structure, which, following Java conventions, is a kind of reverse URL. As a result, the code acknowledges the institutional context that fostered its growth and would later investigate its production. At the same time, the mere act of following that convention is itself an act of affiliation to the larger community of Java programmers, the folk to whom this lore will be legible.

In these ways, the folklore of code points to its communities.

The Lore of the Comments

Jeremy Douglass argues, "Comments are part of a vernacular, with their own folk traditions and lore" (2010). I would push this a step further by saying that comments themselves are lore, and those in the Transborder Immigrant Tool take a form that parallels the embellished instructions of the poetry. Jason Najarro's commentary in the Transborder Immigrant Tool code offers notes for orientation and wayfinding in parallel to Amy Sarah Carroll's poems.[13] Consider this passage from the TBMIDlet.Java code, in which Najarro seems to be leaving trail marks and warnings:

```
184. /* through a lot of tedious testing, I discovered that these
185. constructors of the TextFields were throwing an
IllegalArgumentException
186. when using TextField.DECIMAL or TextField.NUMERIC constraints.
The
187. following is from the javadoc. It seems not to contradict the
188. use of TextField.DECIMAL or NUMERIC given that I was setting
189. the forms to a decimal/numeric value ... hmmmmm ... this must
be an
190. issue in in iden implementation.
```

After this comment, Najarro quotes the following passage from the iDEN documentation:

```
192. "Some constraints, such as DECIMAL, require the implementation
to
193. perform syntactic validation of the contents of the text
object.
194. The syntax checking is performed on the actual contents of
the text
195. object, which may differ from the displayed contents as
described
196. above. Syntax checking is performed on the initial contents
passed
197. to the constructors, and it is also enforced for all method
calls
198. that affect the contents of the text object. The methods and
199. constructors throw IllegalArgumentException if they would
result
200. in the contents of the text object not conforming to the
required
201. syntax."
```

By contrast, the code in this file seems authorless yet authoritative, like an invocation of holy writ or communal law, and yet this comment is something much more mundane, prosaic, and patently incomplete.

Through Najarro's comment, his notes on his own frustration, the code becomes a document of process, spoken in first person to an audience that is trying to make their way through the code. The text takes the form of an oral remark, as he interrupts himself with "hmmmmm" and then offers speculation. Then, he leaves a bit of text from the manual, the document that was supposed to tell him how to interact with the iDEN system, as a sign of the well that was empty. Najarro is like the traveler, attempting to navigate a challenging environ through code, only to leave notes for future travelers.

Throughout this well-documented code, Najarro's voice returns, translating the functioning of the code into straightforward imperatives. For example, before running `getNearbyWaypoints`, Najarro writes, "Offer any available help to user" (line 430). Yet the voice is not addressing a listener but paraphrasing the activity of the code. In another passage, he writes, "We are now returning from a bad signal" (425). The royal *we* here stands in for the code and perhaps also its programmers. The comments use the modal helping verb *may* in a manner that establishes uncertainty and indeterminacy, as in this example: "In these cases the user may still be able to navigate with a magnetic compass" (408-9). Again, such a state of uncertainty or potential is the state of the unexecuted program, paralleling the advice of the prose poems, in which all instructions are offered with contingencies.

This is not to suggest that the comments were all written by one person or in one voice. Consider the text of the TBgpxParser file:

```
147. /* Completely rebuilt this part on may 10th, 2008, in order
to make the class
148. * more robust. Before it assumed that certain elements would
be contained in
149. * a particular order, without any intervening xml tags that
might be added
150. * by various applications. (Such as G7towin, which produced
gpx files that
151. * this class threw up on.) I tried to make it more robust by
looking for tags
152. * and accepting their data if they contained "wpt" data, and
just ignoring
```

```
153. * anything else it finds. Brett.
154. */
```

A class "throwing up" on GPX files does not appear to be the standard procedure for Java. In this passage, this comment returns to the decidedly personal record of the designer's log rather than paraphrasing what the code does. As a further sign of documentation to aid future revisions to the code, Stalbaum even signs this note. In another comment, Brett's informality seems to return:

```
54 ... [the software] should now handle any gpx file containing
55 * waypoints, regardless of other junk in the file.
```

The many voices of the commentary represent not only the multiple authorship but also the heteroglossia of the code, to use Bakhtin's notion, the many genres and styles within even one set of comments composed by the same programmer. While Bakhtin spoke of novels, these code files are likewise full of genres and styles, such as narratives, accumulated fragments, even some autogenerated comments, organized around the particular operational patterns of the instructions.

Walking through the Code

To read the code is to engage in what Dominguez calls a *speculative deployment*, or imagined execution, of the code (UCSBLitCultureMedia 2010a). To trace the code is to test a series of potential use cases, imagining a user—here a mythological border crosser who is about to die. (Note that aside from tests by EDT, there have only been a few public, in situ deployments so far.)[14] So to read this code is to travel with that user across the desert, trying to survive by using the tool. The traveler is left in the state of Schrödinger's indeterminant cat, straddling or toggling between the states of life and death. To aestheticize the plight of the immigrant would be exploitative, but I would argue that because the tool has circulated far in advance of any implementation, it is a rhetorical device even more than it is a survival mechanism. In the context of a border the walls and checkpoints of which Josh Kun (2011) has called "political theater," the tool offers itself as a theater for reimagining the dominant narrative of sovereign nation-states and boundaries through potential narratives about survival and the navigation of challenging geographies. To participate in the ritual of the code is to move with that user, to travel with them, to engage in the subject positions inscribed in the code, which has been framed in a certain logic about the border. A walkthrough of the code will enact this ritual, will stage that drama, while no doubt creating another "text" of the folklore that is the Transborder Immigrant Tool.

At the SourceForge code repository, a reader will first encounter the five main Java files of TBT: DowsingCompass, DowsingCompassListener, TBCoordinates, TBgpxParser, and TBMIDlet. *Midlet* is the name for Mobile Information Device Profile (MIDP) applications designed to be run on small devices, particularly mobile phones. The *let* suffix follows the naming convention of servlets and applets. The primary file, then, is the TBMIDlet file.

The first part of the code declares the variables, setting them to their default states, most of which are null, including the variables that are key to locating the water, nearbyWPList (nearby waypoint list) and targetList.[15] Six poem names are loaded in, as well as the names of the sound files. After this initialization, the code presents the constructor for a transborder midlet:

```
* public TBMIDlet () {
```

In Java, a *constructor* creates an instance of the class (known as *instantiation*)—in other words, a new object, the application itself. *Public* means that any file can call that function.[16]

Before it can help the traveler navigate, the system needs to know where water is, so it runs TBgpxParser as a thread. A *thread* is a process that runs in parallel to and concurrent with the current flow of control in the program. In other words, a thread allows the computer to be working on two processes at once. A commented-out line (or a line of program code that will be "ignored" by machine readers) shows how one implementation of the tool loaded the coordinates from a website:

```
62. // private String URL = "http://internetjunkee.com/transborder/
GPScourseFinal.gpx";
```

In an operational version, according to Stalbaum, the coordinates would be preloaded onto the phone rather than posting them for anyone to find on the internet. Stalbaum said this choice was based on the sensitivity of the water cache data and the project's work to keep it private—not because the water stations themselves are hidden, sitting just off the road in bright blue barrels, but because an opponent of the project might make ill use of the entire list of coordinates (Marino 2011a). As a consequence of this vulnerability, the application does not (and in fact cannot) download the files but will be preloaded with them. This commented-out line of code serves as a reminder of yet another potential threat to the survival of the immigrant: those who wish to sabotage the water stations.

Having loaded the data, the software performs a "freshness test" to see if the location data has expired:

```
302. // make sure the data is not expired
303. if (isExpired) {
304. display.setCurrent(expired);
305. display.vibrate(1000);
306. playAudioFile("expired.wav", true);
307. } else if (expireWarning) {
308. display.setCurrent(expirationWarning, tbDowsingCompass);
309. display.vibrate(1000);
310. playAudioFile("expiration.wav", true);
```

If the data is expired or the warning is already set, the phone vibrates and plays the expiration warning:

```
311. } else if (startUpAlert) { //first time only
312. startUpAlert = false;
313. display.setCurrent(startUpDisplay, tbDowsingCompass);
314. display.vibrate(1000);
315. playAudioFile("startup.wav", true);
316. } else { // we are good to go
317. display.setCurrent(tbDowsingCompass);
318. }
```

Otherwise, if the app has just been launched, it plays its startup audio. The expression of the process that checks the expiration date seems rife with urgency, finality:

```
124. if (exp <= System.currentTimeMillis()) {
125. expired = new Alert(translation.translate("Data expired"),
126. translation.translate("The data is expired, TBTool is not
safe to use."),
127. errorImage,
128. AlertType.ERROR);
129. expired.setTimeout(Alert.FOREVER);
```

```
130. expired.addCommand(exit);
131. expired.addCommand(ignore);
132. expired.setCommandListener(this);
133. isExpired = true;
```

Again, line 124 checks to see if the expiration date is on or before the current date. If it is, then a new alert is created. Lines 130–131 create options for response, including Exit and Ignore options. Finally, the boolean variable registering expiration is set to true.

In this code snippet, the reader encounters the first scenario in which the imagined user would likely die. Reading the code as a kind of procedural narrative creates the sense of two distinct tonal registers. Notice how the more unemotional, mathematical aspects of the code (such as if (exp <=) alternate with a more loaded, natural language of the functions, methods, objects, and data. The lines AlertType.ERROR and expired.setTimeout (Alert.FOREVER) indicate the finality of this state because no additional waypoint information is available (129, 130). Reading these lines of code, excerpted from their coding environment, I find it difficult not to notice the foreboding in the all-caps ERROR and FOREVER or to ignore the terrible resonance that builds with each repeated *expired*. However, those dramatic elements alternate with lines that seem much more understated. The simple variable assignment isExpired = true would most likely spell death for the traveler. In this way, dual registers sound out in the code, one that more directly announces the danger and another that, though delivering equally grave news, proceeds with a bare mathematical calm.

The second such scenario occurs immediately after in the code:

```
158. noNearbyWaypoints = new Alert(translation.translate("No
Nearby Points"),
```

Translated into the traveler's preferred language, this alert plays for ten thousand milliseconds, possibly the last alert the person will hear. Such a statement sounds maudlin, but it is important to remember that this code is not merely a system of causes and effects, of calculations, but a representation of potential real-world moments with dire consequences. Like Carroll's poetry, the code conveys these moments of imminent death without using the conventions of a protagonist, drawn-out scenes, or other devices that typically cue affect, requiring instead that the reader realize the potential peril while processing these instructions. The finality of this scenario does not come across with the sensationalism of twenty-four-hour news but instead with a kind of muted affect, the impact only settling in once the reader has traced through the implications by tracing through the consequences of the code.

Of Witching Sticks and GPS

Although the Transborder Immigrant Tool relies on high-tech navigation equipment, the story of the code does not champion the potential for a technological rescue but instead reverts to folk knowledge, material bodies, and natural environs. Both kinds of scientific knowledge might be considered folk knowledge, but the Transborder Immigrant Tool draws upon the wisdom of Death Valley rather than Silicon Valley.

Although death awaits the traveler who has expired data or cannot find a waypoint, in other versions of the scenario the traveler will find a destination to navigate toward. By default, the system will set the cache as the location, but the user can manually choose another destination, including a beacon or a city. The tool searches for a nearby water station by using DowsingCompassListener, an extension of a WalkingTools method called `NavigatorListener`:

```
206. tbDowsingCompass.addNavigatorListener(this);
207.
208. targetList = new List(translation.translate("Select a
Target"), List.IMPLICIT);
```

When the user is facing a water cache, the software calls `witchingEvent`, a method that begins the primary navigation. *Water witching* or *dowsing* is the name for the ritual of searching for water using a *witching stick*, also known as a *divining rod*. *Witching* is not a term typically used with digital GPS navigation; it was added by Jason Najarro to frame the process. Consequently, this metaphor of witching or dowsing is built into the conceptual framework of the tool through the code. No incidental feature of the code, the metaphor from the ritual of water witching is a centerpiece of Najarro's presentations of the code, indicating its central significance (Najarro et al. 2010). The metaphor returns in `witchingEvent` (when water is detected), `dowsingCompass`, `dowsingCompassListener`, and `tbDowsingCompass`, naming objects, methods, and files.

Introducing this folk practice as a conceptual metaphor of the Transborder Immigrant Tool frames this set of methods to a predigital cultural practice. The high-tech communication and global positioning device is turned into the stick drawn to water through some innate connection. Electronic Disturbance Theater explains this seeming low-tech evocation by situating the app as Mayan technology, as formulated by the Zapatista movement in Mexico. In a folkloric narrative, EDT member Dominguez performs a tale about Mayan technology in which a mere boy uses a simple stick to send an overhead military helicopter away (Marino 2011c). The lesson of the tale is clear: Mayan technology is as seemingly simple as a boy playing with a stick and yet powerful enough to disrupt Western narratives of progress and power, command and control. So too does the witching metaphor organize the sense of meaning within this code, situating this project not in the realm of progress but in the realm of provocation, by embedding a supernatural (or perhaps merely extranatural) folk practice in a contemporary computer program.

In a witching event, the tool begins wayfinding, leading the person to the water cache through a set of audio and haptic cues. If the immigrant is fortunate enough to reach the water, the code celebrates:

```
213. waypointAheadAlert = new Alert (translation.translate("Site Ahead!")
[...]
221. arrivedAlert= new Alert(translation.translate("Arrived at Site")
```

Here we are encountering one of the many potential scenarios embedded in this code. However, toward the end of TBMIDlet, the code raises the specter of another unfortunate outcome. If the traveler stops, the MIDlet plays a message to encourage the person to walk:

```
555. If (isMoving) {// uptdated to moving
556. nearbyWPList =
557. tbDowsingCompass.getNearbyWaypoints (SEARCH_DISTANCE);//so update nearby point
558. }else { //updated nt movingdisplay.vibrate(200).
559. If (moveWarningEnervator % 5 == 0) {//only play this file ~ every 5th time
560. playAudioFile("move.wav", false);//the "move for compass" message can be too frequent.
```

The moveWarningEnervator is meant to push onward the immigrant who may have stopped from exhaustion or perhaps disorientation. The vibrations and the audio output were built around Najarro's research into the state of a dehydrated person. Here is another occasion in the development of this project that demonstrates its primary focus on serving a real desperate human need, rather than merely representing that need. Reflecting on the mental state of the traveler, Najarro realized that their interface must be simple enough to communicate to a person about to pass out or worse (Marino 2011a). Similarly, as the traveler nears the water station, the duration of the periodic vibration increases, just as a dowsing stick would respond to its approach to water in the ground.

To read this code, by my measure, is to emulate the functioning of the code in a variety of use cases. The reader must imagine the effects on the code of a traveler encountering a nearby water station or finding none at all, of navigating toward that station or ceasing to progress out of fatigue or disorientation. In this way, that reading experience is likely to be multiple, but it cannot be vague. In other words, to process the code as the machine does, the reader cannot avoid the question of whether the traveler finds a water cache but instead in each use case must decide whether water is found and, consequently, whether the border crosser lives or dies.

Poetry in Potential

Just as the code presents the use case as instructions suspended around potential states, so too does Carroll's poetry. A second poem demonstrates this combination of instructional imperative, poetry, and potentiality:

> Heat cramps, relatively mild, signal dehydration and loss of sodium. *Drink water, rest in the shade; seek water at twilight.* Heat illness is an injury whose symptoms include fatigue, dizziness, fainting, nausea, vomiting. Redux: *Drink water, rest in the shade; seek water at twilight.* Heat exhaustion produces sweating, clammy skin, increased pulse and respiration rate, weakness, more fainting, nausea and vomiting. *STOP. The choices from now on you make will dictate whether you live or die.* Heatstroke happens when a person pushes on despite heat exhaustion. Trauma ensues—physical collapse, loss of consciousness, rapid pulse and respiration, a skyrocketing body temperature, severe disorientation, impaired motor skills, involuntary urination, dilated pupils. As heatstroke progresses, you will experience chest and arm pain, convulse, go into a coma. You will not be equipped to deal with these symptoms as they present themselves. *Call 9-1-1 or 0-6-6 beforehand.*

Similar to the code that handled the expired data, this poem offers the reader another pair of voices: one delivering data, medical information, in a dry, calm tone, the other offering imperatives, the italics of which underscore their urgency and alarm. The passage begins with the plain tone of a definition followed by instructions on how to combat dehydration. The symptoms list grows, followed by a repetition of the instructions to "drink ... rest ... seek water at twilight," now a refrain. For those who encounter the art project, as opposed to those using the system to survive, the instructions are like the code: something that we read (or hear) as intended for someone or something else to put into action. Like the code, the poetry alternates conditions with instructions. The second symptoms list is repeated, but the pattern is interrupted by an alert: "Stop," followed by a much more stark warning. The symptoms list resumes with elaboration, embellished with images. Through anaphora, Carroll intensifies the impact of the heat. The final list marks symptoms the person will not be able to react to or recover from, followed by a command. This alternation of the symptoms and instructions acts as alternating threads or subroutines, the one depicting the set of effects of dehydration, the other instructions on what to do next. Yet they are not unrelated. The symptoms serve as signs to motivate the responses, like a series of if-then statements. They proceed with increasing severity on a path to dehydration even while they are instructing how to respond to it. The instructions, through direct address, serve as the move-WarningEnervator, to push the perishing traveler to action. Although the code does not list the symptoms in stark detail, the poem fills in details of the additional conditions of the traveler for whom the variable isMoving is set to false. Moreover, the parallels between the code and the poetry have made permeable the border between their two positions in the art project.

The rhetoric of folk wisdom, whether in rituals or prophesies, delivers its instructions with conditions for execution and possible scenarios for outcomes, in ways analogous to the code (Borovoy 2002). In cautionary stories and warning axioms, rules and rhymes, legends and prayers, folk wisdom travels through a set of admonitions that, like the code, carries with it the outcomes when its conditions are not met. The code and poetry of this piece deliver the wisdom of those survival procedures in tones that alternate between calm, methodological instructions and descriptions, on the one hand, and alarming alerts and pressing imperatives on the other. The juxtaposition of those tones, as well as the interplay between the poetry and the code layers, the way they frame one another, disrupts any singular narrative of the transborder traveler's experience, offering instead a journey that proceeds with urgency and yet inevitability, inevitability and yet possibility, leading either to death or to survival.

At the same time, both the code and the poetry defuse the political Molotov cocktail of the border by situating the land not in the context of political boundaries but in a survival narrative. Although we have read the code as deployed by an imaginary undocumented immigrant, neither the poetry nor the code make mention of the traveler's national identity, using *TB* in the naming of files and methods throughout the code to inscribe *transborder* across the project in place of *undocumented* or *illegal*. The criminalization authored by the State hence is supplanted by the moniker of movement across a political fiction. Nor is this piece only about crossing geographic borders. EDT member micha cárdenas, a trans artist, has opened the term *transborder* to other kinds of crossings, specifically the constructions of gender and sex. Her poem "Song of My Cells" culminates thus: "This Bridge Called my Back, my heart, my head, my cock, my cunt, my tunnel. Vision: You. Are. Crossing. Into. Me" (Electronic Disturbance Theater 2010). As she links her work to Anzaldúa's powerful "This Bridge Called My Back," she maps the geography of the TBT onto the biological border between the sexes, as well as the conceptual border between "you" and "me," self and other, opening up this ritual to other frames of reference where borders divide, such as the binaries in identity, sexuality, and gender. Thus, though some texts and paratexts direct our attention to one interpretation of the piece, it is important not to limit our readings of the code to one context and not to privilege denotations over connotations, literal references and designations over figurative ones, even though they do (and must) provide a basis for interpretation. To limit reading in that way reproduces and enforces borders and boundaries to meaning and meaning-making that are even more imaginary than the political borders this piece disrupts.

Just as with any ritual, the procedure is an entryway to a hermeneutic of experience or a meaningful experience designed to be symbolic and evocative, designated with one meaning and yet opening out to others. For example, take the exception toward the end of the program:

```
572. while (running) {
573. try {
574. Thread.sleep(1000 * 60 * (rand.nextInt(19) + 1)); // sleep
random minutes
575. //Thread.sleep(1000 * 60); // sleep one min (test)
576. } catch (InterruptedException e) {
577. running = false;
}
```

If this code detects the app is asleep, the program corrects the state of the program from `running = true` to `running = false`. These lines remind me of the role of this hactavist artwork that is always trying to wake us up, always has its eye on when its audience is lapsing into sleep and then energizes us with some provocations. Just as the program watches for the sleep of the geographic traveler, the many components of this piece—the poems, the code, and the metaphors that they employ and deploy—keep trying to stir us, to keep us moving. The app, in this interpretation, is just as much a process of our minds as it is a program for a phone or an attendant to a progression of feet. The code-becoming-poetry resists our simple assigning of this process of navigation and its encoded methods to mere geography. These powerful methods of `NavigatorListener` and `DowsingCompass` are just as much about physical wayfinding as the internal pathfinding of thought.

Both the code and the poetry therefore are part of rituals, part of this instantiation of the Transborder Immigrant Tool. They are performed in the execution of the tool, but this execution has been mostly an imaginary activity. Most people who encounter this tool have not been dying in the desert. Rather, those who speak of the software and its applications engage in speculative deployments. Some deploy the project only partially based on little more than publicity videos or snippets of poetry, leading typically to reactionary responses. However, tracing carefully through the instructions in the code and the poetry, the reader has the opportunity to imagine the potential outcomes for the traveler and more fully consider the implications separate from the hysterical political rhetoric. Like the person following the steps of a ritual or ceremony, pursuing the processes of the Transborder Immigrant Tool requires faithfully following set paths that others have pursued and will continue to pursue as a form of meditation.

To situate code as ritual is to acknowledge its place in the transmission and production of culture itself. In *Ethnomimesis*, anthropologist Robert Cantwell (1993) writes of the place of ritual in culture, arguing, "Whatever the ontological status of culture as such, it must be embodied, enacted, performed, represented and reproduced in order to have any social reality" (30). The code and the poetry of the Transborder Immigrant Tool present a site of this performance, the enactment of culture through the lore of travelers who live or die while making their way through a desert that they must learn to read. In reading the code, we cross and cross back that same desert, guided by the wayfinding of the comments and advice, encountering and becoming a community attentive not to the political spectacle of national border debates but to the potential loss of life and the conditions of sustenance for our fellow travelers.

4   Climategate

File: briffa_sep98_e.pro

Programming Language: Interactive Data Language

Developed: 1998

Principal Authors: Tim Mitchell, Mark New, Ian "Harry" Harris

Platform: Window, macOS, Unix, VMS, and others

Source File: http://di2.nu/foia/harris-tree/briffa_sep98_e.pro; FOAI.zip (leaked file)

Interoperating Files: Age-banded and Hugershoff-standardized datasets (corr_age2hug.out)

Code

```
1. ;
2. ; PLOTS 'ALL' REGION MXD timeseries from age banded and from
hugershoff
3. ; standardised datasets.
4. ; Reads Harry's regional timeseries and outputs the 1600-1992
portion
5. ; with missing values set appropriately.  Uses mxd, and just
the
6. ; "all band" timeseries
7. ;****** APPLIES A VERY ARTIFICIAL CORRECTION FOR
DECLINE*********
8. ;
9. yrloc=[1400,findgen(19)*5.+1904]
10. valadj=[0.,0.,0.,0.,0.,-0.1,-0.25,-
0.3,0.,-0.1,0.3,0.8,1.2,1.7,2.5,2.6,2.6,$
11.   2.6,2.6,2.6]*0.75          ; fudge factor
```

```
12. if n_elements(yrloc) ne n_elements(valadj) then
message,'Oooops!'
13. ;
14. loadct,39
15. def_1color,20,color='red'
16. plot,[0,1]
17. multi_plot,nrow=4,layout='large'
18. if !d.name eq 'X' then begin
19.   window, ysize=800
20.   !p.font=-1
21. endif else begin
22.   !p.font=0
23.   device,/helvetica,/bold,font_size=18
24. endelse
25. ;
26. ; Get regional tree lists and rbar
27. ;
28. restore,filename='reglists.idlsave'
29. harryfn=['nwcan','wnam','cecan','nweur','sweur','nsib','csib',
'tib',$
30.   'esib','allsites']
31. ;
32. rawdat=fltarr(4,2000)
33. for i = nreg-1 , nreg-1 do begin
34.   fn='mxd.'+harryfn(i)+'.pa.mean.dat'
35.   print,fn
36.   openr,1,fn
37.   readf,1,rawdat
38.   close,1
39.   ;
40.   densadj=reform(rawdat(2:3,*))
41.   ml=where(densadj eq -99.999,nmiss)
42.   densadj(ml)=!values.f_nan
43.   ;
44.   x=reform(rawdat(0,*))
45.   kl=where((x ge 1400) and (x le 1992))
46.   x=x(kl)
```

```
47.    densall=densadj(1,kl)       ; all bands
48.    densadj=densadj(0,kl)       ; 2-6 bands
49.    ;
50.    ; Now normalise w.r.t. 1881-1960
51.    ;
52.    mknormal,densadj,x,refperiod=[1881,1960],refmean=refmean,ref
sd=refsd
53.    mknormal,densall,x,refperiod=[1881,1960],refmean=refmean,ref
sd=refsd
54. ;
55. ; APPLY ARTIFICIAL CORRECTION
56. ;
57. yearlyadj=interpol(valadj,yrloc,x)
58. densall=densall+yearlyadj
59.    ;
60.    ; Now plot them
61.    ;
62.    filter_cru,20,tsin=densall,tslow=tslow,/nan
63.    cpl_barts,x,densall,title='Age-banded MXD from all sites',$
64.      xrange=[1399.5,1994.5],xtitle='Year',/xstyle,$
65.      zeroline=tslow,yrange=[-7,3]
66.    oplot,x,tslow,thick=3
67.    oplot,!x.crange,[0.,0.],linestyle=1
68.    ;
69. endfor
70. ;
71. ; Restore the Hugershoff NHD1 (see Nature paper 2)
72. ;
73. xband=x
74. restore,filename='../tree5/densadj_MEAN.idlsave'
75. ; gets: x,densadj,n,neff
76. ;
77. ; Extract the post 1600 part
78. ;
79. kl=where(x ge 1400)
80. x=x(kl)
81. densadj=densadj(kl)
```

```
82. ;
83. ; APPLY ARTIFICIAL CORRECTION
84. ;
85. yearlyadj=interpol(valadj,yrloc,x)
86. densadj=densadj+yearlyadj
87. ;
88. ; Now plot it too
89. ;
90. filter_cru,20,tsin=densadj,tslow=tshug,/nan
91. cpl_barts,x,densadj,title='Hugershoff-standardised MXD from
all sites',$
92.    xrange=[1399.5,1994.5],xtitle='Year',/xstyle,$
93.    zeroline=tshug,yrange=[-7,3],bar_color=20
94. oplot,x,tshug,thick=3,color=20
95. oplot,!x.crange,[0.,0.],linestyle=1
96. ;
97. ; Now overplot their bidecadal components
98. ;
99. plot,xband,tslow,$
100.    xrange=[1399.5,1994.5],xtitle='Year',/xstyle,$
101.    yrange=[-6,2],thick=3,title='Low-pass (20-yr) filtered
comparison'
102. oplot,x,tshug,thick=3,color=20
103. oplot,!x.crange,[0.,0.],linestyle=1
104. ;
105. ; Now overplot their 50-yr components
106. ;
107. filter_cru,50,tsin=densadj,tslow=tshug,/nan
108. filter_cru,50,tsin=densall,tslow=tslow,/nan
109. plot,xband,tslow,$
110.    xrange=[1399.5,1994.5],xtitle='Year',/xstyle,$
111.    yrange=[-6,2],thick=3,title='Low-pass (50-yr) filtered
comparison'
112. oplot,x,tshug,thick=3,color=20
113. oplot,!x.crange,[0.,0.],linestyle=1
114. ;
```

```
115. ; Now compute the full, high and low pass correlations
between the two
116. ; series
117. ;
118. perst=1400.
119. peren=1992.
120. ;
121. openw,1,'corr_age2hug.out'
122. thalf=[10.,30.,50.,100.]
123. ntry=n_elements(thalf)
124. printf,1,'Correlations between timeseries'
125. printf,1,'Age-banded vs. Hugershoff-standardised'
126. printf,1,'    Region    Full    <10    >10    >30    >50    >100'
127. ;
128. kla=where((xband ge perst) and (xband le peren))
129. klh=where((x ge perst) and (x le peren))
130. ts1=densadj(klh)
131. ts2=densall(kla)
132. ;
133. r1=correlate(ts1,ts2)
134. rall=fltarr(ntry)
135. for i = 0 , ntry-1 do begin
136.    filter_cru,thalf(i),tsin=ts1,tslow=tslow1,tshigh=tshi1,/nan
137.    filter_cru,thalf(i),tsin=ts2,tslow=tslow2,tshigh=tshi2,/nan
138.    if i eq 0 then r2=correlate(tshi1,tshi2)
139.    rall(i)=correlate(tslow1,tslow2)
140. endfor
141. ;
142. printf,1,'ALL SITES',r1,r2,rall,$
143.    format='(A11,2X,6F6.2)'
144. ;
145. printf,1,' '
146. printf,1,'Correlations carried out over the  period
',perst,peren
147. ;
148. close,1
149. ;
150. end
```

Notes

1: A semicolon (;) precedes comments in IDL. Also, John Graham-Cumming (2009) offers a useful gloss of this code on his blog.

2: MXD is *maximum latewood density*, a correlate of regional temperature. *Hugershoff* refers to the Hugershoff function (Warren 1980).

7: The phrase "a very artificial correction" became the smoking gun of climate data manipulation. But as one commentator adds, "Certainly if I wanted to actually fudge something without anyone knowing, a 15-star comment wouldn't be my first thought" (Clark 2009).

9: Creates the list (a.k.a. vector) [1400, 1904, 1909, 1914, 1919, 1924, 1929, 1934, 1939, 1944, 1949, 1954, 1959, 1964, 1969, 1974, 1979, 1984, 1989, 1994]. Findgen creates a floating-point array of the dimensions specified. Note that this array is declared without static typing, arguably a weakness in IDL.

10: Here are the adjustments: down for 1929–1934, 1944, then increasingly upward after 1949, plateauing at a +2.6 adjustment from 1974–1994. Each number is multiplied by 0.75. As noted in chapter 1, because these magic numbers (i.e., unnamed constants) are not further documented in the code, they give off an air of arbitrariness.

11: The *fudge factor* is the offset used to correct the data. This phrase alone fueled much of the Climategate controversy.

12: If the sizes of the arrays do not equal, display an error message. However, no doubt the use of "Ooops" was also read as signaling a larger error—and perhaps, too, a lax attitude toward the code.

14: Load color table 39 ("rainbow and white") for the color display palette.

16: plot draws a line of the vector arguments (0, 1).

17: multi_plot,nrow=4,layout='large'. nrow is the number of rows in the graph. multi_ plot is the method. This line exemplifies the way IDL differentiates the method from the arguments by position only, one of of the complaints about the language. In one critic's words, "It's gross and I don't see any reason it should be structured differently from function calls, which take a more typical name(arg, arg) style" (Elliott 2014).

21: endif ends the first if condition, just as endelse ends an else.

24: See 21.

28: Restores the variables from the reglists file.

29: This array contains the following regions: northwest Canada, west North America, central Canada, northwest Europe, southwest Europe, north Siberia, central Siberia, Tibetan plateau, east Siberia, and all sites (Briffa et al. 2001). The name *harryfn* most likely refers to Ian "Harry" Harris, one of the programmers (with *fn* possibly referring to *file name*).

32: `rawdat=fltarr(4,2000)` creates `rawdat`, a floating-point array of 4×2000.

33–38: Opens the harrfn files and reads in the data.

35. `print,fn`. The first of many print statements is a reminder that the goal of this program is to create a graph, not to alter data. The destination of the changed data is a display, not its repository.

45: The boundaries of the data are 1400 and 1992.

52–53: Notably, this normalization runs from 1881–1960, before the tree data becomes less reliable. Another version of this code contains a commented-out section that applies this normalization to 1881–1940 (http://blog.jgc.org/2009/11/about-that-cru-hack.html).

57: Uses linear interpolation to fill in the data in between the adjusted years.

58: This adjustment is made to data containing "all bands."

71: This reference to an article in *Nature* demonstrates one of the ways intertextual references can appear in code. Nature 2 probably refers to the *Nature* article that Harris did not coauthor (Briffa, Schweingruber, Jones, Osborn, Shiyatov, et al. 1998).

77: Perhaps a typo; the code that follows begins its work after 1400, not 1600.

79: Similar to 77; the code narrows the range to after 1400.

81: Narrows range of adjustment to just years after 1400.

85: See comment on line 57.

86: This second adjustment is made just to the data containing "2–6 bands."

94–95: `oplot` plots points over a previously drawn plot without redrawing the axis.

118: Throughout this code, 1400 reappears as the bottom boundary, and its repetition in the code draws my reflection. This early modern moment may have been chosen because it occurs well after the *medieval climate anomaly* (c950-c1250; Mann et al. 2009), which saw unusually high temperatures; however, even that anomaly appears tiny compared to late-twentieth-century temperature increases.

124: `printf, 1` prints to an open file (1).

128: With expressions like `where((xband ge perst) and (xband le peren))`, IDL appears almost like an English phrase, with the abbreviations ge (greater or equal) and le (less than or equal) presenting only minor obstacles to comprehension as natural language. Chapter 5 will take up the quest for programming language legibility.

Functionality

This code primarily draws a chart and plots the lines of data related to tree ring density and temperature change. However, rather than plotting the data as recorded, it makes a series of adjustments to the data, sometimes upward, sometimes downward. The results are multiplied by 0.75. These adjustments, labeled as a *fudge factor*, will be the source of the claims of evidence tampering. At first, the code makes those adjustments to the data every five years; then, through linear interpolation, it makes adjustments to the intervening years (in between the five-year increments; Graham-Cumming 2009).

In the first part of this code, `yrloc` creates an array, or *vector* in this programming language, that begins with 1400 and continues with 1904, 1909, 1914, all the way to 1994. In other words, after the first two terms, it increases the years by five. The next line creates an array of numbers, each of which are multiplied by 0.75, the so-called fudge factor, and then a comparitor checks to see if there are the same number of elements in the two arrays. Now we have a set of years and a list of discrete adjustments. The `yearlyadj` array will become the source for the curve for the graph for the entire range (1400–1994), using linear interpolation, essentially connecting the dots. Subseqently, the yearly adjusted numbers are added to the densall data.

Extreme Climate

In 2009, this computer source code, along with other code and a bundle of thousands of emails and other documents, was leaked to the public and reposted on the internet, bringing what had previously been code developed in the context of a research group before an audience that was ignorant of its context, including a group of readers who were deeply suspicious of its programmers' motives. So began an episode known as the Climatic Research Unit email controversy, or *Climategate*, the *-gate* suffix commonly appended to political scandals in the United States since Watergate. This source code began as a working document, an in-progress visualization tool that had been circulated among researchers all working on the same problem at the same institution, the Climate Research Unit (CRU) of East Anglia in the United Kingdom. However, its meaning changed as it was passed into the hands of a group for whom the code would become if not the smoking gun of the deception of climate change science, at least a political football. With its significance in play, it was tossed around by pundits on message boards and news outlets, where what mattered most was not its place as a stopgap measure but the digital deception it seemed to represent and even acknowledge in its very comments. The discussions that followed, though driven by misreading the intent of the code, gave this code a new meaning that would shape its significance thereafter, demonstrating another way that code accrues meaning through its circulation.

To understand the story of this code, it is worth remembering the political climate of the time. The year 2009 in the United States was an intense moment in the culture wars over climate change, largely due to a change in the political landscape. President George W. Bush, son of President George H. W. Bush, whose family's fortunes had grown largely out of a century of involvement in the oil industry (Phillips 2004), had been replaced by President Barak Obama, whose political platform largely centered on regulation of pollutants and whose campaign speeches promised to combat the effects of climate change (Grist Staff 2007). Only a few years earlier, director David Guggenheim had released the film *An Inconvenient Truth*, which presented Al Gore's documentation of climate change, including the much-contested hockey stick graph (figure 4.1), which showed the relatively recent skyrocketing of global temperatures after prolonged periods of gradual change. In addition to talk radio and twenty-four-hour cable news fomenting debate, a vibrant and contentious blogosphere was fraught with hobbyist climate scientists combing through the science behind the claims from the opposing side. Into this tense climate, this code was released, and it was through the hot magnifying lens of distrust that it would be read.

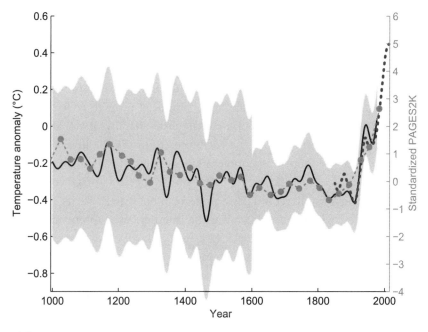

Figure 4.1
The dark line that begins just above 0.2 is the original hockey stick of Mann, Bradley, and Hughes (1999), with its uncertainty range (grey). The sharply rising line that overlaps the end is the global mean temperature, according to HadCRUT4 data from 1850 onward. The connected large dots represent correlated data from the PAGES2K initiative, a community-based research project that confirmed the hockey stick graph (PAGES2k Consortium 2017). Graph by Klaus Bitterman. CC-BY-SA 4.0.

This code was developed by Tim Mitchell and then updated by Ian "Harry" Harris, both of the CRU, whose job it was to bring disparate climate databases into alignment.[1] Harris documents his four-year-long saga in the Harry_Read_Me.txt file, and many of his exasperated comments became fodder for the tempest (in a teapot or no) about the code. Through this expression of his struggles, far beyond the frustrations Jason Najarro mentions in the Transborder Immigrant Tool (see chapter 3), Harry even earned the sympathy of some of his detractors, one of whom refers to him as "the poor sod who seems to have been landed with the responsibility of reworking the code after (I think) the departure of Tim Mitchell and/or Mark New who apparently wrote much of it."[2] At the time of the 1998 code, Briffa, Harris, and others published a paper entitled "Trees Tell of Past Climates: But Are They Speaking Less Clearly Today?" (Briffa, Schweingruber, Jones, Osborn, Harris, et al. 1998), which presents graphs similar to the ones produced by this code in which they discuss the disconnect between the tree ring data and directly measured temperature data. They propose a way to adjust for the tree ring data's lack of reliability post-1960. The code offers an attempt to graph temperatures that includes this adjustment, labeling it as a correction.

However, in the moment of bombastic blog posts reporting this so-called scandal, the all-caps comment "VERY ARTIFICIAL CORRECTION," a kind note-to-self, became the bold-faced evidence of a large-scale hoax, produced through code that appeared to falsify data to create the illusion of a climate crisis literally of global proportions. With allusions to the false weapons that were used to justify the invasion that began the Iraq War, one blog commentator, jorgekafkazar, writes, "CRU caught with weapons of math destruction" (jorgekafkazar, comment on Greiner 2009b). Of course, the fact that this deception was allegedly taking place in hidden (read secret, surreptitious) source code made it all the more juicy for the internet-based forums determined to produce an uproar. Here was the black box magically opened—the computational charlatans exposed with code, that secret and powerful mechanism of manipulation exposed for what it is, an elaborate shell game. Here was code studies as performed by those who distrusted the coders, a group of readers playing what Peter Elbow (1973, 145) calls "the doubting game," a hunt for underlying assumptions, driven by skepticism.

There was only one problem, one obstacle to the frenzied reading: the code was hardly a smoking gun. Rather, the "fudged" code represented work in progress, a placeholder while the programmer was awaiting a finalized data set or settling on a more standard model for marking the difference in data. The label of the artificial correction did not mark a site of deception but a site of provisional adjustment, marked as "artificial" so as not to falsify the data even in the code. Indeed, this code-in-progress is another sign of the always-in-progress nature of code and of the crucial role of context in discussing the meaning of code. Nonetheless, this file exemplifies how code's meaning depends on context and how its cultural meaning grows not solely from what it does but also how it is perceived by its varying audiences. In linguistic discourse, we specify the way the object of analysis is framed for its readers. In this chapter, I examine the way the meaning of code changes as it moves before different and often unexpected audiences in a case that illustrates what Jeremy Douglass has called code reading "in the wild" (2011).

The Climategate affair represents an example in which code entered the mainstream and circulated beyond its intended readers to a new group, which then assigned it an alternative meaning, largely by taking it out of context, and continued to purvey that meaning even after it was proven incorrect. In that way, this example may offer a case of misreading of code. On the other hand, reading this code more closely against the backdrop of this misinterpretation offers a glimpse into the social life of computer source code, the contingency of its meaning, and the ways code signifies differently to unexpected and unintended audiences.

Recontextualizing Code

Code's meaning, arguably, begins when it is first designed. The authors of the Climategate code were Ian Harris, Tim Mitchell, and Mark New, though the code seems to support and illustrate other work at the CRU, particularly that of Keith Briffa, whose name this file bears. CRU's primary function is to study climate directly, through measurements of climate over time, and indirectly through changes in tree ring density (a.k.a. dendroclimatology; Oxburgh 2010, 2). The CRU is a relatively small unit with one part-time and three full-time "academic staff members," along with about a dozen research associates (ibid., 1). In the fall of 2009, this ten-year-old code, along with over one thousand emails from a thirteen-year span, was hacked and then posted on the internet (Eilperin 2009).

Immediately, the conspiracy theory websites ate up the story, which was a veritable platter of red meat for those who had already suspected a climate change hoax. The *Telegraph* headline read: "Climate Change: This Is the Worst Scientific Scandal of Our Generation" (Booker 2009). The *Climategate* moniker, attributed to *Telegraph* blogger James Delingpole, quickly caught on as it played into the salacious tone of the story. Taking at least partial credit for the term, Delingpole would later write an article for the *Spectator* titled "Watching the Climategate Scandal Explode Makes Me Feel Like a

Proud Parent" (2009). The rest of the credit he gives to a commenter on his blog who posted under the handle Bulldust.

Code changes its meaning when it is recontextualized. To be clear, I am not arguing that code means what people say it does or that anyone can decide the meaning and even function of code. Rather, I am arguing that like other semiotic forms, when code is recontextualized for a new audience, its meaning changes. It is once again more than what it does. It is an object of analysis and interpretation and, in this case, fuel for debate. Those who recontextualize the code cannot change what it does, but they do add to how the code signifies. However, unlike other sets of signs, such as films or poems, a source code file from a functioning piece of software contains contents that have an empirical, often discernible, unambiguous, and typically irrefutable effect. For that reason, these debates often lead to someone countering another interpretation by asserting the authority of the "true" functioning of the code. That is not to say the assertion of the empirical effects of the code is the final word in a discussion of the meaning of code (nor should it be). Just because someone can say what code does, that does not give them the final authority on what it means. Nonetheless, heated discussions about code tend to funnel toward a confirmation of the technical and empirical effects of the code and then invert the funnel as they broaden back into the implications of the code.

In the case of Climategate, even in posts that do not center on code, a commentator will invariably bring up a line from the code somewhere in the middle of the thread, which ultimately reverts back to discussing at a more abstract level, or at least a level that does not require reading the code. Take, for example, the post about Climategate on *Wizbang* (Laprarie 2009) called "The Heart of ClimateGate," which begins with a graph of the rapidly rising increase in temperatures known as the *hockey stick*, which was originally presented in an article by Michael Mann. The post largely offers context of the scandal from the point of view of climate change skeptic Michael Laprarie. His initial post is followed by about thirty comments (which is a bit low for a post about Climategate). The early comments react mostly to the post and its discussion of the context of the scandal. Then, almost exactly halfway into the exchange, on the thirteenth comment, a reader named Andrew offers a line of code, line 10, with its fudge factor introduced as "the human contribution to global warming." Afterward, the comments return to discussing the context. Although many of the chains of blog comments discuss the code for a bit longer, the pattern tends to repeat itself: commentary, a turn toward the code, and then a turn back into commentary—largely, I suspect, at the point at which the code turns out not to be proof of deception at all. In any event, the code serves as a means of debate, but not an end.

The public outcry over the code was enough to lead to an investigation of the programmers, analogous to the way the provocations of the Transborder Immigrant Tool led to an investigation of Electronic Disturbance Theater and then group member Ricardo Domiguez. When code talks, people listen. Or should I say, as a sign of its status as a powerful, mysterious mechanism, when people generate hysteria around code, investigations follow.

Adjusting the Numbers

At the heart of much of the debate over Climategate is a passage in the code that adjusts the temperatures over a series of years in the twentieth century. To be clear, the code adjusts the temperatures based on proxy data, maximum latewood density (mxd), up or down, depending on the sign of the adjustment (positive or negative):

```
9.  yrloc=[1400,findgen(19)*5.+1904]
10. valadj=[0.,0.,0.,0.,0.,-0.1,-0.25,-
0.3,0.,-0.1,0.3,0.8,1.2,1.7,2.5,2.6,2.6,$
11. 2.6,2.6,2.6]*0.75          ; fudge factor
```

Essentially, the valadj numbers are an array of adjustments to be made to the temperatures in five-year increments. Those values are then made continuous, filling in the intervening years through linear interpolation. Then, the adjustments are applied to the original data to create an array of data that will be used for plotting graphs. The code adjusts two different versions of the data, densall and densadj:

```
57. yearlyadj=interpol(valadj,yrloc,x)
58. densall=densall+yearlyadj
```

This first adjustment applies the correction to all the temperature data, whereas a second run of the changes applies only to the two- to six-rings group:

```
85. yearlyadj=interpol(valadj,yrloc,x)
86. densadj=densadj+yearlyadj
```

However, the interpolation function can be described with a more sinister edge. For example, blogger Robert Greiner (2009a) writes, "The interpol() function will take each element in both arrays and 'guess' at the points in between them to create a smoothing effect on the data. This technique often is used when dealing with natural data points, just not quite in this manner." With scare quotes and some innuendo, the blogger can characterize a fairly standard graphing function with a malicious intent as it tries, in Greiner's words, to "skew" the data toward the `valadj` values. The question regarding this code is not what it does but why.

Why does this code adjust the data? One commentator sums up many, writing, "The code certainly does suggest the data was manipulated, and therefore does invalidate the conclusions drawn from you nitwits by the CRU data set" (Wheeler 2009). Again, alarmists saw the adjustment as an attempt to manipulate the data. One such claim of foul play was lodged by Eric S. Raymond, author of *The Cathedral and the Bazaar* (2001), a much-celebrated account of the development of an open-source software project, a progressive gesture regarding an alternative model of development. However, in his post on Climategate, Raymond (2009) seems much more reactionary: "This, people, is blatant data-cooking, with no pretense otherwise. It flattens a period of warm temperatures in the 1940s 1930s—see those negative coefficients? Then, later on, it applies a positive multiplier so you get a nice dramatic hockey stick at the end of the century." Later in this comment, Raymond characterizes the code, writing it is not "just a smoking gun, it's a siege cannon with the barrel still hot."

Raymond's reading is colored by passages in the leaked emails. He later comments on his blog, quoting from those emails: "Reminder: Here's Phil Jones writing to Ray Bradley and friends: 'I've just completed Mike's Nature trick of adding in the real temps to each series for the last 20 years (ie from 1981 onwards) amd [sic] from 1961 for Keith's to hide the decline'" (Raymond 2009). Mike refers to Michael Mann, the much-maligned climate scientist who in April of 1998 published a coauthored article in *Nature* that demonstrates the adjustments to the graph. Mann would become the target of much criticism for what people claimed were arbitrary manipulations of the data.

This use of the word *trick* became another piece of red meat for climate change conspiracy theorists. Here was a climatologist admitting to using deception, caught red-handed, although apparently the "trick" Jones was referring to was using twenty years of directly measured temperatures rather than proxy data (Heffernan 2010). In other words, the trick was not a deception but a method for moving to measured temperatures rather than proxy data when that data was not reliable. *Trick* here carries the sense of *clever technique* rather than foul play.

"Hide the decline," however, sounds like an unquestionable deception. In an interview, Mann responds to the use of the phrase:

The "decline" refers to a well-known decline in the response of only a certain type of tree-ring data (high-latitude tree-ring density measurements collected by Briffa and colleagues) to temperatures after about 1960.

In their original article in *Nature* in 1998, Briffa and colleagues are very clear that the post-1960 data in their tree-ring dataset should not be used in reconstructing temperatures due to a problem known as the "divergence problem" where their tree-ring data decline in their response to warming temperatures after about 1960.

"Hide" was therefore a poor word choice, since the existence of this decline, and the reason not to use the post 1960 data because of it, was not only known, but was indeed the point emphasized in the original Briffa et al. Nature article. (Grandia 2009)

Just as the decline was underlined in the article by Briffa and his collaborators, the decline or divergence is clearly marked in the code, as the years before 1960 are grouped together and normalized separate from the corrected years. The following code implements a normalizing function on the data between 1881 and 1960:

```
52.mknormal,densadj,x,refperiod=[1881,1960],refmean=refmean,refsd=
refsd
53.mknormal,densall,x,refperiod=[1881,1960],refmean=refmean,refsd=
refsd
```

This normalization occurs just before the "artificial correction." But why use this label if the scientists are attempting to enact a deception?

One commentator asks a similar question, wondering why the scientists would plot both the MXD and corrected temperatures (and label the adjusted graph) if they were trying to perpetrate a hoax. Raymond replies, "The output of this program may have been their check to see if a visualization of the cooked data wouldn't look obviously bogus before they shopped it to the politicians and funding sources. That's the only way I can think of to explain plotting both crocked and uncrocked datasets in the same visualization." Raymond's repeated use of the loaded terms *cooked* and *crocked* data continue his characterization of the scientists as charlatans.

In a more detailed discussion of the adjustment, Gavin A. Schmidt (2009), a climate modeler, says: "So, we leave the data alone from 1904–1928, adjust downward for 1929–1943, leave the same for 1944–1948, adjust down for 1949–1953, and then, whoa, start an exponential fudge upward (guess that would be the 'VERY ARTIFICIAL CORRECTION FOR DECLINE' noted by the programmer). Might this result in data which don't show the desired trend or god forbid show a global temperature 'DECLINE' after 'VERY ARTIFICIAL CORRECTION' turn into a hockey schtick—I mean stick? and 'HIDE THE DECLINE'? You bet it would!" Note how this reader dramatizes his interpretation of the code: "whoa" and "exponential fudge upward," juxtaposed with the facetious "guess that would be" and the pun "hockey schtick." In performing his incredulity when reading the code, the interpreter attempts to insinuate the duplicitous intentions of the programmer in a way that engages his readers as confederates, with a bit of ire toward the scientific elite who have tried to dupe them. At its base, the comment describes the literal functioning of the code, adjusting the numbers, but this reading demonstrates the way the interpreter reads into the code an ulterior motive. Put simply, reading an extrafunctional significance of the code has become the means for this commentator to make an argument.

Fudge Factors

Without question, this code makes a correction. However, the nature of the correction has more to do with established inconsistencies in tree ring data than in the manipulation of temperatures, and the CRU scientists themselves were key in establishing that lack of correlation. Tree ring data is a proxy measure for climate. In a series of articles (particularly Briffa, Schweingruber, Jones, Osborn, Harris, et al. 1998 and Briffa, Schweingruber, Jones, Osborn, Shiyatov, et al. 1998), the scientists at CRU spelled out the inconsistencies between the tree ring data and other sources of temperature data. Consider, for example, their article in *Nature*, "Reduced Sensitivity of Recent Tree-Growth to Temperature at High Northern Latitudes," which was accepted for publication a year before the date on the leaked code. In this article, the scientists do not attempt to inflate temperatures but to demonstrate that particular tree ring data does not correspond accurately with measured temperatures. As the authors explain, "Although temperatures rose again after the mid-1960s and reached unprecedentedly high recorded levels by the late 1980s, hemispheric tree growth fell consistently after 1940, and in the late 1970s and 1980s reached levels as low as those attained in the cool 1880s. Over the hemisphere, the divergence between tree growth and mean summer temperatures began perhaps as early as the 1930s; became clearly recognisable, particularly in the north, after 1960; and has continued to increase up until the end of the common record at around 1990" (Briffa, Schweingruber, Jones, Osborn, Shiyatov, et al. 1998, 681).

In defense of the code, one scientist, posting under the name Dendrite (2009), explains that he typically encouraged the use of terms such as *fudge* and *fiddle factor* for a reason:

They fostered an ethos in the lab of self-criticism and self-skepticism which I regard as entirely healthy. In computer code, they drew the attention of new or unfamiliar users to steps in the analysis that warranted close scrutiny. I felt it was good to wear our problems and weaknesses on our sleeves.

Would these expressions be embarrassing in the hands of an unscrupulous hacker or rival—undoubtedly yes. Were they evidence of falsification of data—absolutely not. On the contrary, they were intended to make sure that the assumptions and corrections in our analyses were never concealed, forgotten or overlooked.

Ironically, to label a fudge factor may be a sign of methodological rigor.

As with reading other texts, an interpretation of code is influenced by whatever other texts are juxtaposed with it. The CRU leak contained many files, and people's readings were shaped by whichever files they read. One critic comments on another CRU file in which they "went looking for the divergence using principal component analysis." The code comments describe the procedure:

```
; Reads in site-by-site MXD and temperature series in; 5 yr
blocks, all correctly normalised etc. Rotated PCA ; is performed
to obtain the 'decline' signal!
    (http://di2.nu/foia/osborn-tree6/briffa_sep98_decline2.pro)
```

On his blog, Graham-Cumming (2009) discusses the code, adding:

So, they appear to have replaced their hacked-up adjustment above with actual analysis to try to understand what part of the MXD data is caused by some unknown "decline" causing the difference. The 1998 paper speculates on what might be causing this difference, but the PCA is done just to find it statistically without knowing why.

So, given that I'm a total climate change newbie and haven't been involved in what looks like a great deal of political back and forth I'm going to take this with a grain of salt and say this looks OK to me and not like a conspiracy.

Another commentator reads another code file, calling the reactions "way overblown. Everyone knows (since it was published in Nature) there is a problem [with] the MXD proxy post 1960" (Schmidt 2009). The commentator is referring to the article in *Nature*, written by CRU scientists, that identifies the divergence between the MXD and global temperatures after that year. The code file this commentator responds to begins with this comment:

```
; On a site-by-site basis, computes MXD timeseries from 1902-
1976, and; computes Apr-Sep temperature for same period, using
surrounding boxes ; if necessary. Normalises them over as common
```

```
a period as possible, then ; takes 5-yr means of each (fairly
generous allowance for; missing data), then takes the difference.;
Results are then saved for briffa_sep98_decline2.pro to perform
rotated PCA; on, to obtain the 'decline' signal!
     http://di2.nu/foia/osborn-tree6/briffa_sep98_decline1.pro
```

Based on this source code comment, the reader offers an overall reaction to the code vis-à-vis the alleged scandal:

> I guess the initial reason to do this would be to see if there is a spatial pattern to the divergence that might reveal something about it's [sic] cause. The weighting of that pattern (the 'yearly-adj' PC weights) could be used to correct for the decline, but I'm not sure what use that would be. More importantly, I have no idea if that was used in a paper (I have no access from home), but since the graph would have read "Corrected MXD", I don't see how anyone would have been misled. It certainly has nothing to do with Jones' comment or the 1999 WMO plot, nor the published data. This is just malicious cherry picking.—gavin] (Schmidt 2009)

As perhaps a sign of that cherry picking, bloggers and commentators on the blog discussed finding the code in question by searching the leaked files for the word *artificial* as they followed the breadcrumbs left by other bloggers. In other words, rather than reading through the code to see what it does, they used the word *artificial* as a shortcut to locating code self-labeled as deceptive.

Throughout the debate, regardless of their perspective on climate change, skeptics and supporters alike gesture toward the code as the ultimate evidence of what was really going on at the CRU. One blogger titles his response, "CRU Emails 'May' Be Open to Interpretation, but Commented Code by the Programmer Tells the Real Story" (Watts 2009). The narrative is repeated throughout the blogs: the code holds the truth. However, such assertions rely on establishing one meaning of the code, and in particular its comments. By this logic, discovering that one, true meaning is an act of unveiling what has been hidden.

Hidden in Plain Sight

Except it is not hidden. At the beginning of this chapter, I mentioned how excited the blogosphere gets about discovering this hidden code, opening the black box. The posting of the code and emails has the sensational flare of publishing the Pentagon Papers during the Vietnam War, only in this battle it is not the politicians and soldiers who are hiding their true assessment but instead the scientists and coders. However, despite the suggestion of emails that "hide the decline" or use "tricks," the code tells a very different story.

First, the software the code produces proves to be less surreptitious in action. Most of the versions of this software clearly label the graphs, indicating the correction. One version of the graphing code even delivers this message:

```
Data4alps.pro: 'IMPORTANT NOTE: The data after 1960 should not be
used. The tree-ring density records tend to show a decline after
1960 relative to the summer temperature in many high-latitude
locations. In this data set this 'decline' has been artificially
removed in an ad-hoc way, and this means that data after 1960
no longer represent tree-ring density variations, but have been
modified to look more like the observed temperatures.
```

That comment does not speak to some sort of scientific shell game but instead to an open acknowledgement of the methods used to generate the graph. Such code hardly makes for dramatic blogging.

In the code of Climategate, even when data is being transformed (which bloggers would characterize as falsification), the moves are clearly marked. Both times that the temperatures are being adjusted, the code clearly labels the changes:

```
; APPLY ARTIFICIAL CORRECTION
```

This passage of code even begins:

```
; PLOTS 'ALL' REGION MXD timeseries from age banded and from
hugershoff
; standardised datasets.
; Reads Harry's regional timeseries and outputs the 1600-1992
portion
; with missing values set appropriately. Uses mxd, and just the
; "all band" timeseries
;****** APPLIES A VERY ARTIFICIAL CORRECTION FOR DECLINE*********
```

Again the climate change skeptics admit that key to their hunt through the CRU code was to search for the words *fudge factor* and *artificial* (or *artifical*, as it is misspelled in one of the variations on this code). This code comment became a tool of their discovery. However, as one commentator explains, "Comments are put in code only for a couple reasons: To remind yourself of it in the future, or to inform the rest of your team about something. If you have comments in all-caps like 'VERY ARTIFICIAL', ending with '!!', and using words like 'fudge' it means you're trying to caution your team about something. You wouldn't put those kinds of comments in code when you're trying to obfuscate wrongdoing. That was most likely a rudimentary, probably temporary version of the code" (Joseph, comment on Graham-Cumming 2009a).

Thus, the very words that called attention to this code, that drew these critiquing eyes, are words that label the changes in the code. Although ill-intentioned programmers may try to encode their machinations, it is unlikely that they will so clearly document it. When the black box was opened, its contents revealed the work of a team of programmers trying to carefully document (sometimes a bit too frankly in the case of the Harry_Read_Me file) their process and their progress.

Even the Programming Language Was Critiqued

This controversial code was written in a programming language called Interactive Data Language, which some of the bloggers initially mistook for FORTRAN.[3] David Stern developed Interactive Data Language in the late 1970s when working with a group of scientists at the University of Colorado to study the Mariner Mars data (Stern 2000). IDL has been adopted as a data-visualization language by terrestrial researchers as well, including this group working on measures of climate change. The language often is used for graphing data in ways similar to MATLAB. Still, a language for manipulating arrays is not immune to mockery. In fact, perhaps even more than this climate-graphing code written in it, IDL has received some withering scrutiny in the court of online opinion, further demonstrating the way in the world of programming that meaning can be made through public lambasting in sarcastic online critique, which I call encoded chauvinism.

Melissa Elliott (2014; a.k.a. @0xabad1dea) offers one scathing critique of the language on her Tumblr blog *PHP Manual Masterpieces*. At first, she allows for a reason that people used IDL in the first place; as she puts it, "It is a language oriented to efficient transforms of entire arrays, which is exactly what scientists working on datasets want." Then she begins an unrelenting critique of its failings ("intential misfeature" as she calls them) from the syntax to integer size, which she criticizes for being arbitrarily set to 16 bits. In another example, she adds, in this language that at least offers array handling, when scalar values are "out of bounds," the language both produces an error message and clips them to the minimum or maximum index value. As Elliott puts it, having both error-handling methods, an error and an adjustment, in the same language, means it responds both ambiguously and unambiguously. At the end of her post, she exclaims in all caps, "WE RUN ENTIRE LABS ON THIS."

Elliott is hardly the only critic of IDL. Elsewhere on the internet is a Stack Overflow page dedicated to comparing IDL to Python, largely to IDL's detraction. Among a litany of weaknesses, the initial poster includes "narrow applicability," "slower for large arrays," "array functionality less powerful," and "table support poor" (Fry 2008). Various complaints use the word *awkward* to characterize its features. It is also closed source and comes with an expensive license. Another respondent to the thread can only attribute its longevity to the persistent use of it by scientists (in this case astronomers) who either don't want to learn a new language or consider other languages to lie in the realm of programmers. Like many languages, IDL receives the benefit of longevity through legacy and inertia. But the smack talk against the language replicates the kind of personal grudge match found on blogs about sports, politics, and, as we have seen, climate science and code. In the discussions of Climategate, IDL gets further derided. Greiner (2009a) calls IDL simply a "pain to go through."

The beating that IDL takes has tones of street basketball trash talk, an expression of a particular kind of male-dominated culture that extends the boy culture of hackerdom that Douglas Thomas (2002) characterized in *Hacker Culture*. At its best, it takes the form of a sharp but necessary critique, as in Elliott's riposte on IDL. At its worst, it performs the behaviors that Anastasia Salter and Bridget Blodgett (2017) characterize in *Toxic Geek Masculinity in Media*. The kind of vitriol that accompanies Climategate is not just outrage over a presumed CRU cover-up (and the larger-scale deception it seems to epitomize) but an example of common online code critique: it is tribal (with allegiances to programming paradigms), it is chauvinistic (with little tolerance for newbies or outsiders), and it tends to devolve in explosions of snap judgments, posted quickly during angry moments stolen from frustrating coding or during time people used to give to resting. I will explore the effects of this culture of encoded chauvinism in chapter 5.

In the End

An investigation into the CRU by its university would ultimately exonerate the programmers, but not before the research group became synonymous with the scandal. The damage had been done. Although the scientific researchers were cleared of wrongdoings in a panel chaired by Sir Muir Russell (2010), the skeptics through the noisy posts had reinforced the caricature of deceptive scientists manipulating data through the hidden means of code. In effect, the source code in question would always be tied to this scandal. What was communicated by the bloggers quoted in this chapter was that the unseen source code hides machinations that promote nefarious agendas.

With all the code taken together, after a few deep breaths, all the noise over Climategate appears to be much ado about null. The code does not manipulate data but merely its presentation. It does not create a graph for a scientific paper, but instead prints its results to the screen. As a result, several of the commentators remarked that the code is most likely designed as an exploratory enterprise. Whether that exploration was being done in the name of scientific research or deception depends on the reader of the code. But as it is labeled so clearly, it hardly appears to be designed to deceive.

Ultimately, this code was a placeholder code appearing in an experiment, one that would be replaced by two other files: briffa_sep98_decline1.pro and briffa_sep98_decline2.pro. These files go about the correction using a mathematical process. The first set of code (in decline1) normalizes and stores the data in a file, using the range 1902–1976:

```
kl=where((timey ge 1902) and (timey le 1976),nyr2)
mxd5yr=allmxd(*,kl)
temp5yr=alltemp(*,kl)
```

The second performs principal component analysis (PCA): rotates PCA on the data to derive the "'decline' signal" alluded to in the code. In this second set of files, there is no "artificial correction," merely some statistical modeling to explore the divergence between the MXD and temperature data. The fudge factor therefore was a placeholder in use until the researchers could apply the appropriate statistical models: nothing to see here.

Climategate represents a case in which code was removed from its original context and circulated with a different frame. Combined with stolen emails that seemed to speak of a cover-up, the code was not so much a smoking gun as a match discarded in a dry forest. Although the fudging of the temperature changes did not turn out to be manipulations of weather data, this code will be forever linked to this scandal. Like other cultural objects, code gains meaning as it is circulated. However, unlike most sign systems, because most code has a definitive functioning, its effects are not up for debate. What is contested then is the intention behind its design. The Climategate episode demonstrates the ways in which code has become a text in public discourse, a battleground for political debate. More importantly, it demonstrates the need for more code literacy,[4] not merely at the level of functionality but with a rich understanding of context. The expert programmers like Eric Raymond who saw scandal in this code were not misunderstanding what the code did but why. This incident marks the moment at which code emerges as a medium for political discourse. The debates that ensued after the leak of this code reveal the urgency for code literacy at a level of reflection, much more like the reading of literature or history, with thoughtful critique rather than reading for function alone.

5 FLOW-MATIC

File: FLOW-MATIC demo
Programming Language: FLOW-MATIC
Developed: 1958
Principal Authors: Grace Hopper et al.[1]
Platform: UNIVAC II Data-Automation System
Interoperating Files: INVENTORY FILE, PRICE FILE

Code

```
0. INPUT INVENTORY FILE-A PRICE FILE-B ; OUTPUT PRICED-INV FILE-C
UNPRICED-INV FILE-D ; HSP D .
1.    COMPARE PRODUCT-NO (A) WITH PRODUCT-NO (B) ; IF GREATER GO
TO OPERATION 10 ; IF EQUAL GO TO OPERATION 5 ; OTHERWISE GO TO
OPERATION 2
2.    TRANSFER A TO D .
3.    WRITE-ITEM D .
4.    JUMP TO OPERATION 8 .
5.    TRANSFER A TO C .
6.    MOVE UNIT-PRICE (B) TO UNIT-PRICE (C) .
7. WRITE-ITEM C .
8. READ-ITEM A ; IF END OF DATA GO TO OPERATION 14 .
9. JUMP TO OPERATION 1 .
10. READ ITEM B ; IF END OF DATA GO TO OPERATION 12 .
11. JUMP TO OPERATION 1 .
12. SET OPERATION 9 TO GO TO OPERATION 2 .
13. JUMP TO OPERATION 2 .
```

```
14. TEST PRODUCT-NO (B) AGAINST ZZZZZZZZZZZZ ; IF EQUAL GO TO
OPERATION 16 ; OTHERWISE GO TO OPERATION 15 .
15. REWIND B .
16. CLOSE-OUT FILES C ; D .
17. STOP . (END)
```

Notes

0: Reads two files (A and B) and writes two files (C and D). HSP D tells the machine to print that file using the UNIVAC high-speed printer.

1: Compares the product number of A & B. If A is greater, it moves to operation 10. If PRODUCT-NO (A) equals PRODUCT-NO (B), the program moves to the next step. If less, it goes to operation 2. The programming language uses both GOTO and JUMP TO. FLOW-MATIC introduced the if-then concept into programming languages, according to Jean Sammet (1969, 325).

2–4: If the product number of A is less than the product number of B, for that particular item then it must not have a price, so it is placed by the next few operations into the unpriced file. WRITE-ITEM records the product number on magnetic tape.

5–7: Follows the same pattern as 2–4, but uses C as the destination. In line 6, not only is the data in B moved to C, but the items are assigned the name UNIT-PRICE.

8: Reads a new item from the A file. If this is the last item, it moves to the end. If it is not, it goes back to the comparison operation at the top of the program.

10: This set of instructions advances B to the next value, unless the program has reached the end of the file, in which case it moves to the ending.

12: In a very unusual bit of syntax, if the program has reached the end of list B without reaching the end of the file, it needs to advance item A and do more comparisons. Line 12 rewrites operation 9, presumably until the program finishes executing, to GO TO OPERATION 2 and then goes there, essentially advancing the product number until it reaches the end of the list of products.

14: Presumably this is a test to see if the end of the file has been reached. If so, it skips ahead two steps, if not; it goes to 15. zzzzzzzzzzzz follows the format that the Univac II programming manual refers to as a *sentinel block*, which is placed "at the end of the last tape of a file." Sentinel blocks were ten characters long, but only the first six were significant. This full sentinel block was otherwise a command to rewind the tape (Sperry Rand Corporation 1958, 13). Here is another sign of the hardware shaping the code.

15: Rewind B. Physically returns file B to the start so it can be accessed from the beginning again.

16: These instructions close out the two output files. Unlike file B, these output files do not need to be rewound, merely closed.

17: In a bit of seeming redundancy, this code stops the execution of the program and marks the end of the program. STOP rewinds the instruction tape. As Damon Loren Baker (2014) phrases it, "end was a non executable marker at the end of all programs and subroutines."

Functionality

This sample program reads and compares items from two lists, containing inventory and price, respectively, and from these creates two lists, one that lists products that have prices and one that lists products without a price.[2]

Interoperating Systems

Writing programs in a natural language, whether spoken or written, has been a dream of programmers perhaps since the advent of the digital state machine, and yet the pursuit of that dream has revealed subtle (and not so subtle) distinctions between the natures of programming languages and human languages. Paradoxically increasing accessibility with respect to one aspect, such as readability to those who know English, can raise obstacles to others. Furthermore, as computer languages distance themselves from the binary of the machine and the hardware-dependent assembly, as they develop syntax and vocabularies that resemble the language of everyday interaction, the sources of meaning, attending the code, proliferate. Top that off with the vast social histories of languages, so tied to culture and identity, and code reveals itself to be (always already, as the philosophers like to say) political.

On its surface, the code example that opens this chapter may seem the most accessible example in this book, seemingly written in everyday imperative English. Yet what makes this program and its programming language, FLOW-MATIC, interesting is its own internal contradiction. On the one hand, the language was created to give business people, meaning nonprogramming managers and nonprogramming military officers, an accessible language for programming newly arrived business and tactical machines.[3] On the other hand, the very symbols that make this language (potentially) easier to read for some make it cumbersome for others, especially those more comfortable with mathematical symbols who would feel more at home in other languages of the time, such as FORTRAN or MATH-MATIC. Surely the desire to make computer languages and computer programming seem more familiar is a deep and persistent one.

However, because language, culture, and epistemologies are so closely intertwined, to choose one specific natural language for a base language has significant implications for those who will use it, particularly for those who come from different linguistic backgrounds. That choice can have colonizing effects as those who wish to program in the new language are subject to it, and if the tokens or syntax of the base language are not familiar, these programmers will be at a disadvantage in the computational economy. Consequently, the choice of a natural base language on which to model a programming language has implications for the cultural meaning of code that tie into the long legacy of linguistic imperialism. Language, to put it mildly, is the fabric of a community, tribe, and modern nation-state. On the one hand, to make a programming language is to create a means of communication for a community of users. On the other hand, to make a programming language similar to any one language makes it potentially more accessible to some, yet less hospitable to others. To explore this contradiction, I will first turn to the origins of FLOW-MATIC, which emerged at the dawn of high-level computer programming languages.

This chapter, which begins with Grace Hopper's efforts to bring business managers into programming, considers the costs and benefits of making computer programming more accessible—*cost* in terms of programming affordances and also in terms of cultural exclusions—while touching upon the origins of the current gender imbalance of professional programming. Hopper was a pioneer in computer language development whose legacy has been recovered by historians. Nonetheless, digital media scholar Marie Hicks (2017) warns against focusing too narrowly on a few luminary women in computational history—namely, elevating particular groundbreaking women above all of the many other women who worked in early computing, often to little notice and even less remuneration (232–233). This recovery work is a key component of critical code studies.[4] Although I will focus on Hopper's contributions because they are so pivotal to the development of programming languages, Hicks's critique is key to this chapter, which sees the rise of programming languages that will displace many of the computers (meaning those who did computing, who were mostly female), or at least those who did not transition into programming. Moreover, the issue of inclusion and exclusion is key to this chapter, which ultimately is about access to programming and how coding languages themselves can facilitate or inhibit that access (or do both simultaneously).

In this chapter, I will draw together several critical approaches to explore the porous border between so-called natural languages and programming languages. With the border-transgressing ethos of the Transborder Immigrant Tool (see chapter 3), meaning-making systems and discourse cultures will travel back and forth across this boundary, transforming both sides through their interactions. Discussing these imbricated realms requires an equally interwoven set of reading practices. I will specifically draw upon practices of feminist historical recovery, postcolonial code studies, and what I might call the ethics and algorithms movement. The feminist historical recovery follows the work of Hicks (2017), whose *Programmed Inequality* explores the denigration and supresssion of the technological and mathematical contributions of women. It draws upon as well the work of N. Katherine Hayles (2005), whose *My Mother Was a Computer* shows how feminism can be applied to reading computational technology. Other works include *#WomenTechLit* (Mencia 2017) and Anastasia Salter and Bridget Blodgett's (2017) *Toxic Geek Masculinity in Media: Sexism, Trolling, and Identity Policing.* Roopika Risam, Amit Ray, and Adeline Koh (2014) have modeled postcolonial readings of code, drawing upon theorizations of global English. My reading will also be informed by the approaches of algorithms and ethics exemplified by Safiya Noble's (2018) reading of bias in search algorithms in *Algorithms of Oppression: How Search Engines Reinforce Racism.* Lastly, my reading in this chapter draws upon the work of Jason Edward Lewis, Outi Laiti, Ramsey Nasser, and Jon Corbett (whose work is featured in figure 5.1), who have been exploring the power of coding in one's mother tongue—or at least closer to it. Just as a piece of code draws upon various libraries of methods, I combine these emerging reading practices to create an examination with the complexity of its object of study and as a reminder that meaning is never happening merely in one dimension but emerges out of the interaction of many complex, interrelated, interoperating, fluctuating systems.

The program at the center of this chapter seems quite simple by today's terms, producing that kind of operation that could be done with a simple macro in a spreadsheet program, such as Microsoft Excel. As Baker (2014) has written, "Apparently this was just the sort of whiz-bang killer app that made a late 50's business exec sit up and take notice about your new computer gizmo." However, the simplicity of this program should not render its utility trivial but rather accentuate that in many ways spreadsheets have become the most accessible of the business programming environments with their formulas, pivot tables, and built-in functions, a site of programming that often goes unnoticed in discussions of programming languages because of their ubiquity and perhaps because of their interface, which produces an IDE that seems more distant from a modern language, such as Python, than FLOW-MATIC is.

On further consideration, the way spreadsheets disappear in conversations of "real" programming languages offers a parallel to the second-class status that once-cutting-edge languages like FLOW-MATIC and its descendant COBOL possess when new developments render large portions of them obsolete. I do not wish to further expand this divide, but just to note it as another hierarchy in an economy in which certain programming skills are valued more than others and in which the more priestly class of

Figure 5.1
Computer-generated beaded still image of Jon Corbett's grandmother, produced by his code. Image courtesy of the artist.

programmers maintain a degree of status that those working in data-entry environments, such as Excel, even while programming them, do not.

In fact, this hierarchy ties directly to a recurring theme of this chapter, *encoded chauvinism*, the name I give denigrating expressions of superiority in matters concerning programming, which I see as a foundational element of the toxic climate in programming culture, a climate which often proves hostile—particularly to women and other minority groups—and is a kind of technological imperialism. The playful competition that leads programmers to support paradigms like sports teams, that fuels arguments that real coders don't use x, be it COBOL or BASIC or JavaScript, sees in its mirror the tendencies to chauvinism, factionism, and a blindness to cultural imperialism. In other words, in this case study, issues of gender division and technocultural imperialism come together in an analysis of code in an English-like language written by one of the pioneering women in computer science. She collaborated with others to explore ways to make programming more accessible to more people, even as coding was in its transition from clerical work performed by women to a lucrative profession in a culture dominated by men. This experiment demonstrates quite a bit about the nature of language in code, and this exploration is continued by those who look to include even more people by creating code based in languages other than English, including indigenous languages.

FLOW-MATIC

Grace Hopper and her team developed FLOW-MATIC (a.k.a. B-0 or B-Zero) in the mid-1950s as an alternative to MATH-MATIC and FORTRAN.[5] The name is a portmanteau that combines the *flow* of *flowcharts* with the *matic* of *automatic*, the latter a trendy suffix of the 1950s. As one brochure for the language advertises: "The English-like pseudo-code of Flow-Matic causes the Univac system to automatically compile and write its own compiler code. Thus, both flow charts and codes are made intelligible to the non-programmer as well as to the programmer" (Remington Rand 1957). The order of the intended audiences (i.e., nonprogrammers first) in that last sentence reveals which was primary. In *History of Programming Languages*, Richard Wexelblat (1981) classifies MATH-MATIC and FORTRAN as scientific, numeric-oriented languages and FLOW-MATIC as a business, data-processing language. More notably as FORTRAN's tokens emerged from the symbolic representation of mathematics and science, FLOW-MATIC drew from English, which for the primary customers of Remington Rand was the language of business (Remington Rand 1957). However, the distance between the appearance of English and the processing of natural language offers a valuable lesson in the dangerous temptation to read code by merely imposing reading strategies from other semiotic systems.

Throughout her work, Grace Hopper combatted "the dull labor of writing and checking programs" (1952, 243). However, harder than dealing with programs apparently was convincing business managers and other supervisors to learn to read programs. Hopper developed FLOW-MATIC out of her experience with two different potential users of programming languages. As she explained in an interview, "One was people who liked using symbols—mathematicians and people like that. There was another bunch of people who were in data processing who hated symbols, and wanted words, word-oriented people very definitely. And that was the reason I thought we needed two languages" (Hopper 1980). To address the preferences of these two audiences, early developers created two of the most pervasive languages of the mid-twentieth century: COBOL and FORTRAN. FORTRAN (for *for*mula *trans*lation) language was designed by IBM for those who preferred or had to process more mathematical symbols, and COBOL (*co*mmon *b*usiness-*o*riented *l*anguage) was developed for those who preferred, or, perhaps more accurately, needed, words in their programming languages.

FLOW-MATIC was an "ancestor" to COBOL (Hopper 1980). Also known as B-Zero (or business language version 0), FLOW-MATIC used English-like tokens even for arithmetical operations (e.g., EQUAL for =). Jean Sammet notes that limitations of the UNIVAC system kept these instructional words under a twelve-character limit. Hopper developed this language to be used on the UNIVAC II for Remington Rand by nonprogrammer users from the business world, for whom mathematical notation was daunting. COBOL, by contrast, was a standard that did not depend on a specific machine. Hopper and her team developed FLOW-MATIC while working for Sperry Rand's Automatic Programming Department. However, developing the language was not enough. Hopper, a talented salesperson, would have to convince people, particularly in business, to use it. As she explains, "We finally got it running, and there we were, research and development group, with a product, and nobody to use it. We had to go out and sell the idea of writing programs in English" (quoted in Beyer 2009, 274). In her work on both software development and software sales, Hopper strived to invite more people into programming. However, though programmers were using English "tokens," FLOW-MATIC did not process natural language. The language examples foregrounded its ability to handle common activities such as comparing and calculating data rather than processing scientific formulas (pers. interview, Sarah Lehne, May 21, 2019). This difference is probably the principal reason that it was such a hard sell for the programmers who preferred FORTRAN and even FLOW-MATIC's sister language, MATH-MATIC.

Because FLOW-MATIC was built for the UNIVAC II, understanding this mainframe computer is key to understanding the language. First, there is no terminal for the UNIVAC II. Without a terminal, the programmer must wait until all the code is processed to determine if the program functioned properly. There was no screen interface. Programming was input via ninety-column punch cards (Walker 1996). Second, the machine had no direct access storage, but rather used magnetic tape that would be physically moved forward and backward and had to be rewound when the end was reached. Much of what seems unusual about the language can be attributed to physical constraints, such as the lack of lowercase letters, which would have consumed too much memory. Despite, or perhaps because of, these hardware constraints, FLOW-MATIC was a breakthrough language.

One brochure advertising FLOW-MATIC played up its English-like aspects, calling FLOW-MATIC "the most far-reaching development ever offered for automatic computer programming." *Automatic computer programming* here refers to a compiler that transforms this higher-level language into machine code as "the instructions cause the computer to generate for itself the various subroutines required to process the problem." Note that in this formulation, UNIVAC is given agency, autonomy even, as though it were taking over the difficult task of dealing with itself. The emphasis was on ease of programming: "To program a new application, the user merely describes his systems flow chart in the English-language instructions of FLOW-Matic." The system "drastically reduces training time," requiring "just a few days" for training users. Perhaps its most radical intervention, however, was not bridging the gap between humans and computers but breaking "the communication barrier between programming and management groups" because "the programming is intelligible to all who understand the application." That includes not just managers but also the "clerical workers," to whom the "method of pseudocode" can be easily taught (Remington Rand 1957).

Although the FLOW-MATIC name may be obscure to contemporary programmers, its core concepts and structures reemerge in a much more recognizable language, COBOL. In 1959, a group of thought-leaders in the world of computers gathered at the Pentagon for a summit to discuss the potential for a common business language (CBL). Sammet spells out the goals in creating the language, quoting a report from the conference:

a. Majority of group favored maximum use of simple English language; even though some participants suggested there might be advantage from using mathematical symbolism.

b. A minority suggested that we steer away from problem-oriented language because English language is not a panacea as it cannot be manipulated as algebraic expressions can.

c. The need is for a programming language that is easier to use, even if somewhat less powerful.

d. We need to broaden the base of those who can state problems to computers.

e. The CBL should not be biased by present compiler problems. (Marcotty, Sammet, and Holberton 1981, 201).

Released in 1958, FLOW-MATIC was one of the languages the group used as a model, and it clearly informed these specifications (Marcotty, Sammet, and Holberton 1981, 202). FLOW-MATIC appeared to be "easier to use" and made use of twenty keywords of "simple English language." However, even for Sammet, FLOW-MATIC represented a bridge too far in the efforts to offer a crutch to those who could not read programming languages. She went on to write, "Perhaps the only disadvantage that accrued from the experience [of developing FLOW-MATIC] was what can be defined as bending over backwards to provide English-like language. In other words, the Remington Rand people felt that no businessman or person concerned with business data processing was really interested in writing symbolic formulas and that if he actually wanted to compute. ... he would prefer to write it as a series of individual statements" (Sammet 1969, 323–324).

Perhaps the clearest modern-day heir to this project (other than COBOL) is the spreadsheet. Considering the vast volume of formulas regularly programmed into spreadsheets today, business has become computational in a way that might even have been inconceivable then. In any event, FLOW-MATIC was a language born out of the frustration of trying to teach managers and other supervisors these daunting new symbolic forms. It stands as a memorial to efforts to make programming languages more readable on the surface level, even when their symbols obscure some of the flow of the program itself.

English-Like

FLOW-MATIC may look like English, but the code is not exactly fluid prose. In Sammet's estimation, "The language is stilted and the English is not very natural" (Sammet 1969, 322). FLOW-MATIC uses English-like tokens and a syntax that resembles English sentences in an imperative structure. In imperative structure, the code takes the form of instructions issued to the computer, as it would in other imperative languages, from BASIC, another clear heir of FLOW-MATIC, to C to Python. Due to memory limitations, the language uses all caps (which again will show up in BASIC and other languages) and so cards and key punches did not even support lowercase. Nonetheless, these phrases read like sentences that end in periods or can be joined by using semicolons. For example:

```
READ-ITEM A ; IF END OF DATA GO TO OPERATION 14 .
```

This line reads like two sentences joined by a semicolon. In English, we might expect a few more words in the second clause, something like "if you have reached the end of the data," but the meaning is still fairly clear. Another example:

```
CLOSE-OUT FILES C ; D .
```

While FLOW-MATIC resembles English, this line uses the semicolon to append a second clause (CLOSE-OUT FILES D), most of which is elided through what grammarians call *zeugma*, or a yoking together with the repeated words omitted. There are spaces before the ending punctuation (whether semicolon or period), but that distinction seems negligible, compared with assembly, which performs a similar operation:

```
mov  ah, 3eh mov  bx, handler  int  21h
```

On closer inspection, the language has opportunities for confusion in what natural language instructors call *false cognates*. For example, in operations 8 and 10, the conditional statement involves identifying whether the program has reached the end of the data. However, operation 14 seems to offer a second means of testing for the end of the data. COMPARE and TEST seem synonymous, as operations 1 and 14 seem to offer similar operations. Nonetheless, the TEST ... AGAINST syntax offers affordances not found in COMPARE ... WITH because it primarily tests conditions, looking for the figurative constant that is the marker of the end of the file or the end of the tape, and here the physical platform reasserts itself in the code.[6] On the other hand COMPARE was used with two data values, a mathematical comparison (<, >, =, etc.). Still, the English words *compare* and *test* do not, by themselves, foreground that distinction, so, despite the familiar appearance of the tokens, programmers must still learn unique and unambiguous references, as they would with any tokens.

Go to versus Jump To

Throughout FLOW-MATIC, the ambiguities and synonymous vocabulary of English cloud distinctions in related operations. For example, FLOW-MATIC has both GO TO and JUMP TO instructions, both of which seem to send the flow of the program to another operation. JUMP TO appears at the beginning of statements, whereas GO TO is used in conditional statements. In the second part of operation 2, the code reads:

```
IF GREATER GO TO OPERATION 10 ;
```

Whereas operation 6 reads:

```
JUMP TO OPERATION 8  .
```

The only difference seems to be the syntax of the statement. And even that distinction is not absolute because operation 12 changes a JUMP TO operation into a GO TO operation without adding a condition to the syntax. In the documentation, GO TO is not listed as a separate instruction, but is only included in the possible format for READ-ITEM and NUMERICAL-TEST as part of conditional statements. Conditional statements (if this, do that), likewise only appear as part of other statements, not as standalone commands. For example, in the specification of READ-ITEM, the list of commands reads as follows:

(h) △READ-ITEM△f1[;IF△END△OF△DATA△GO△TO△OPERATION△h1△].△[7]

In this line, the △ represents a space and the brackets represent optional code. The characters f1 and h1 are variables. Again, note that both GO TO and IF are part of the formulation of a READ-ITEM command, rather than standalone commands. Note, too, that the IF ... THEN conditional was new with FLOW-MATIC, according to Sammet (1969, 325). On closer inspection, the distinguishing feature appears to be that GO TO is conditional, whereas JUMP is unconditional—or, rather, does not require a condition.

It is hard to know what linguistic concept led to the choice of JUMP TO as a command and GO TO as an operation within other commands. Perhaps JUMP TO sounded more like a standalone imperative, while GO TO seemed to be more provisional. The choice of JUMP likely developed from assembly's jump operation (JMP). GO TO is a verbal representation of the branching instructions in assembly. GO TO would live on in GOTO, only to be evicerated by Dijkstra's famous "GOTO considered harmful." English's need for a preposition after "jump" and "go" expands the character count. Note, too, the verbosity of the language, which requires the word OPERATION before each line number. Nine letters might not seem much in a twenty-line program, but put this requirement into a program hundreds of thousands of lines long and the managers had better worry about their workers' repeated-stress injuries rather than the legibility of the programming language. Of course, line numbers would also disappear from languages, which arguably also led to greater legibility and flexibility with the advent of object-oriented languages and other paradigms.

It is not clear whether FLOW-MATIC's English-like tokens are actually easier to read because so much, if not all, of reading imperative code involves following the flow of the processes. Compare these two versions of the operations written in a more simplified version. First, we have one that is more like FLOW-MATIC:

```
3. COMPARE A WITH B; IF GREATER GO TO OPERATION 4; IF EQUAL GO TO
OPERATION 9; OTHERWISE GO TO OPERATION 6 .
4. WRITE-ITEM A
5. GO TO OPERATION 10 .
6. TRANSFER B TO D .
7. WRITE-ITEM C .
8. GO TO OPERATION 10 .
9. TRANSFER SUM OF PRODUCT OF B AND 3 AND A TO D .
10. WRITE-ITEM D.
```

Here is a second, rendered in Python:

```
if a > b:
    print(a)
elif a == b:
    d = b
    print(c)
else:
    d = b * 3 + a
print(d)
```

Which of these versions is easier to read depends ultimately on the reader. Even though the first version of the code uses more English-like tokens, the second is arguably easier to follow because it can essentially phrase all of the operations in the equivalent of one sentence: *if* this, *do* this; *else if* that, *do* that; *else do* something different. The first uses symbols that are more like prose, but the second uses a syntax that is less awkward. On the other hand, to understand the penultimate line in FLOW-MATIC one can read the order of the words, but to understand the Python version, one would need to know the order of precedence to know that the multiplication must come first.[8]

The legibility of programing is subjective. Baker (2014) argues that FLOW-MATIC's COMPARE syntax offers a more intuitive evaluation structure because it can begin a comparison and then offer a series of branches without continuing to repeat the items being evaluated, unlike the Python example and also unlike its immediate heir, COBOL. Baker argues that this structure makes FLOW-MATIC more like English, in which once a topic is raised, the listener assumes that topic persists until a new one is introduced. FLOW-MATIC's branching comparisons rely on that persistence and offer an affordance for multiple branching right from the initial comparison, reducing verbosity despite its longer tokens (COMPARE vs. IF, OTHERWISE vs. ELSE). A further exploration of these different ways of drawing comparisons demonstrates the challenges to making a language legible.

The language has two ways of comparing values without any surface-level difference, the first of which is COMPARE:

```
1. COMPARE PRODUCT-NO (A) WITH PRODUCT-NO (B) ; IF GREATER GO
TO OPERATION 10 ; IF EQUAL GO TO OPERATION 5 ; OTHERWISE GO TO
OPERATION 2
```

Later the code introduces the TEST operation:

```
14. TEST PRODUCT-NO (B) AGAINST ZZZZZZZZZZZ ; IF EQUAL GO TO
OPERATION 16 ; OTHERWISE GO TO OPERATION 15 .
```

FLOW-MATIC uses COMPARE when drawing items from a file and TEST when dealing with a constant. This branching syntax seems to parallel the comparisons in assembly—for example, blo (branch if lower). Like assembly, this syntax calls for the comparison operation only the first time, followed by the two values to be compared. Then the code tells which operation to check followed by the conditional outcomes. Again, following assembly, FLOW-MATIC and COBOL then can handle multiple branches based on the outcome of that comparison. However, the use of the semicolon and the word OTHERWISE in the conditional branch evoke for readers of English a formal diction. Subsequently, OTHERWISE would be replaced in many high-level languages (including COBOL) with ELSE, as in COBOL's IF-THEN-ELSE, a well-known construct in contemporary programming. Contrasted with these lighter, shorter words, OTHERWISE seems to hail from another register of diction, an example of a token that colors the code, not only making it legible to managers but also giving it formal character to flatter their sense of importance.

Whether using OTHERWISE or ELSE, the question persists: Is FLOW-MATIC's formulation actually easier to read? Compare FLOW-MATIC's handling of comparison to a simple, more symbolic language, such as Java. For example, examine this passage in J2ME from the Transborder Immigrant Tool (chapter 3):

```
111. if (width < 150) {
112. errorImage = loadImage("error_sm.png");
113. tbImage = loadImage("tb_sm.png");
114. } else {
115. errorImage = loadImage("error.png");
116. tbImage = loadImage("tb.png");
}
```

In this formulation, the evaluation happens with the `if` statement, and then the series of resulting actions are held together in curly brackets. The *otherwise* option is preceded by an `else`. Or consider this example of the somewhat more visually awkward syntax of IDL, drawn from chapter 3:

```
18. if !d.name eq 'X' then begin
19.     window, ysize=800
20.    !p.font=-1
21. endif else begin
22.    !p.font=0
23.    device,/helvetica,/bold,font_size=18
24. endelse
```

Which is easier to read? In contrast to J2ME, IDL requires `begin` at the start of its conditional operations, which seems comparatively verbose. The run-togethers `endif` and `endelse` are both more challenging to parse visually and more verbose compared to the curly brackets, but at least both of these languages do not need to declare that they are comparing but rather let the comparison begin with the conditional `if`. Others might prefer `begin`/`endif` because it can be easier when debugging to look for these longer verbal markers rather than matching up brackets. On the other hand, in both J2ME and IDL, if they were evaluating numbers in their initial condition, they would need to repeat the evaluation for all further branches (other than the opposite of the first condition). FLOW-MATIC, like assembly and COBOL, does all its numerical comparisons at the same time, essentially by storing the difference of the two values being compared.

Ultimately, the legibility of code does not depend primarily on the symbols but rather on the ease of tracing its functioning. One element that makes FLOW-MATIC especially difficult to read to contemporary eyes is its omission of a basic trait of programming languages: loops. If, for example, the code could specify that an operation repeats *while* the product number is less than the last entry, there would be no need for the JUMP TO or GO TO statements. However, as Evan Buswell (2014) notes, FLOW-MATIC also lacks another important feature used in most while loops, a simple means of counting and incrementing. Of course, the language lacks many of these features because they had not yet become conventions of programming languages. Grace Hopper and her team were innovating with FLOW-MATIC at the birth of these languages.

This example illustrates the ways legibility is not dependent on similarity to natural language but overall clarity of expression. That is to say, legibility grows not out of just the syntax but also the phrasing, indentation, and, in many languages, other uses of white space; not in individual tokens but from their use in a system. Programming languages and paradigms are built from powerful constructs that combine syntax, grammar, and convention to express ideas. This example also underscores the way affordances of programming languages, such as loops, offer not just a means of expression but organizational and architectural concepts. Which is to say that a programming language's clarity grows not from its similarity to spoken languages but its ability to render its operations obvious at a glance against the backdrop of symbolic representation (including written language and mathematical notations), as well as the prevailing programming languages and paradigms. Arguably, programming conventions and paradigms are more important to the question of meaning than symbolic representation (whether in words, numerals, or other symbols) because to understand the latter requires only a translation dictionary; to understand the former requires a grasp of organizational and operational constructs.

Although *otherwise* and *jump to* might seem unnecessarily verbose, a few words, notably *if, then, else, for,* and *while,* have proven to be preferable to symbolic synonyms. Meanwhile, the arithmetical symbols (+, -, /, *, =, <, >) have largely won out over their verbal equivalents (plus, minus, divided by, times, equals, less than, greater than), with the exception of the abbreviations eq and ne for equals and not equals found in IDL and other languages, such as early FORTRAN, which many languages represent symbolically as = and !=. Of course, such symbols can also be misleading as the programmer must decide whether = will be used for assignment or evaluation (Vee 2017, 108). Sammet (1969) notes, "The question of whether people prefer to write *equals* or *equal* *to* instead of = is one that requires solution by a psychologist rather than by programmers" (324). Why do some natural language words turn out to be more useful than others?

In FLOW-MATIC, the English-like code foregrounds the conceptual metaphors being employed for these mnemonics. Consider READ in line 8:

```
8. READ-ITEM A ; IF END OF DATA GO TO OPERATION 14 .
```

READ-ITEM here means "get the value of." On the surface of it, the command identifies the action of checking a value with the human activity of reading. Programming languages that use *read* in this way include FORTRAN, C, and Haskell, although these instances are not all exactly the same. For example, in Haskell, the read class "provides operations for parsing character strings to obtain the values they may represent" (Hudak, Peterson, and Fasel 1999, 37). This multiplicity of meaning demonstrates just one aspect of the ambiguity of natural language tokens. However, even when using the same fundamental meaning of read, as Barbara Marino (pers. interview, June 23, 2018) points out, this activity is actually quite distinct from the more common human notion of reading: "If you asked someone to look up a value on a table, you wouldn't consider that reading," she explains. "Reading requires taking something's meaning in context." By context, here she is referring to *sequence* or what Saussurian linguistics refers to as the *syntagm*, the meaning a word has based on grammatical sequence and syntax. In other words, "reading" for humans is much more analogous to parsing commands than it is accessing values of variables or in arrays. By that logic, READ-ITEM is much more analogous to "look up the value of" than "read," or perhaps "read" in the limited meaning "to draw input from data storage," such as a tape in the case of the UNIVAC II. Other computer languages use the token *get* instead.

Such conceptual metaphors persist in later languages—for example, the use of PRINT in BASIC. That command is used to display content on a screen, yet it uses an ink and paper metaphor as a kind of remediation in the code (Montfort et al. 2013). In this case, the use of *read* in READ-ITEM anthropomorphizes the process, but in a way that obscures the operation. The effects on the disinterested manager who is the target audience for programs in FLOW-MATIC may seem minor until it is necessary that this manager understands how the computer is working. For example, because our notion of reading generally entails some amount of comprehension, the manager might wonder why the computer does not comprehend or evaluate this value once it is read, why that is a subsequent operation. The selection of natural language tokens for computational operations offers a clarification of one aspect of the operation that at the same time obscures or even obfuscates others.

Not all the words are so metaphorically employed, as some of these reserved words are tied to actual material contexts—for example, REWIND, which is connected to tape storage. Most contemporary high-level languages deal with storage more abstractly, as in the case of arrays, using values to control the place in the array rather than directing the hardware to move physical memory—though this renders mostly invisible the electronic manipulation of physical memory. This distinction is a reminder of the physical referent because modern storage is not on physical tapes. The REWIND example in this FLOW-MATIC program occurs in a place of paradox in the code. For the UNIVAC II, the system for which FLOW-MATIC was designed, ZZZZZZZZZZZ causes to machine to rewind the tape:

```
14. TEST PRODUCT-NO (B) AGAINST ZZZZZZZZZZZ ; IF EQUAL GO TO
OPERATION 16 ; OTHERWISE GO TO OPERATION 15.   REWIND B .
```

So operation 14 is in effect testing whether or not the tape has already been rewound. If so, it skips the REWIND operation. But to understand that set of operations, the reader has to know that ZZZZZZZZZZZ represents the rewind instruction. Otherwise, this would appear to be a fairly meaningless operation. This example then demonstrates the contradictions of this English-like programming language because the program essentially uses both ZZZZZZZZZZZ and REWIND to indicate that instruction.

This moment of the code also demonstrates how the English in FLOW-MATIC is not language, in the sense of natural language, but symbolic representation. The token ZZZZZZZZZZZ stands for rewind, just as B stands in for the PRICE-FILE (see line 0 of the code). By continuing to use B for PRICE-FILE and ZZZZZZZZZZZ, the program offers its paradox, revealing the limits of its dedication to legibility. Some tokens are translated; others are not. Whereas B is specified in the code, a command such as ZZZZZZZZZZZ would require prior knowledge of what we might call a specialized vocabulary. According to its marketing materials, FLOW-MATIC was designed to minimize the need for that kind of specialized vocabulary. In so doing, FLOW-MATIC addresses the human reader as its primary audience—or, perhaps more accurately if we represent the audience as a spectrum between human and machine, FLOW-MATIC is closer to the human side, but, as this example demonstrates, it is still quite close to the specific machine on which it was implemented.

In many ways, FLOW-MATIC is not using English. Instead, as Todd Millstein (pers. interview, June 14, 2018) puts it, FLOW-MATIC "pretends" to use English. In other words, FLOW-MATIC does not parse the English words for their meaning, but instead uses English words for discrete operations, reducing the word to one meaning, changing these ambiguous signifiers into more limited, simple symbols. However, because the readers of the language use those same symbols as words in spoken and written language, they can conflate the two. In fact, these are not words in the same sense at all.

What makes FLOW-MATIC deceptively legible to someone who knows English are the use of what linguists call *false cognates*. These are words in a second language that resemble those in the first but mean something different. In a natural language instruction class, they are pointed out as imposters, deceivers, likely to confuse the second-language learner. Arguably, almost all English tokens in programming languages are false cognates because words in code simply do not behave the way they do in spoken or written language, except perhaps through the use of metaphor, as in the case of performative language as framed by J. L. Austin (discussed in chapter 1). Mathematical operators may be the closest (plus and +) to their natural language equivalents, but to call them the same erases their distinct status in a computational system as opposed to a system of spoken or written discourse. Such confusion has led Ben Allen to speculate that rather than call this a "higher-level language," a better classification of FLOW-MATIC may be "pseudocode in English" (Marino 2014). Likewise, perhaps assembly's formulation of code as mnemonics better captures the sense of these tokens that are symbols built to help humans remember what they do.

FLOW-MATIC's English-like tokens seem like natural language, but the question remains: Assuming such distinctions are useful, just how high level is FLOW-MATIC? On the one hand, many of the operations seem to be merely verbal representations of assembly commands, leading Nick Montfort to call the language *assembly++* (Marino 2014). For example, consider the JUMP and MOVE operations. On the other hand, FLOW-MATIC uses an architecture that is quite sophisticated in which the data is modeled separately from these instructions—or, as Samett (1969) puts it, there is "the realization that the data designs can and should be written completely independently of the procedures to be executed. Thus, it was possible to write ... a complicated description of a file quite independently from a specific procedure to be executed on that file" (316, 322). That distinction has led some critics, including Buswell (pers. comm. October 21, 2018), to argue that FLOW-MATIC is more high level than C or FORTRAN. Regardless of how one assesses the language, FLOW-MATIC makes it clear that the level of the language, how abstracted it is from the machine, is not determined merely by the degree to which its symbols resemble a natural language.

COBOL's Global Reach

Despite FLOW-MATIC's relatively short life, its DNA would live on in its descendants—most notably in COBOL, developed by the Conference on Data Systems Languages (CODSYL), which included Hopper. In fact, Hopper (1980) once said, "If you take the FLOW-MATIC manual and compare it with COBOL 60 you'll find COBOL 60 is 95% FLOW-MATIC" (37). Unlike the machine-dependent FLOW-MATIC, which required the UNIVAC II, COBOL was a standard that could run on whatever machine it was installed on. COBOL would become an industry standard in the so-called military-industrial complex when the Department of Defense announced that it would not "lease or purchase a computer" that did not have a COBOL compiler on it (Vee 2017, 109). Thus, the language spread by institutional fiat.

COBOL has since grown to become one of the most pervasive languages, if not the most widely used language, today thanks to legacy systems (Allen 2018, 18–19). Even in the early twenty-first century, despite great advances in language design, massive amounts of software written in COBOL drive key operations—particularly in the world of finance, in which programmers must continually be trained to maintain it. In a very material way, language is money: the cost of replacing these systems outweighs the benefits of replacing them. Despite numerous criticisms against COBOL, such is the persistent reach of a language embedded in legacy software, what we might call the inertia of programming languages. Like all languages, COBOL, and by extension FLOW-MATIC, has its critics. As Dijkstra (1982) wrote, "The use of COBOL cripples the mind; its teaching should, therefore, be regarded as a criminal offense" (130). Hyperbole is a hallmark of encoded chauvinism, and comments such as these, which could constructively contribute, instead reinforce divisions and hierarchies among the cultures of programming languages and paradigms.

In 1984, Richard L. Connor wrote a critique of the language in *Computerworld* in a piece with a title that taunts the language in a strangely gendered manner: "COBOL, Your Age Is Showing." In it, Connor writes, "We got it backwards. We failed to recognize that mastering another programming language is duck soup for someone who understands programming. So we taught a generation to write COBOL statements, and we left to chance the education of that generation in programming" (15). Connor's critique parallels the critique of FLOW-MATIC, wherein the drive for easy-to-learn tokens gets priority over the ease of programming or following the flow of the language.

The Drive for Natural Languages

Although learning the tokens may only be a small part of learning to program in a language, the desire to program in natural language, especially one familiar to the programmer, is as old as programming itself, especially once compilers made possible the move from machine and assembly language into higher languages. If programmers could choose the symbolic registry for communicating with the machine, why not choose a language in which they were already fluent? COBOL presents merely one of the attempts to reach that goal. Others include BASIC and Inform 7.

However, the initial move toward higher-level languages had its resisters. Famously, John von Neumann, creator of the eponymous computer architecture ubiquitous today, called developing these programming languages a waste of time and resources. When he heard about the development of FORTRAN, von Neumann was reported to have said, "Why would you want more than machine language?" (quoted in Toal et al. 2017). When a student of von Neumann's developed an assembler so he wouldn't have to "hand-assemble programs into binary," von Neumann allegedly remarked, "It is a waste of a valuable scientific computing instrument to use it to do clerical work" (paraphrased in Lee 2009) Considering the number of women computers who did the mathematics that would become programming (Hicks 2017), this remark shows how a social hierarchy enters by analogy into the world of programming. When stating that computation time should not be wasted on this clerical work, he was essentially saying "leave it to the computers," a group of workers largely made up of women.

A hierarchy is already present in the concept of higher- and lower-level programming languages, drawn from an imaginary vertical tower of babel that puts the machine on the bottom-most level and the humans and their languages at the top. However, the status of those using the languages tends to fluctuate. At first, the original computers, the women who programmed the machines, had lower status than the men who gave the orders.[9] At the time of Hopper, program designers had high status, while those who had to encode instructions into the machine had low status (a division that still persists in the industry). However, once programming and coding became more deeply intertwined through higher-level languages, then programming became a higher status and more lucrative job, which historically coincides with when the gender divide favoring men emerges.[10] And while managers, to whom FLOW-MATIC was marketed, might earn more money, the status of esteem has become a currency in programming circles. Of course, that turn would have dire consequences well into the twenty-first century; the gap has rapidly widened as unequal hiring practices have proliferated. By one measure, in 2018 women accounted for only 26 percent of professionals in programming positions in the United States, although recent efforts in computer science have begun at least to increase enrollments in undergraduate programs (Thompson 2019).

At the time of the emergence of higher-level languages, programming in something abstracted from assembly was seen as inferior. Consider the way early programmers regarded FORTRAN: "FORTRAN was proposed by Backus and friends, and again was opposed by almost all programmers. First, it was said it could not be done. Second, if it could be done, it would be too wasteful of machine time and capacity. Third, even if it did work, no respectable programmer would use it—it was only for sissies!" (Hamming 2014, 26). The gendered language of this quote reflects a moment in which, despite or as a result of the rise of the image of the geek or boffin, programmers take on the language of male bravado, awarding the highest status to the one who could work at the level of the machine. Using assembly becomes the programming equivalent of changing your own oil in your car or fixing your own engine. And long before the advent of brogrammers, it casts in the language of chauvinism the hierarchy of computer languages.

However, many years of high-level language development have increased the status of those who use them to program, while leaving the lower-level languages only to those whose resource-sensitive operations require it. Meanwhile, the attempts to build even higher-level or more "natural" languages persist. Perhaps the most English-like specialty language is Inform 7, which was developed for the production of interactive fiction. Inform 7 can accept instructions such as "There is a door in the room," which creates a door object in the room object. However, it cannot accept the instruction "The door in the room needs to be fixed," or at least it cannot accept it without additional code. I offer this as merely one small example of the way natural-seeming programming languages can lull a newbie into thinking the language can understand a statement rather than process it. This example highlights the difference between understanding and parsing and processing, and the sheer amount of ambiguity tolerated in natural language exchanges. In natural language, meaning proliferates in the flow between connotation and denotation. In computer languages, connotation is singular, one-to-one. The natural language is interpreted, the synthetic language parsed and processed. Ask a smart speaker like Google Home or Alexa something more complex than to turn on the lights,[11] and you will experience that same brittleness of the interface language.

All these movements toward natural language seem like progress, except when your native tongue is not being included. Through that perspective, the colonizing force of natural languages embedded in programming languages becomes clear.

Natural Language in the Postcolonial Age

Although I have been discussing "natural language," all my examples have involved English—which is not coincidental. Not only is English my own native language, but also these early languages were being developed primarily in English-speaking locations. When Hopper and her team in the United States decided to make programming more legible, they created an English-like programming language. Though Hopper did also write compilers for FLOW-MATIC in French and German, these European-language versions were discarded. As Ben Allen explains, given the number of contracts they had with the US government, "Remington Rand management was ... distinctly disinterested in the French and German versions" (2017, 58). Higher-level languages were not the first to introduce English; assembly language already had English-language mnemonics, such as *MOV* for *move*. Even the first known assembly language, developed by Kathleen Booth (which ran on the ARC 2 at Birkbeck, University of London, developed in 1947), used abbreviations or mnemonics based in English. Programmers could type "E" for *end* and "T" for *tape* and "M" for *memory*. Although other languages emerged with a more symbolic or mathematical base, as developers built further languages with signs tied to human languages, they tended to draw from English.[12]

For the decades to follow, to the present day, the majority of higher-level languages would be built around English-like tokens, making English, along with, of course, Arabic numerals (or rather, Hindu-Arabic numerals), the de facto lingua franca of programming. As Toal (pers. comm., September 26, 2018) notes: "We are at a point in history where things took off in an English-speaking milieu. Python was designed by Guido von Rossum whose native language was Dutch. Ruby by Yukihiro Matsumoto whose native language was Japanese. Lua came from Brazil. Erlang from Sweden. José Valim from Brazil did Elixir. To make a widely used programming language right now, English is where to go. Most of the keywords and function names start looking the same." Toal's point about keywords demonstrates the force of inertia in developing programming languages. Because early languages had English-like tokens, new programming languages adopted similar attributes to render themselves legible. However, of the non-English programming languages registered by the online Historical Encyclopaedia of Programming Languages (HOPL; http://hopl.info), many of them are either pedagogical languages, primarily designed to introduce beginners to programming, or localizations of languages that are at root in English—for example, Chinese localizations of C++ or the Russian localization of Python.

For Toal and others, the differences in language paradigms far outweighs any resemblance to English. In Toal's words, the pervasiveness of English is nothing more than the privilege of "naming rights," the just due to those who arrive, or at least do the naming, first. In Western culture, he offers, constellations have Arabic names. English relies on a Latin alphabet. However, I would argue that the prevalence of English in the most widespread contemporary programming languages represents more than a legacy of who came first and instead operates as a form of digital postcolonialism, or the manifestation of a colonizing force beyond the forms of historical, geographical, or territorial colonialism.

The pervasiveness of English in programming languages demonstrates the hegemony of what has been called "global English" and "global Englishes." Global Englishes "broadly means the linguistic variations of English that arose with the British Empire, the term has also been fruitfully used to examine the intersections of language, knowledge-production, power, and representation" (Risam, Ray, and Koh 2014). Drawing on the work of Edgar Schneider, Roopika Risam, Adeline Koh, and Amit Ray, I frame the spread of English in programming languages as a postcolonial manifestation of this phenomenon, which compels speakers of other languages to learn English due to its "cultural capital."[13] Their response to the language, including adaptations of dialects, leads to the postcolonial legacies of varied Englishes. Rita Raley (2003) notes the way English's role in colonialism parallels the colonizing force of computer languages: "With Global English as a precursor network and medium of late twentieth-century communication, computer languages maintain a parallel currency and legitimation. ... The old economy of English studies has itself been made new as the market focus for corporations, governments, and schools alike has shifted to functionality and efficiency, and specifically to the means by which information is retrieved, exchanged, and transmitted" (207).

Jessica Pressman (2014) continues this line of critique by reflecting on the World Wide Web, structured by HTML which "sits on top of an Apache web server that sits on top of C++, which sits on top of assembly," languages "structured by English" (149). The prevalence of English in high-level programming languages and the basic tokens of programming intertwine the cultural legacy of the natural language with synthetic language.

However, some programmers have offered resistance to the hegemony of English. For example, programmer-artist Ramsey Nasser created قلب (or 'alb), as an Arabic programming language, the full name of which is "a recursive acronym" of r لغة برمجة قلب:,

"pronounced 'alb: lughat barmajeh, meaning "alb: a programming language'" (see https://github.com/nasser/---). In essence, the language adapts a LISP-variant, Scheme, into Arabic tokens. Such a translation might seem trivial in computational terms; but consider, even just at a visual level, the impact of Nasser's "Hello, World" example:

قول   "مرحبا يا عالم (" ! (

The word قول at the beginning of this statement, which of course seems to be at the end to English speakers, means *say*. So the program reads: say hello, world. This defamiliarizing effect of using an Arabic script calls attention to the unmarked influence of English on many high-level languages, as well as the unmarked centrality of English in most higher languages, such as JavaScript. That centrality constitutes the latent postcolonial imperialism of programming languages that spread English implicitly. Laila Shereen Sakr argues that even moving from highly mathematical C++ to more verbal Java (a language with "more English-based vocabulary") represents a challenge to non-English natives. And yet, with respect to قلب, she also warns against treating Arabic as a monolithic language community, writing, "Even though the Arabic is written in Modern Standard Arabic (MSA), I could tell the author was of Levantine background (Lebanese, Syrian, Jordanian, or Palestinian) because of the use of the greeting 'مرحب' in the 'Hello, World' statement as opposed to 'ahlan or labaas or essalaam 3laykoum'" (vjumamel, comment on Risam, Ray, and Koh 2014). Nasser's project could be seen as the opposite of a localization project, for rather than simplifying programming by rendering one programming language with another language's tokens, this language introduces complexities by gesturing to the language cultures at the heart of much symbolic interaction with computers. However, as Allen points out, قلب still has to engage with libraries written in languages based in English, rendering the language "a difficult-to-read mixture of Arabic and English" (Allen 2018, 29), showing how difficult resistance to an embedded language can be when developing for a computational platform. The computer compels compliance.

This desire to have a language in one's native tongue, or in a tongue at all instead of more mathematical, symbolic representations, points back to the moment when Grace Hopper was developing FLOW-MATIC. She describes the rationale behind its development:

> I used to be a mathematics professor. At that time I found there were a certain number of students who could not learn mathematics. I then was charged with the job of making it easy for businessmen to use our computers. I found it was not a question of whether they could learn mathematics or not, but whether they would. ... They said, 'Throw those symbols out—I do

not know what they mean, I have not time to learn symbols.' I suggest a reply to those who would like data processing people to use mathematical symbols that they make them first attempt to teach those symbols to vice-presidents or a colonel or admiral. I assure you that I tried it. (quoted in Knuth and Pardo 1980, 270)

Hopper's frustration perhaps reflects a challenge of teaching programming languages to adults who would obviously have little inclination and background to learn them. In fact, it is perhaps more remarkable that Hopper is trying to teach programming to vice presidents and admirals than to the women who had done the programming and been the computers or the emerging group of specialists who would do the programming in the ensuing years. Nonetheless, Hopper's remark is also a reminder of the challenge that reading formal notation presents in the moment when these computer languages are emerging—an intimidation factor that doubtless confronts any newcomer to programming. How much is that intimidation intensified when the root symbols or even epistemology does not match that of one's culture of origin?

In response to this growing awareness of the effects of basing programming languages on any one spoken language, more researchers have been turning their energies to creating programming languages in mother tongues, resisting a pervasive technocolonialism spread through global English.

In the ʻAnuʻu project, a Hawaiian team is working to translate the C# programming language into ʻōlelo Hawaiʻi "as a move to initialize and support decolonial processes in the development of digital media."[14] The team includes Kari Noe, Nathan Nahina, Kauwila Mahi, Noe Arista, and Jason Edward Lewis, who met while participating in the Skins Workshops on Aboriginal Storytelling and Video Game Design codirected by Lewis and organized under the Aboriginal Territories in Cyberspace research network.[15]

In the words of the ʻAnuʻu project team, "When a person processes thoughts within their own language, they feel, speak, and create through it. Giving Hawaiʻi the opportunity to create through ʻAnuʻu, lets the speakers breathe and exhale through ʻōlelo Hawaiʻi." If programming is thinking, then the programming language is the medium of thought. Being able to program in one's mother tongue and more importantly in an indigenous language in this postcolonial moment is to be able to compute through one's own cultural paradigms. The ʻAnuʻu project team hopes "to plant the roots for a new programming language and to extend the power/usability of ʻōlelo Hawaiʻi. In addition to this, we aim to have the implementation of ʻAnuʻu to extend to Hawaiian Language Immersion school programs, as well as to any organization or person who would like to express themselves with code in ʻōlelo Hawaiʻi." This pedagogical goal offers another component of the colonizing force of programming languages. For even if the language is not being used in the same sense as spoken or written language, to use the characters and tokens of those languages in programming is to reenforce them, particularly in the erosive context of a lingua franca, as global English is today in programming.

Although the team is just beginning to develop this translation, its members present their process through one of the ʻŌlelo noʻeau, or Hawaiian proverbs: "O ke kahua mamua, mahope ke kūkulu," or literally, "the site first, and then the building." As they explain, "The lesson is to learn all you can before practicing. Our project will be what comes before future structures that will support our language and culture." The ʻAnuʻu project, similar to ʻalb, translates programming largely at the level of the symbols. However, the selection of tokens has led them to the conceptual level, for example, as they reimagine the IF-THEN-ELSE conditional structure into concepts and words from Hawaiian (kahawai, makawai, muliwai) to represent the stream, a diversion, and their rejoining. As I have attempted to demonstrate in the case of FLOW-MATIC, the tokens affect one aspect of programming, while the underlying conceptual logic determines another. Although the tokens can be translated into different languages, they are not necessarily informed by the cultural perspective of that language community as they are in this case. Could a programmer engage that level of logic to write code in a dominant language to express concepts or worldviews from another culture—for example, an indigenous one?

Wrestling with this question, Jon M. R. Corbett, a programmer of Métis heritage, has been asking what it would mean to code from an indigenous perspective. In "Four Generations" (2015), he created a program that would produce beaded portraits in the traditional Métis manner of his grandmother, his father, himself, and his son. His program was later featured in the Smithsonian's National Museum of the American Indian. He described his approach in an interview with me (pers. interview, Google Hangouts, August 24, 2018):

> So I thought at the time I was writing the program (for my MFA), I have this physical process of beading and the thread does not break. It continues in a loop, not end to the end. So I rewrote the program to reflect the cultural practice to make sure that all the beads are connected to one another—a metaphor for connection. The logic of the computer is not a reflection of my physical experience, and I felt it should be. Why shouldn't the program also be reflective of the action?

Corbett explains how he attempted to encode the Cree epistemology into the beading program: "The loop doesn't start over at the beginning but does a serpentine if it's at the end of the row."

In this work, for which he created portraits of his family members (figure 5.1), Corbett was working in the language Processing, a popular contemporary language known for its affordances for creating visuals. Corbett changed the following code:

```
1. For(int x = 1; x<= NumberOfRows; x++){
2.    placeBeadAt(x, currentColumn);
3. }
```

into a more complex expression:

```
1. For(int x = 1; x <= NumberOfRows; x++){
2.    switch(x % 2){
3.      case 0:
4.        For(currentColumn = NumberOfColumns; currentColumn > 0;
currentColumn--){
5.          placeBeadAt(x, currentColumn);
6.        }
7.      break;
8.      default:
9.        For(currentColumn = 1; currentColumn <= NumberOfColumns;
currentColumn++){
10.          placeBeadAt(x, currentColumn);
11.        }
12.      break;
13.    }
14. }
```

In this example, Corbett is attempting to change the way beads are placed. As he explains, "So odd rows go left to right, and even rows go right to left."

Corbett also wished to encode the spiral pattern, but did not want to use the Western Cartesian mathematical model for the spiral because it does not exist in the Cree framework:

> I set the electronic beading on a spiral. But that set up a different problem because of the unique perspective of Indigenous mathematics. Using the center point as the eye I had to figure out where to put the second bead and the third bead. How do you make a spiral that doesn't use a radial calculation? I do a bunch of xy nudges until the previous bead location plus its radius isn't touching the placement of the current bead. Each iteration gets a little shaky because the

xy starting point of the second bead is never the same. When there's 8000 beads on a screen, you don't notice it—it isn't until you get a hundred completed images you can compare side by side that you see how dramatically different each design is. (pers. interview, August 24, 2018)

Corbett is still developing his code in a language heavily inflected with English. However, his use of the language tries to work around the default system of creating spirals by using one that reflected a Cree perspective on mathematics. That project led Corbett to try to develop a programming platform that allows speakers of Cree to tell traditional stories in a system that would also produce images.

Corbett characterizes his desire to program in Cree as an attraction to *ethnoprogramming*, which Outi Laiti coined to name "a cultural approach to computer programming," calling the practitioners "ethnoprogrammers" (2016, 9). For Laiti, ethnoprogramming is about more than merely creating programs in a native tongue. As she explains, "Ethnoprogramming can be seen as a way to increase cultural knowledge among computer programmers. It can also mean a way to teach programming from a cultural point of view. Ethnoprogramming can be a way to save and make the current information society aware of traditional knowledge" (ibid). Inherent in this formulation is the idea that culture is embedded in language, so to create in a form of that language is to engage with cultural production and preservation.

Corbett's current project demonstrates this concept further: he is trying to create a Cree story-making platform, whereby one can use Cree to tell a story that then produces an image, illustrating the intimate relation between visual and oral representation of tales in the Cree culture. Corbett illustrates an example of Cree in code:

> One of the first things I built in was the concept of ceremony. At Blue Quills (University nuhelot'įne thaiyots'į nistameyimâkanak Blue Quills), in the beginning of each class, we do a smudge, lighting sweetgrass or an herb and wash it over you and blow the smoke trails over you, to clear your mind, clear your eyes, and you want to speak truthfully.
>
> I do this in programming all the time, zeroing out variables, cleaning out an array, so the very first function you call is smudge as a function. Your opportunity to set up any arrays or variables. The concept of what it does is a cultural practice, creating a digitally encoded version of that cultural practice. (pers. interview, August 24, 2018)

For Corbett, to intervene in the nature of a language also requires intervening at the level of logic:

> For example—a simple For-next loop. Really there is only one way to do it. (Or I could do a Do Until.) But ... my language has the flexibility to let them put those together in different ways. So they don't have to go in a particular order. Sure the start of the loop and end need to be defined, but the inner contents can be in any order as long as the underlying story describes it

as such—like say I wanted to write a loop to show a crow flying, and it is currently perched—logically I would first check if it was already in flight before starting the routine to make it fly. But in story if I said, "The crow flew east, far far away, from where he was perched." This might translate in code to:

```
{start} the crow is flying, move right, from stationary {end}
```

This is a rudimentary mock-up but I could rearrange the internal statements in any order and still retain the same operation I want to see happen on screen. (ibid.)

Corbett frames his efforts as a parallel to Hopper: "Similar to Hopper, I have that same kind of idea, that might be a little naive, but I believe you should be able to program in a language that can be understood by an 'average' person and then converted into code that can be understood by the machine" (ibid.).

Whereas Hopper's intended average user for FLOW-MATIC was a business manager or military supervisor who would be at home in English, Corbett's intended average user has grown up in the Cree tradition, a tradition that informs her thinking at a level he hopes to amplify with a culturally homologous programming environment.

Hopper's Intervention

This analysis of FLOW-MATIC may seem to cast that particular programming language as something of a failure. Rather than judging an early experiment in programming language by today's standards, I intend instead to examine FLOW-MATIC in the context of the larger questions about the way code creates meaning. Perhaps Hopper's greatest intervention with regard to facilitating human and computer languages was her development of the first compiler in 1951. By transforming high-level language into machine code, compilers make possible every kind of high-level language, regardless of whether the language favors linguistic or nonlinguistic symbols. First used in FORTRAN before spreading to other languages, these programs that write other programs would be the key component to the development of many languages to come.

What was Hopper's greatest contribution, if not her insights into the potential for moving between languages? She demonstrated that ability also in dealing with humans, with whom she could move between realms of discourse. In an interview, she explains, "I could switch my vocabulary and speak highly technical for the programmers, and then tell the same things to the managers a few hours later but with a totally different vocabulary. So I guess I've always been innately a teacher. So that again was what made me want to get user-friendly languages out so people could use them" (Hopper 1980, 12). Just as Hopper sought to make programming legible to those in the world of business, through the development of compilers, Hopper opened the doors to a proliferation of higher-level languages, creating the possibility for even more paths to access.

Underlying this reading of FLOW-MATIC, therefore, is a consideration of the questions of inclusion and exclusion. Hopper, an innovator in programming languages, worked to make a computer language that was accessible to corporate managers, a language that seemed to be speaking their language. Corbett, Nasser, and the developers of 'ōlelo Hawai'i are working on interventions to open programming to developers from more cultural and linguistic backgrounds. The legacy of Hopper, as a woman working in the field of computer science, has been obscured and to some extent recovered, at the start of a larger wave of recovery, as historians document a process of exclusion and direct and indirect discouragement of women studying and working in the field of computer programming—an inequity that many are working to redress today. If Hopper was opening programming to people of nonprogramming backgrounds, this chapter asks, What does it mean to make programming culturally inclusive, and how can that process grow out of more accessible languages? Also, what is the role of encoded chauvinism in silencing and excluding or creating a hostile work or learning environment? However, because programming is evolving with hardware innovations, what is accessible today can be unwieldy tomorrow. What is accessible to one group can be foreign to another. Similarly, tales of innovations can obscure or obfuscate exclusions and erasures. Computer history is never simply science because such a notion is a fantasy. By reflecting on historically situated code objects, asking about not just audience and authorship but also accessibility and access, we trace the edges of more complex sociotechnological histories.

But there is also a trap in drawing too strong a parallel between human and computer language, the trap of trying to fit human languages into the systematic model of programming languages. David Golumbia weighs in on this point in *The Cultural Logic of Computation*, writing:

> Computers invite us to view languages on their terms: on the terms by which computers use formal systems that we have recently decided to call languages—that is, programming languages. But these closed systems, subject to univocal, correct, "activating" interpretations, look little like human language practices, which seems not just to allow but to thrive on ambiguity, context, and polysemy. Inevitably, a strong intuition of computationalists is that human language itself must be code-like and that ambiguity and polysemy are, in some critical sense, imperfections. Note that it is rarely if ever linguists who propose this view; there is just too much in the everyday world of language to let this view stand up under even mild critique. But language has many code-like aspects, and to a greater and lesser extent research programs have focused on these. (2009, 84)

For Golumbia, the conflation of computer and natural languages is an expression of a contemporary ideology that reduces the complexity of natural language by assessing its ambiguities as failures.

Critical code studies can be seen as the inverse operation. Rather than trying to make ambiguous language behave according to the systematic standards of programming languages, critical code studies seeks the ambiguous (and unverifiable) connotations of programming languages as they interact with and travels through other systems of meaning read by humans and machines, or what Bruno Latour calls *actor-networks*.

Whereas this chapter examined the way Hopper used FLOW-MATIC to bring programming closer to the level of human language, the next chapter explores how a media theorist, Friedrich Kittler, used programming in C and assembly to get closer to the machine.

6 Kittler's Code

Author: Friedrich Kittler

Years: Early 1980s–2000s

Hardware: Pentium IV,

x86 family of processors,

x87 family of floating-point coprocessors

Languages: C and assembly

Interoperating Files: xgraf.c, ray.s

Files: xsuptrace.c (excerpt), matrices.s (excerpt)

Code

```
1.  /*
2.  v. 3.57
3.  31.07.11
4.  PTRACE.PAS (c't 1/93,167ff.) extended
5.  Superelliosoid, rotational body and procedural textures from
povray3
6.  DOS-version no longer supported
7.
8.  COMPILE:
9.  Normal: xgraf xsuptrace ray.s matrices.s
10. // Option -DNEWFRESNEL: simplified Fresnel lanterns from
povray3
11. Option -DJITTER:    blurred (and time-consuming) shadows
12. Option -DGAMMA:     gamma correction
13. SVGALIB or DGA:   change bild.i ".equ XWINDOW,1"!
14.
```

15. RUNTIME.

16. <xsuptrace 1>: reproducible noise for runtime tests

17.

18. FEATURES:

19. All reflecting surfaces are adaptable on ReflectionMapping: what then appears on the surface is a picture to be loaded. This feature

20. first has to be demanded by user on the standard interface.

21.

22. Prompts (':') for scalars and vectors you can confirm with either use of <w[eiter]>

23. or <n[ein]> or answer with a new input

24.

25. 3 constant objects: Heaven, hell, ground (which only allows plein-air images)

26. Any number of variable objects (limited only by RAM)

27. As variable objects by default 2 balls and each 1 other object are predefined.

28. But standard objects can be deleted again.

29. If an object requires more than the standard number,

30. a prompt will ask for new coordinates.

31. All objects are editable (constants only by reassigning the color to normal procedure, variables also by location and size).

32. Some exotic objects are scalable and rotatable. This will be expanded further.

33. Any number of lamps, the first 2 are predefined.

34. Surface 1. global, 2. can be edited individually after assignment to objects.

35. LINUX: Arbitrary size *.24f-pictures as 2D-textures loadable.

36.

37. Objects as ranking for quick intershade() (cf. Foley, p. 784);

38. Lamps as a simply linked list.

39. Left-handed coordinate system: left < x < right, front < y < back,

40. below < z < above.

41.

42. NEW:

43. 01.04.97: AttCol()-acceleration path - transparencies get worse

44. 07.04.98: Individual Fresnel coefficients with individual dullness for

45. opaque, but metallic surfaces (so that the coefficients TransC and dullness can overwrite transpar). This is physically correct

46. and mirabile dictu, better than in POVRAY3. Color chart (ColTabT) globally editable

47. 22.11.98: ReflV() by Glassner, image synthesis, p. 726, again in

48. Light() pro lamps calculates

49. 24.12.98: object window selectable; unzipped DOS-*.24f-files loadable

50. 08.03.99: Experimental support for Ohta/Maekawa-algorithm

51. 01.09.01: DOS no longer supported

52. 13.08.04: Init_Ohta() different, still untested

53. 24.10.08: Stahl new for /usr/ich/laptop/xsuptrace.c

54.

55. BUGS:

56. Change of stei, sup, sor very empirically calculated

57. 2DMapping on Steiner, Agnesi, SuperQuadrik und rotation body only as reflection map

58. implemented: the transformation (x, y, z)->(u, v) would be difficult

59. MapProc () and Init_Fresnel() not prepared for multiple calls

60. Editing of boxes and pyramids still inconsistent

61. lambda and thin global, also not pro surface variable

62. No transparency shading as in CALCNEW.C

63. For freely placeable objects, null pointer errors are inevitable; man

64. Change a midpoint coordinate by small amounts

65. SOR-Umkugel will be calculated in Edit_Sor() instead of Gravity()

66. Computation indicators do not depend on wavelengths of light

67. 08.04.99: intershade() now correctly returns L->Shad, but the object coherence

68. cuts repeatedly, thus rather hindering

69. 30.12.00: xgraf (gcc with optimization) can falsify the SOR-curve, if

70. in SorInput the difference quotient Dy/Dx (thus, the curve gradient between the two x-fixed points) is too large.

71. 09.09.03: Change in transformation matrices only works when gcc-g. Dark

72. 31.07.11: QuColProc() debugged

73.

74. HINTS:

75. Between internal data structures and user display complex conversions take place;

76. So do not patch global data!

77. */

78.

79. #define   SUPTRACE

80. #define   COLTABSIZE   127   // unter DOS ggf. kleiner

81. #define   PIII   // bei schlechterer CPU dringend aendern!

82.

83. // CompileTime: Globale Zaehler, bei neuen Objekten oder Oberflaechen erhoehen

84.

85. #define SurfCnt   27

86. #define FormCnt   16

87.

88. #include <time.h>

89. #define   SPALTEN 640

90. #define   ZEILEN   480

91. #define   RAY

92. #include "xdefines.h"   // SVGALIB: defines.h

93. #include "ray.h"   // SVGALIB: #include bild16m.c || lock16m.c

Notes on xsuptrace.c

Note that this entire passage of code was translated by the Hammermann family at my request.

2. v. 3.57: Kittler is systematically updating his revisions to the code. This is version 3, update 57.

3: 31.07.11: Dates appear throughout this piece. This update seems to be from July 31, 2011. Note that Kittler published *Optical Media* in 2010, published "Computer Graphics" in 2001, and gave the lectures *Optical Media* was based on in 1999. The earliest update in this code is noted as 01.04.97 in line 43. However, there may have been earlier versions.

4: The core of this program is based on a Turbo Pascal program called PTRACE.PAS, originally published in c't 1/93,167ff, *Magazin für Computertechnik* (Claussen and Pöpsel 1993), which indicates when Kittler likely began work on this project.

5: A second mention here of povray3, another one of the sources for functions in this code. It is a raytracer the first version of which appeared in 1991. *POV* in the name refers to Dali's "Persistence of Memory" and the concept of persistence of vision in biology (Buck 2001).

6: Kittler shows how he is wrestling with the software upgrades that affect his code, showing how code studies is also software and platform studies. While developing this software, Kittler was using Intel machines that had DOS installed.

8: COMPILE precedes a list of software that Kittler drew from.

9: See a further discussion of matrices.s later in this chapter.

19: In *reflection mapping*, the software creates the illusion of reflection by applying an image (the reflection) to the reflective surface, mapping the image onto the contours of the reflective object. The technique was developed in the early 1980s by two independent groups, Gene Miller with Ken Perlin, and Michael Chou with Lance Williams (DeBevec 2006).

22–23: In German, *weiter* means "continue" and *nein*, of course, means "no."

25: Heaven, Hell, and ground here originally, "Himmel, Hoelle, Boden," which could also be translated as "sky," "hell," and "ground." *Plein-air* refers to images painted outside "en plein-air," a technique that dates back to the eighteenth century (Malafronte 2009). Here, Kittler seems to be referring to images created outside of the program itself, which becomes the "inside," mapping a historical artistic dyad (inside the studio, outside the studio) onto the software (inside the program, outside the program).

26: "Limited only by RAM": Notice Kittler's attention to hardware in his code's documentation.

33: "Any number of lamps": as a ray tracer, the software works to model the movement of light from light sources, or "lamps."

38: In the foreword to *Gramophone, Film, Typewriter* (Winthrop-Young and Wutz 1999, xxxi), the translator notes the irony of Kittler's use of "simply" (*einfach*) for things that to others are hardly simple.

42–53: *New* begins a section of documented updates from January 1997 through October 2008. Kittler used the English word here.

46: *Mirable dictu*, happy to relate. Yes, it is a bit uncommon to find Latin in computer source code comments. See how Kittler's voice persists even in the technical documentation.

55–72: Documents a series of *bugs*. Kittler used the English word here.

74–77: This word, *hint*, also appeared in English.

Functionality

This is a translation of the header comment at the beginning of a raytracing program. The majority of this code is merely documentation of the development of the file itself, the entire contents of which can be found at this book's website (http://criticalcodestudies.com), republished with permission of the archive.

There Is No Software, Except …

Friedrich Kittler is the media theorist known for his provocative declaration titling his essay "There Is No Software" (1992), in which he makes the argument that code is a kind of illusion, for in the end, everything done in code is reduced to electronic signals. Given that position, it might be surprising to have a chapter of this book devoted to the analysis of his computer code, of which he reportedly wrote over one hundred thousand lines (Parikka and Feigelfeld 2015). What happens when the man for whom there is no software writes code? One scholar, his assistant Paul Feigelfeld, calls Kittler a liar for making that claim—but in the sense of Odysseus, more of a trickster in the face of myopic, or cyclopic, brutality, a provocation meant to help his readers to see a point about the "materiality behind the code" (2013, 1). Therefore, rather than dwelling on this irony, through the exposition of Kittler's code, I trace a reciprocal process through which an influential media theorist used code as a means to explore technology to inform his theoretical writing, and, subsequently, that exploration in and through code shaped the way he theorized. Furthermore, I will argue that for Kittler, programming was a kind of theorizing, an activity of philosophical labor, involving interfacing with a machine and tracing ideas by expressing them in code.

Following in the footsteps of the philosophers he idealized, Kittler used code to understand the physics, mathematics, and programming of the media forms he was interpreting. Once, when giving a lecture on the evolution of programming languages (Kittler 2011a), as he explains the history of computing, Kittler stops short of commenting extensively on computer languages because, as he admitted, he had never developed one. Such was his sense that to understand a medium was to understand its most intricate workings. To build was to know. Although he may not have built from scratch a gramophone, film projector, or typewriter, the subjects of one his most famous works, he showed a dedication to understanding intimately the workings of the media he theorized. At the same time, his work in code, in this unambiguous realm of signification, reinforces a critical practice that prefers accurate technological and scientific description to interpretation and reflection. Though he conjures meaning through his wry, allusive writing style, he seems reluctant to interpret beyond drawing analogies and demonstrating the impact of technology in his signature move of technological determinism.

This chapter interprets the code he developed for a type of graphics software known as a *raytracer*. An examination of Kittler's code reveals his engagement with the algorithms of raytracing and his understanding of the affordances of the Pentium IV. Exploring his C and assembly code in his raytracer leads to a more complex understanding of Kittler's critical positions and demonstrates the way critical making informs his theory. In this chapter, I will identify ways writing this raytracer seems to have informed his own sense of the models, metaphors, and machinery operationalized in the processes he would interpret. By coding to understand, Kittler engages in a kind of epistemological programming, thinking through media and its relationship to culture.

More importantly, this chapter will bring together the techniques of critical code studies, software, and platform studies, along with, of course, media archaeology, of which Kittler can rightfully be called a father, to demonstrate the interdependence of all these approaches. Here is a preeminent media archaeologist writing code with attention to *platform*—creating *software* that combines high and low languages to create, through algorithms, a *medium* (on the medium of all media, the computer) that models the physics of vision.

In writing code to understand media, Kittler is modeling through performance his own notion of media-technological a priori, putting the technology before the theorization of it. If, in Kittler's formulation, the workings of technology transform our understanding of the world, by developing a more intimate understanding of the software and hardware by writing and assembling code, Kittler was bathing in the waters of our technological moment while testing, to extend the metaphor, buoyancy and the effects of submersion. Furthermore, I would argue that just as we read the drafts, journals, and letters of philosophers to understand their writings, so too can we read their code, which is another expression of their thought and critical practice, even if it is an assemblage of code derived and adapted from other sources. For what is critical writing but an assemblage built from our own thoughts and the thoughts of others? This is a long way of saying that through this example, we can see how code becomes a channel of discourse, a means of critical thinking and exploration, a writing process of drafting and revision, and a mode of theoretical practice that is theorizing through making. This chapter advances the project of critical code studies by showing how reading code is examining a symbolic manifestation of a person's understanding. To make this argument, as with all code readings, I will need to offer a bit of context.

// One Brief Comment on Authorship

One small note before we begin, however. As I have mentioned previously (see chapter 2), authorship is a slippery notion when it comes to code. Any given line in a body of code may have many sources of origin: a textbook, another program, a community posting board, et cetera. In that way, lines of code are a bit more like nails or screws and a bit less like sentences. For this reason, a more thorough media archaeological exploration of this code may turn up sources for many aspects of the code that I will attribute to Kittler. To this concern, I offer two responses. The first is that there is documentation in and out of the code linking Kittler to the code. Regardless of the source of any given method, it appears Kittler was at least joining these segments together in his own program. Further, Paul Feigelfeld, who assisted Kittler with, among other projects, his programming classes, and who with Peter Berz has taken on the task of curating the code, attests to his authorship.[1] Feigelfeld also asserts that Kittler's training in the humanities had built in him the habit of citing his sources, even to the extent of giving him pride in acknowledging them, a habit that manifests itself in the code (pers. interview, Google Hangouts, January 21, 2019). Take, for example, his references to povray3 throughout his code, particularly in the comment on line 5, which attributes to povray the Superellipsoid, the Rotationskoerper (rotation algorithm), and the texture procedure. Susanne Holl (2017) has also explored Kittler's code and notes the difficulties of attribution, but cites various insertions of German in file names that seem to point to Kittler's interaction with the code, which was stored on his computers.

The second response borrows a lesson from literary critical theory, the notion of the *author function*, which postulates that all that constitutes the epiphenomena that we call authors—regardless in many ways of its authenticity, so much of which can never be verified—has an effect on how we read works. Further, the author function stipulates that the concept of any author is a historical and social construction. Our sense of any author—for example, William Shakespeare—including any historical data we have about him or any other texts we attribute to him, shapes how we read plays and sonnets that bear his name. For this reason, in reading this code that we are attributing to Kittler in light of his other writing, I am actually reading one textual body through the lens of another under an umbrella concept, itself a bit of an assemblage—this notion of a theorist Friedrich Kittler, a conceptual field that I am further reifying by writing this chapter.[2] In other words, rather than fall down the rabbit hole of the quest to prove authorship, I will read one text, this code, in light of other texts, including the corpus of Kittler's prose-based theoretical works, his books, articles, and lectures, under the presumption that the same author worked on both, understanding that such an assertion is an operational fiction, a frame of convenience.

What this example helps to emphasize, more importantly, is that authorship has a different meaning when it comes to code. Kittler may not have created most of the lines in his raytracer. He may have collected and connected it from many different sources, including computing magazines and even other programmers. In fact, it would be difficult to prove without question that he knew what each line of this code did. Nonetheless, programmers do not need to build every light bulb to experience their illumination, and as the many volumes of hobbyist programming magazines show, such as the one that published the basis for Kittler's raytracer, the process of inputting code someone else has written can be educational. What is important for future critical code studies is to resituate authorship not as something that necessarily emerges out of whole cloth from the genius poised at the computer but instead as an act of reading and writing, cutting and pasting, patching together and reworking. Thus, though Kittler may not be the source for much of this code, there is evidence he got it working and even did some debugging. In the world of programming, as opposed to the world of expository writing, that is authorship enough—not to recreate the myth of the author but to explore the code that was at least handled by this media philosopher.

The Man behind the Code

Friedrich Kittler is one of the most well-renowned media theorists of the twentieth century. He is one of the originators of what is called *media archaeology*, particularly in what's known as the Berlin school, and his theories express the notion of *media determinism*, an idea that the technologies of the age determine the way we conceptualize the world (Winthrop-Young and Wutz 1999, xii). Fundamental to the concept of media determinism is the *technological* a priori, adapted from Foucault's *historical* a priori (1982, chapter 5), which describes the way technological developments shape how we understand and envision our world and its future.[3] His most famous works are *Discourse Networks* and *Gramophone, Film, Typewriter* (*GFT*; originally published in 1986), though "There Is No Software" is often cited in scholarship about software or code.[4] In Kittler's media archaeology, the advent of media technologies shapes the way people, particularly philosophers and other artists, view the world. In *GFT*, Kittler demonstrates the effects of the "terror" of the introduction of the three technologies of the title on the psyche of those living at the time. As an example of the technical a priori, he explains how the advent of the gramophone led to people thinking of memories as recordings. With the advent of film, people perceived time as something with cuts and jumps. With the advent of the typewriter, as writing is no longer connected to the hand (as in manuscripts), the act of writing continues on a progression (which leads to computer code) away from the intimate connection with the writer.

For Kittler, these varied examples of new technologies, particularly new communication technologies, demonstrate the way media forms shape our mental constructs. In the oft-quoted first line of his preface to *GFT*, Kittler writes, "Media determine our situation" (1999, xxxiv). However, the implications of that understanding only multiply in the age of the machine that can imitate all other machines, this *uber medium* (my phrase), the digital computer. In the introduction of *GFT*, he begins not with any of the three technologies of the title, but with one connected to computational machines: "Optical fiber networks. People will be hooked to an information channel that can be used for any medium—for the first time in history, or for its end" (1). This quote shows not only Kittler's increasing fascination with digital technology but also his dark, droll sense of humor that takes a scientific claim into ominous teleological realms. It is this combination of scientific observation and resonant allusion that marks Kittler's critical writing, his ability to gesture to the transcendental without sacrificing his attention to technological specificities, that we can also see at play in his code and his writing about it. In fact, I would argue that the code of this acclaimed media determinist and the exercise of his writing it shape his philosophy and his thinking on computational media beyond merely giving him the bona fides to write about it. Simply put, the code precedes, expresses, and extends his theory.

Is There Really No Software?

To write that "there is no software" in 1992,[5] well into the so-called digital age, over a decade after the advent of home computing and its spread thanks to user-friendly operating systems and the graphically browsable World Wide Web, is to make a very counterintuitive claim. In fact, this intentionally provocative claim runs so counter to conventional wisdom that the title alone has become a kind of shorthand for Kittler's contribution to what would become software, platform, and code studies. In the article, Kittler explains how the "tower of babel" of programming languages must in the end be reduced to machine language and, in turn, electrical signals. Consequently, every human expression of any important idea circulated on computational media can ultimately be reduced to electrical signals. For practical reasons, assembly language is about as close to these signals as a programmer can get. This argument does not so much eradicate the notion of software as it shows its ultimate ends, the translation into the language via which it is connected to the machine, as the assembly instructs the CPU to write to and read from specific registers. Unlike these higher languages, because it deals with assigning material registers, assembly language is a direct linguistic extension of the machine.

Because Kittler envisions the important work of computers happening at this electronic level, as he seeks a full understanding of the workings of computational media, he is frustrated by anything that blocks his access to the machine. In his essay "Protected Mode" (2014), Kittler makes the claim that design choices in microchip architecture block programmers from accessing and thereby controlling certain aspects of the digital machine. He claims that chip makers have erected a new Berlin Wall in between the user and the microprocessor: "And so, software—a billion-dollar enterprise based on one of the cheapest elements on Earth—used everything at its disposal to prevent said 'humans' from having access to hardware" (209).

Kittler longs for "the good old days—when microprocessor pins were still big enough" to operate on with "simple soldering irons" and when "even literary critics could do whatver they wanted with Intel's 8086 Processor" (2014, 209). Here Kittler alludes to his own work on software and hardware as he worked with his brother Wolf to build their own Moog synthesizer (Feigelfeld, pers. interview, January 21, 2019). Instead, end users have been "duped by strategically produced illusions" that block their access to hardware, becoming "subject[s] or underling[s] of the Microsoft Corporation" (Kittler 2014, 209). Kittler despised this subjectivity.

In "Protected Mode," Kittler writes with the fury of a worker who sees how he has been cordoned off from the means of production. He bemoans the loss of the time when the programmer translated code into the binary of operation code by hand, left only with the mnemonics of assembly "as the outer limit of what users might understand or want of machines" (Kittler 2014, 210). As a media theorist dedicated to understanding these a priori technological media, Kittler desires access to the inner workings of the machine and sees the denial of that access as a stupefying manipulation of Silicon Valley and Seattle.[6]

As his argument progresses, Kittler traces a path to a workaround using MS-DOS that lets him access Real Mode, allowing him to directly address registers rather than virtual memory. As he notes in a later lecture (Kittler 2011a), a programmer could "cheat DOS" to get around this barrier, particularly by running multiple programs at once and accessing Real Mode. For Kittler, then, anything that blocks access to the machine is subjugating and subordinating the programmer, denying agency in the form of direct interaction with the machine. This drama, in *Tron*-like fashion, places the programmer in a struggle with the software corporations that wish to maintain control of the technosocial realm. In the age dominated by Google, Facebook, and Apple, it is hard to contest such arguments. Kittler raised similar objections to object-oriented programming: "For Kittler, ultimately, object-orientation (a programming paradigm he abhorred) meant the necessary escalation towards our being subjects of media technologies" (Parikka and Feigelfeld 2015). Accessing the machine through code and through hardware was a way for Kittler to free himself from this subjectivity to the lords of Silicon Valley. Programming, especially at the level of the hardware, was a means of achieving agency.

For Kittler, writing code was also continuous with the evolution of writing and discourse itself, only it was even more demanding. On one hand, code writing offered a fulfillment of the dream of romantic poetry, a language that makes things happen. To illustrate, Kittler tells what he calls a joke, the story of Sappho's poem Fragment 1 in which she calls to Aphrodite to bring her lover back to life. For Kittler, this is the sign of the oldest desire of lyric poetry—namely, language that can do things, language that can be executed, a dream he sees finally fulfilled at the command line, where a person can "kill" a program by merely typing the word and pressing Enter. Upon telling this joke, Kittler (2011a) further quips, "It's rather nice to know something about poetry and something about computers." His poetic sense likewise informs his code.

On the other hand, code, as anyone who has tried to program knows, is an unforgiving, inflexible communication environment. Kittler tells another story of breaking a program he was writing by using a colon instead of a semicolon in his code. As he explains, there is a "higher responsibility you take on your shoulders when you write a program" (Kittler 2011a). This higher responsibility applies to the duty to put every semicolon in its place, yet Kittler's engineering mind seems also to extrapolate from his endeavor the duty to explain technological media with accuracy and precision. His encounter with the realm of the unambiguous has informed and reinforced his own tendency toward exactness.

Kittler wrote code in assembly, as well as his "favorite language," C, preferring it because it could cooperate with assembly (Kittler 2011a). C is a language of the Algol family, born of Bell Labs in 1972. There is "a small 'semantic gap' between C and the computer hardware," meaning "its data types and operators are closely related to the operations provided by most computers" (Harbison and Steele 1994, 3). Among his many programs in C, Kittler's crowning achievement was his raytracer, the subject of this chapter, the writing of which gave him insights and authority to theorize about this specular medium. Reading this code not only illuminates his theoretical writing about optical media but also attends the extension of his theorization in code form. This case study demonstrates the ways reading code and other critical writing can be part of a continuous process of understanding a person's philosophy.

Kittler and Computer Graphics

Before publishing his work on computer graphics, Kittler had written extensively on optical media in a book by that title (2010). However, prior to that book (published in German in 2002), based on lectures he gave in 1999, he had "implemented all the knowledge about optical media, the physics of light and optics in code" (Feigelfeld, pers. comm, March 27, 2019). That book traces the development of visual recording media from the camera obscura to film and television and finally to computers. He addresses computational image production specifically in his essay "Computer Graphics: A Semi-Technical Introduction" (2001), which expresses the theorization that emerged out of his coding. In that essay, he writes, "From the *camera obscura* to the television camera, all these media have simply taken the ancient law of reflection and the modern law of refraction and poured them into hardware" (34–35). By contrast, computer graphics reproduce these processes mathematically. As he explains, "Computer graphics are to these optical media what the optical media are to the eye. Just as the camera lens, literally as hardware, simulates the eye, which is literally wetware, so does software, as computer graphics, simulate hardware" (35). Through such a claim, Kittler demonstrates the ways in which his software and code studies are also enacting forms of hardware studies and by extension media archaeology, though he does not use those terms. He is recreating hardware processes in software. In creating the program, he explores the software that "transposes such optical laws ... into algebraically pure logic" (35). However, because code is a specific historically bound implementation of an algorithm, full of choice, what Saussurian linguists call paradigms and sequences, or syntagm, his code is not "pure logic" but an expression of his attempt to manifest it. Similarly, he writes, "Computer graphics, because it is software, consists of algorithms and only of algorithms" (36). However, as evident from even the extensive code comment that begins this chapter, the source code of those algorithms contain much more than only algorithms, including development notes, bug reports, and hints. More importantly, the entire implementation of this code was never inevitable but instead shows the traces of its own development and the evolving understanding of its programmer.

Anticipating today's discussions of "fake news" and digital media manipulation, Kittler argues that computer graphics are prone to falsification to a degree far beyond photography. He explains that because "a single pixel" on a screen can be addressed and altered without going through all the ones before or after it, "the computer image is thus prone to a falsification to a degree that already gives television producers and ethics watchdogs the shivers" (Kittler 2001, 32). The deception for Kittler goes beyond the manipulation of images produced or edited on the machine and into the interface of contemporary operating systems. Kittler points to the ways, unlike the older display of "white dots on an amber or green background," that operations become invisible in the graphical user interface. The operating system presents its interface as transparent "windows" or a background "desktop," even though it is a construction of graphics. These windows are hardly transparent as they keep users, especially those who cannot pass through the windows, subjugated to Microsoft and Apple.

In "Computer Graphics," Kittler (2001) explores two specific means for creating images on computers: raytracing and radiosity. *Raytracing* is a method for modeling the path a ray takes from the eye to the object, as well as the path light takes from its source, reflecting off objects and then reaching the eye (or its surrogate, the computer screen). It models the process of refraction and reflection, tracing photons as they illuminate or are transformed into shadows or refracted. Kittler seems disappointed with raytracing as a means of image production, writing, "Unfortunately ... the optical option called raytracing shows both more and less than straightforward perception. Simply because the ray of light is infinitely thin and thus zero-dimensional, all local effects are maximized to the same extent that global effects are suppressed" (39). Thus, the raytracing process simply cannot replicate human vision completely. Due to limitations of raytracing, the process does not create very realistic images. As Kittler put it in a lecture, "The computer apple," or as he jokingly calls it, "Apple's apple," has "a more brilliant appearance than ... the biological apple. ... Raytracing apples are perfect" (Kittler 2011c). Kittler does not use *perfect* as a compliment but instead to mark a shortcoming in computer graphics: the "imperfect" apple is the kind you can eat, the stuff of life. He refers to these images as *ideals*—not in the positive sense, but in the sense of Platonic ideals, lacking reality (Kittler 2001, 36). Kittler explains that given time enough and the correct programming, computers would be capable of producing "such miracles" as visually realistic images but, at the time of his writing, to achieve this level of verisimilitude, programmers would need "a capacity to waste time that would rival that of good old painters" (36). However, "It is only in the name of impatience that all existing computer graphics are based on idealizations—a term that functions here, unlike in philosophy, as a pejorative" (36). Ideals, imaginaries, are deprecations when compared with the real.

If technology is insufficient, who can intervene? Philosophers. Specifically, philosophers who are willing to enact processes to understand reality, also known as *phenomenology*. Philosophers experiment to understand reality. For example, Kittler presents Kant's formulation of Beauty, the "optical gestalt," as a "mechanism of recognition," to ruminate on the conditions of aesthetic representation. As he explains in the essay "The World of the Symbolic" (Kittler 1997), unlike humans, "angels have no need to reflect on temporo-serial and spatio-discrete data; machines have no possibility of doing so. The former skip over the problem; the latter over its solution" (131). Angels have access to the entirety of the thing, presumably inside and out and consequently have no need to dwell on the details (incidentally, where the devil is purported to be) of technologies to capture images. By contrast, machines are not in the business of contemplation, nor are they capable of a solution, so they skip over its solution by relying on partial processes. Thus, in the world of idealized images, the human philosopher must report for duty.

Answering that call, Kittler's examination of the raytracer leads him beyond the "pure logic," into the cultural history, which then leads to military history. Consistent with his other views of media development, Kittler does not seem surprised that the innovation of computer graphics is driven by the necessities of military operations. He cites Axel Roch, who demonstrated that raytracing "derives not at all from computer graphics, but rather from its military predecessor: the tracking of enemy airplanes with radar" (Kittler 2001, 37). Kittler notes that the histories of computers and computer images "lie not in television, but in radar, a medium of war" (31). He traces computer graphics to early-warning systems, "even if [technology] has replaced the polar coordinates of the radar screen with the Cartesian coordinates" of the computer monitor (32). However, we wouldn't have Cartesian coordinates at all without René Descartes.

Descartes provides not only a coordinate system for computer graphics but also a model for tracing the path of light, as well as a model of the philosopher scientist. In the early 1600s, Descartes had studied the "play of light" of the rainbow by commissioning "a glassblower to create a simulacrum of a single raindrop one hundred times enlarged" (Kittler 2001, 38). Descartes then imagined the journey of a ray of light through every path through the globe. Note a bit of Kittlerian sleight of hand, as the ray of light becomes the Cartesian "subject" moving through the globe: "The subject itself thus enacted as a ray of light coming from the sun through the raindrop and executing every imaginable reflection and refraction until the simplest sunlight finally disintegrated, according to trigonometric laws, into the spectrum of the rainbow" (38). If it was not already, Kittler then makes this process of subject formation through simulation crystal clear by writing, "The Cartesisan subject comes about through self-application, or, to put it in terms of computer science, through recursion" (38). Thereafter, Kittler refers to this thought experiment as the "Cartesian raytracer." In this historical example, Kittler has found the model he will emulate, the philosopher-programmer who creates a system for simulating a process to achieve a deeper understanding. Kittler's own glass globe was the raytracer he built, although rather than let his mind and mathematics trace the path, he would share those processes with the machine.

The Raytracer of Heaven and Hell

A *raytracer* recursively follows the path of a vector or ray from the eye of the imagined viewer, or camera, through the screen (or image plane) to the image in order to determine the color of any given pixel on the screen. It also traces the path of rays emanating from light sources in the visual space back to the eye. Depending on the sophistication of the raytracer, the system may calculate for reflection, refraction, and diffusion. Kittler's code uses a number of these effects. For some context, raytracing, albeit a very sophisticated and computationally expensive version of raytracing, is at the heart of the software Pixar uses for creating its popular animated films, such as *Cars* and *Toy Story*.

At first glance, the interface of Kittler's raytracer (figure 6.1) seems a bit stark. The program proceeds as a series of yes or no (*ja* or *nein*) and numerical questions. Responding in the operating system's terminal, the user sees unformatted white text on a black background, the staple of pre-Windows DOS computing, offering parameters for configuration: lights, objects, and surfaces. The user can choose to edit the lamp, or light source, or set additional lamps. Because raytracers trace the path of light reflecting off objects and into the eye or screen, the choice of light sources and light position is critical. Kittler's user can also select from a torus, ellipsoid, or agnesi, also known as the *witch of agnesi*, the name of which derived from that of mathematician Marie Agnesi. According to Feigelfeld (pers. interview, Google Hangouts, January 21, 2019), Kittler was particularly proud of his mobius (moebius) object because the curious shape is not an illusion but the instantiation of mathematics that he had to render in code. The user can also choose surfaces, whether materials such as wood or chrome or natural phenomena such as clouds, storms, rain, or a pond. The main file for this interface, xsuptrace.c, is over five thousand lines long, which in itself may be a sign of the idiosyncratic or amateur nature of this code, as Kittler seems to have added

```
~/Documents/ich/usb > ./xsuptrace
Raytracer Himmel und Hoelle
Lampe edieren?              [j/n] : n
Noch eine Lampe setzen?     [j/n] : n
Fertiges Bild speichern? [j/n] : n
Moegliche Objekte:
   0: Himmel     1: Boden      2: Hoelle      3: Kugel      4: Moebius    5: Steiner
   6: Torus      7: Ellipsoid 8: Kegel       9: Pyramide 10: Quader    11: Agnesi
  12: SuperEll 13: Rotation 14: Scheibe    15: Lemnisk.
Moegliche Oberflaechen:
   0: Wolken     1: Hoelle     2: Grau        3: Marmor     4: Wasser     5: Glas
   6: Spiegel    7: Messing    8: Feuer       9: Holz     10: Fourier   11: Kupfer
  12: Iris      13: Teich     14: Ziegel     15: Sand     16: Schach   17: Wabe
  18: Achat     19: Quilt     20: Regen      21: D2Map    22: Sturm    23: Silber
  24: Gold      25: Chrom     26: ColQuilt 27: Stahl
Oberflaechen global edieren?           [j/n] : n
Oberflaeche fuer den Himmel            [ 0]  : 0
Oberflaeche fuer die Hoelle            [ 1]  : 1
Oberflaeche fuer den Boden             [ 4]  : 4
Noch ein Objekt anlegen?               [j/n] : n
Objekte [in Eingabefolge] edieren?     [j/n] : n
Betrachter edieren?                    [j/n] : n
Sekunden: 0.284
```

Figure 6.1
Interface questions for Kittler's Raytracer Himmel und Hoelle.

to it as he learned new procedures, lengthening the file rather than reorganizing or refactoring it.

Despite his attraction to material technical minutia, an evocation of the transcendental always attends Kittler's technological explanations. On the topic of raytracers, he explains, "Whenever you encounter a computer image whose shining highlights are a close second to heavenly Jerusalem's and whose stark shadows are a close second to Hell's, you are dealing with elementary raytracing" (Kittler 2001, 39).

As Kittler wrote these words about computer graphics, gesturing toward Heaven and Hell, he was not paying compliments to digital graphics: just the opposite. These otherworldly qualities of images are signs of their distance from reality. They are idealistic, not in the positive sense of philosophy, but in a negative sense, marking their distance from photography, which can capture the continuous nature of the visual spectrum of light. Nor does Kittler gesture toward the supernatural in these discussions of images to bring religion into the discussion of media studies, but instead to focus his discussion of images and machines on the realm of humans, whose vision or perception is being represented, recreated, or replicated.

However, this "divine comedy of computer graphics," as Stephanie Boluk has called it,[7] was not a fleeting allusion to the media theorist who knew well his Dante. In fact, the name of the raytracer itself is "Raytracer Himmel und Hoelle," based on the program PTRACE.PAS, published by Ute Claussen and Josef Pöpsel in the computer hobbyist journal *c't* in 1993, which Kittler credits in his opening comment. The article in which the code appears is titled "Himmel und Hölle," and that program uses "Himmel" for the area above the ground and "Hölle"[8] for "den Untergrund" or the area "underground." Unlike Kittler's various geometric objects, in this source program the user can only work with a small or large ball. Note that Kittler labels his raytracer (written in C) as an *erweitert* or "extended" version of this Turbo Pascal program, which is less than five hundred lines long, compared to his, which is over five thousand lines. Kittler not only converted the program to C, he developed it over the course of many years while he learned new techniques as, I would argue, a proving ground for his explorations.

Nonetheless, this program, published in 1993, appears to have given him not just the foundational algorithm for his raytracer but also its central metaphors, Heaven and Hell. Those terms appear frequently throughout Kittler's raytracer's code, representing the upper and lower halves of the visual space. They are evident in the documentation of his xsuptrace.c file:

```
25. 3 constant objects: heaven, hell, ground
25. 3 konstante Objekte: Himmel, Hoelle, Boden
```

The word *Boden* means "ground," which represents the space between Himmel and Hoelle. Each is instantiated as one of the forms that the raytracer can manipulate:

```
133. int    normal[FormCnt] = {0,1,4,7,2,11,10,7,6,11,3,14,12,5,2,2
3};
134. char   ObjStr[FormCnt][32] = {
135.    "den Himmel         ",
136.    "die Hoelle         ",
137.    "den Boden          ",
```

These terms reemerge throughout the code as primitives or `Prims`:

```
161. Prims *Boden,*Hoelle,*Himmel,*Ring,*Last;
```

And then again as the upper and lower limits of the images' frame throughout the code. For example, this function that calculates the dispersal or interreflection of light first checks to see the ray's relation to these primitives:

```
1436. static Prims *
1437. interref (VCT3 *p, rayT *ray) // liefert *p
1438. {
1439.    float l,lmin,opak;
1440.    Prims *Return,*Obj = Ring;
1441.    int   i;
1442.    pyrT  *py;
1443.    boxT  *bo;
1444.
1445.    if (ray->n.z >= 0)
1446.      {
1447.      if (ray->p.z > 0)
1448.        Return = Himmel;
1449.      else
1450.        Return = Boden;
1451.      }
1452.    else
1453.      {
1454.      if (ray->p.z < 0)
1455.        Return = Hoelle;
1456.      else
1457.        Return = Boden;
1458.      }
1459.    if (Return != Boden || ray->n.z == 0) // Null-Div abfangen
1460.      lmin = Infinit;
1461.    else
1462.      lmin = -ray->p.z/ray->n.z;
```

Throughout the file, the code returns to these Prims or "primitives," foundational objects of Heaven and Hell, except here Heaven is not a place that delivers light but an object, a construction, off of which rays return so the computer does not have to track them endlessly into infinity. How must the chronic punster have delighted in the layers of significance, the libraries of signification if you will, that he evokes by including these primitive constructs of Heaven and Hell, which operate not as the infinite, and hence incalculable, Heaven and Hell, but as limits to the path of rays, offering sources of reflection in the mathematical sense.

I do not want to read too much into these terms, as elsewhere in the code Kittler seems to imagine, following John Lennon, that above us is only sky. See the comment on this conditional check:

```
1.  if (Obj->form < ground)        // sky oder hell
```

The sky is not below the ground (`<ground`) but rather has been assigned a lower number in the list of objects. Although Himmel may be at times "sky," Hell, on the other hand, seems to remain Hell, as in this excerpt from a method called `FlameProc`, presumably short for flame procedure:

```
2513.  switch (Obj->form)
2514.  {
2515.    case sky:                  [...]
2517.    case hell:                 [...]
2519.    case ground:
```

I should note that the words *sky* and *hell* in this code comment are written in English, while the word for "or" (*oder*) is written in German, which invites readings from a comparative literatures approach. The code follows a distinction whereby objects are named in German (*Himmel, Hoelle,* and *Boden,* but also *Pyramide*) and code regarding surfaces (*Oberflaechen*) tends to use the English names even of the objects (sky, hell, ground, pyramid). This distinction is also true in PTRACE.PAS, which refers to surfaces in the code in English (sky, hell, simple), while the interface offers German (*Wölken* or "clouds"; Hölle; *Grau* or "grey"). In both cases Hell is an object and a surface, so users could choose Hoelle to be the surface of Himmel, if they so chose. One explanation may have been that the source of the textures in PTRACE.PAS, which the code attributes to Ken Perlin's textures, uses English names.[9] Another possibility is that the code is distinguishing between the objects and the surfaces. However, as I mentioned, even the objects, such as Himmel, are referred to by their English names in the code that handles surfaces.

Regardless of whether they appear in English or in German, these naming conventions offer a wry reflection of Kittler's universe. Here I will perform a very un-Kittlerian "reflection."[10] What does it mean to have Kittler working with these (borrowed) constructs of Himmel and Hoelle in code? On the one hand, his raytracer seems the software implementation of Psalm 139, which in the 1912 *Luterbibel* reads, "Führe ich gen

Himmel, so bist du da. Bettete ich mir in die Hölle, siehe, so bist du auch da." Translated into English, by Google of all sources, the line reads, "If I go to heaven, you are there. If I went to hell, behold, you are there too." It is a testament to the ubiquity of God that speaks of a creator's absolute knowledge of every inch, every word, of their creation, not unlike a programmer and their code. But let us not be silly. Kittler is a disciple of Nietzsche, a fan of what John Durham Peters (2009) calls the "method of perversity," challenging always the "unquestioned moral monopoly" of "the ruling good." Against that image of the author, this code that creates Heaven and Hell as primitive objects to be manipulated by the user, boundaries rather than infinities, the Heaven and Hell raytracer offers a bit of cosmic humor, as the media theorist wrestles with his own creation in the simultaneously exalting and humbling position of the self-taught programmer.

Kittler's critical writing does not dwell much on theology or teleology, but he had labored in code and no doubt the academy enough to recognize a hell. Nonetheless, not every hell is worth consideration. A later segment of the code reveals this comment:

```
5008.  Edit_Predefs (void) // verwaltet global deklarierte Objekte[11]
5009.  {
5010.     Prims *P;
5011.     char  frame[3],Normal[3];
5012.
5013.     for (P = Boden; P != NULL; P = P->prev) // nur von Boden
bis Himmel
5014.        {                                    // Hoellennormale
uninteressant
5015.           *frame = *Normal = 'x';
5016.           if (P->form > ground)
```

This comment appears in an `Edit_predefs` method, which applies to everything *nur von Boden bis Himmel*, between the ground and heaven or the earth and sky. As the code explains, *Hoellennormale uninteressant*, or normal hell, is uninteresting, meaning it will not be addressed by this code. It is hard for me not to see Kittler smirking as he typed that comment, as a philosopher uninterested in normal hells. In any event, reading the code of Kittler's version of the Heaven and Hell raytracer allows us to trace his Cartesian thought experiment as he reproduces mathematical models of image production in code.

Such an interpretive lightness might upset many purists, who find such a nonliteral reading of the hells in Kittler's code to be heretical. Surely, Kittler's comment is referring to the object Hoelle in the raytracer, and I would agree. When I am commenting on this code, I am aware that these terms have particular, unambiguous referents with regard to the program. But when a comment about Hell appears in the code of a theorist who loved to swing from the mundane to the sublime, sometimes mid-sentence, I cannot help but note the resonance beyond its literal reference within the code itself, the extrafunctional significance. I have no reason to believe that Kittler ever arrested, or "killed," the process of playing with language, even (or especially) when also attending to a strict, literal denotation in the unambiguous realm of code. Throughout his critical writing, to which I would add his coding, Kittler was walking, or, perhaps more appropriately, tracing that line between the strictly technological and the transcendental, attending in the allusions and echoes, between the sky of Heaven and the depths of Hell, whether interesting or not.

Encoded Allusions

Kittler's C code is itself a lesson in autodidactic programming, which means that it is full of both epiphanies for the programmer and challenges for the reader. To read through the over five thousand lines in the main raytracer file, xsuptrace.c, is to read the progress of Kittler's understanding, but it is at times like navigating the Winchester Mystery House. Most of the code is made up of functions for either manipulating the objects or modeling the play of light on various objects, built of methods that respond differently depending on the object or surface, sorted out through lengthy case switch statements—for example, in this excerpt from the `Gravity` method:

```
363.    switch(Obj->form)
364.      {
365.        case moebius:              [...]
373.        case steiner:              [...]
390.        case torus:
```

In C, `Obj->form` notation would be rendered in other languages as Obj.form, so this switch is applied varyingly dependent on the form of the object—in other words, its shape.

In addition to the C code, Kittler's raytracer includes comments in German, English, and even a bit of Latin when he throws in a *mirable dictu* (line 46) at his discovery of a superior method for handling metallic surfaces. We should not be surprised by the mixture from the man who includes allusions to Faust in the programming manual he wrote: "The filling routine is pained—in contrast to Mephisto—especially by nibbled pentagrams."[12] Kittler's writing and coding move through planes of discourse from the mathematical to the mythical, from the literal to the literary, without pause.

The comments in Kittler's code display an ongoing wrestling match with the mathematics, physics, and algorithms of raytracing. For example, in a method called `intersect_superellipsoid`, the comment reads:

```
733.        Although there was no sign change, we may actually be
approaching
734.        the surface. In this case, we are being fooled by the
shape of the
735.        surface into thinking there isn't a root between
sample points.
```

The commentor is careful not to be "fooled ... into thinking" something by a calculation, an expression of the cat and mouse game he appears to be playing. Many of these comments read like "notes to self," similar to the comments we saw in the Transborder Immigrant Tool and the Climategate code:

```
805. Home in on the root of a superquadric using a combination of
secant and bi-
806. section methods. This routine requires that the sign of the
function be diffe-
807. rent at P0 and P1, else it will fail drastically.
```

However, it is not clear why the comments alternate between German and English, a question future scholars may answer. Although many of the shorter comments appear in German, there are large portions of the code that include lengthy comments in English. These comments tend to cluster around specific methods that Kittler may have been working on as a unit—again, as in the case of the procedures that treat surfaces. Still, the question remains, Is this even Kittler at all? The line immediately following this comment reads:

```
808. FAK: corrected a severe bug. v3 and v2 were not copied into
v0 and v1.
```

Because FAK (presumably Friedrich A. Kittler) only appears one other time in the code (line 1191), are we to understand that Kittler only wrote these two notes? Based on the evidence I have seen, that is unlikely, but the distinction certainly invites further exploration by future scholars.

Let us turn away from the question of authorship then to treat the code as a text that Kittler interacted with. In that light, while the code brought him repeated mentions of Heaven and Hell, it also brought him continued reminders of the scientists, philosophers, and mathematicians making all this reflection on vision and light possible. The processes encode their contributions, and some of the comments mention them by name. For example, before a function called check_hit2, he comments:

```
906. // Try to find the root of a superquadric using Newton's
method
```

Similarly, the methods and objects bear the names of the scientists who developed them, reminding us of the way history embeds itself into science and math—for example Fresnel, named after French physicist Augustin-Jean Fresnel, who described the reflection of light on surfaces. To engage in mathematics is to speak a language embedded with history, a kind of history Kittler relished—for example, when he traces the word *algorithm* back to its roots with the Persian mathematician, al-Khwārizmī, native of Khwarezm (Kittler 2011a). To create the raytracer, Kittler would have to render in code the mathematical and physical models developed by these giants of scientific philosophy, standing on their shoulders, as it were.

matrices.s (excerpt)

```
1. # povasm.asm-Teil nach LINUX-float portiert
2. # Compute_Axis_Transform nur formal getestet
3. # braucht ray.s
4.
5. FL=4     # 8 for double
6. .version "1.30"
7. # 05.02.11
8. .equ    PII,1
9. .equ    ONE,0x3F800000       # change for double
10. .equ    NEGATIVE,0x80
11.
12. .data
```

```
13.  .extern Epsilon
14.  mat00:      .fill      4,FL
15.  mat01:      .fill      4,FL
16.  mat02:      .fill      4,FL
17.  mat03:      .fill      4,FL
18.  mat10:      .fill      4,FL
19.  mat11:      .fill      4,FL
20.  mat12:      .fill      4,FL
21.  mat13:      .fill      4,FL
22.  degrees:.float      180.0
23.
24.  .text
25.  .extern vcross              #void f(VCT3 *d,*s1,*s2)
26.  .globl     MTimes           #void f(MatrixT *d,*s1,*s2)
27.  .globl     InvertMatrix      #int  f(VCT3 out[3],in[3])
28.  .globl     MIdentity        #void f(MatrixT *s)
29.  .globl     MTranspose       #void f(MatrixT *d,MatrixT *s)
30.  .globl     MITranspose      #void f(MatrixT *s)
31.  .globl     MTransPoint      #void f(VCT3 *d,*s,TransformT *t)
32.  .globl     MInvTransPoint       #void f(VCT3 *d,*s,TransformT
*t)
33.  .globl     MTransDirection      #void f(VCT3 *d,*s,TransformT
*t)
34.  .globl     MInvTransDirection   #void f(VCT3 *d,*s,TransformT
*t)
35.  .globl     MTransNormal         #void f(VCT3 *d,*s,TransformT
*t)
36.  .globl     MTransNormalize      #void f(VCT3 *d,*s,TransformT
*t)
37.  .globl  MInvTransNormal         #void f(VCT3 *d,*s,TransformT
*t)
38.  .globl  Create_Transform    #void f(TransformT *t)
39.  .globl     Compute_Scaling_Transform   #void f(TransformT
*d,VCT3 *s)
40.  .globl     Compute_Translation_Transform #void f(TransformT
*d,VCT3 *s)
```

```
41. .globl   Compute_Rotation_Transform   #void f(TransformT *d VCT3
*s);
42. .globl      Compute_Axis_Transform      #void f(TransformT *d,VCT3
*s,float w)
43. .globl      Compose_Transforms      #void f(MatrixT *Original,*New)
44.
45.     .align 8
46. MTimes:    pushl    %esi                # clobbers ecx; eax+edx
free
47.      pushl    %edi
48.      pushl    %ebx
49.      movl     (12+12)(%esp),%esi
50.      xorl     %ecx,%ecx
51.      movl     (8+12)(%esp),%ebx
52.      movl     $mat00,%edi
53.      movb     $4,%cl
54. mat2:    flds     (%esi)
55.      flds     1*FL(%esi)
56.      flds     2*FL(%esi)
57.      flds     3*FL(%esi)
58.      flds     (%ebx)
59.      fmul     %st,%st(4)
60.      movb     $3,%ch
61.      fmul     %st,%st(3)
62.      fmul     %st,%st(2)
63.      fmulp    %st,%st(1)
64.      .align  4
65. mat1:    addl     $FL,%ebx
66.      addl     $(4*FL),%esi
67.      flds     (%ebx)
68.      fld      %st
69.      fmuls    (%esi)
70.      faddp    %st,%st(5)
71.      fld      %st
72.      fmuls    1*FL(%esi)
73.      faddp    %st,%st(4)
74.      fld      %st
```

```
75.      fmuls    2*FL(%esi)
76.      faddp    %st,%st(3)
77.      decb     %ch
78.      fmuls    3*FL(%esi)
79.      faddp    %st,%st(1)
80.      jnz      mat1
81.      fstps    3*FL(%edi)
82.      fstps    2*FL(%edi)
83.      subl     $(12*FL),%esi
84.      fstps    1*FL(%edi)
85.      addl     $FL,%ebx
86.      fstps    (%edi)
87.      addl     $(4*FL),%edi
88.      loop     mat2
89.      movl     $mat00,%esi
90.      movb     $(4*FL),%cl
91.      popl     %ebx
92.      movl     (4+8)(%esp),%edi# result
93.      rep
94.      movsl
95.      popl     %edi
96.      popl     %esi
97.      ret
98.
99.      .align  8
```

Notes on Matrices.s

The % before register names is required by the GNU assembler (a.k.a. gas).

1: Comments are proceeded by #. This assembler code was written for the x86 Intel processor, using the GNU assembler. This line means that povasm.asm was ported to Linux with floating-point arithmetic.

2: Compute_Axis_Transform was only formally tested.

4: This appears to be the date February 5, 2011, perhaps the last time Kittler worked on the code. Kittler died October 18, 2011.

8–10: .equ "sets the value of." These statements assign values. For example, the first sets PII to 1.

12: .data assembles what follows to the data subsection.

13: .extern imports the symbol only if it is referred to. This is a bit unnecessary as the GNU assembler treats all undefined symbols as external ones. This is perhaps an old habit or a sign that this code was adapted from a different version of assembly.

14–21: Creates empty matrices. .fill reserves the space to fill with values.

22: float converts the floating-point number (flonum—in this case, 180.0) into a binary floating-point number.

24: The other subsection to complement .data is the .text section. This code assembles what follows to the .text subsection.

26–43: Global variable declarations, naming the various matrix transformations.

45: .align places the next byte at an address evenly divisible by eight. The process of aligning accelerates memory access, a sign of Kittler's programming priorities.

46: clobbers, a term from assembly, overwrites ecx; registers eax and edx are free.

47: pushl means put the long operand (l, meaning thirty-two bits) onto the stack.

48: movl, move the long operand from the stackpointer (esp) to esi.

50: xorl clears ecx, changing the operand to 0.

54–57: flds loads the product onto the stack. *Fl* refers to *floating point*.

73: Add the contents of register st to register 5 after st.

77–80: In between the two commands decb (decrement) and jnz (jump so long as counter is not zero), Kittler has added instructions to buy time for the processor to catch up. See a full discussion of this process later in the chapter.

Functionality

The assembly code simply follows the mathematical operation of multiplying two matrices. However, because it is at the level of the machine, the code has many steps for moving data to storage locations, performing operations on it, and moving it back.

Assembling and Understanding of the Machine

Speaking of uninteresting hells, writing an entire raytracer in assembly would have been a task worthy of Sisyphus. Although Kittler loved the connection with the machine that assembler offered and translating assembly into binary, even he did not write this program entirely in assembly. As he once said, "Everything beautiful can be encoded, but it doesn't make sense ... to encode for eternity" (2007b). Instead, Kittler wrote his raytracer in C, which he preferred because it allowed him to work also with assembly language, or assembler, as he called it. Kittler's preference demonstrates how attitudes toward programming can be expressed productively without the encoded chauvinism discussed in chapters 4 and 5. The majority of the raytracer's code is written in C. Nonetheless the files of the raytracer include some very necessary operations in assembler, specifically GNU assembler, which, of course, continued his preference for open-source software. That assembler works with the 8086 Intel architecture with an 8087 floating-point microcontroller, which Kittler accessed through his Pentium IV machine.

According to Feigelfeld, Kittler wrote most of his assembler code early on, and it became a skeleton on which to form his later programs. He was obsessed, as Feigelfeld puts it, with optimizing the processes of his assembler, writing the code in such as way as to make maximum use of the CPU. By the time Kittler was polishing his raytracer, he was no longer working in assembler (pers. interview, January 21, 2019). Nonetheless, as assembler brought the media archaeologist closest to the hardware of the machine, reading his assembler can reveal the depths of his understanding of the machine.

Kittler liked writing in assembly because it engaged the machine directly, with speed, but even he found it difficult to reread his own code later on. The raytracer code "was written by someone with a peculiar understanding of code," according to Feigelfeld. Kittler's disciple Wolfgang Ernst has said, "Kittler wrote in a 'polemic style' of Assembly—You have to know what I'm saying already" (pers. interview, September 18, 2013). Kittler could not explain all of his code or "retrace his steps": "it was irreconstructable" (Feigelfeld, pers. interview, January 21, 2019). For Kittler, "His assembly writing was so close to subconscious ... A kind of 'automatic programming.'" He described the process: "Kittler always spoke about coding in assembler as a deep psychological and analytical process. He would enter a kind of trance. Afterward, he couldn't really tell you how he came to write it that way. He would mostly work on it at night" (ibid.).[13]

Feigelfeld also warns against attributing particular lines of code to Kittler because his method was more of a bricolage, noting that Kittler would frequently draw code from the German computing enthusiast's publication *c't*, which, like the American *Computer* and *Popular Computing*, regularly published sample code, such as the source for Kittler's raytracer, for readers to type in on their own.

A close reading of assembly requires an identification of the hardware on which the assembly operates because the assembly directly manipulates registers. Kittler preferred a thirty-two-bit processor. This code is written in GNU assembly for an x86 family of Intel processors with an x87 family floating coprocessor. Kittler wrote for a computer with a Pentium IV processor, and he wrote that code without a contemporary code IDE but instead using EMACS without even syntax highlighting, at least in the beginning (Feigelfeld, pers. comm., March 27, 2019).[14] This code would work on any system with an x86 processor due to backward compatibility. In his 2010 lecture on the evolution of computing languages, Kittler (2011a) talks about the importance of backward compatibility, which is the principle of technological advancement that allows new models to run the code of previous ones. Because assembly addresses physical registers, new systems must still maintain at their core the physical register structure of former ones. As Kittler explains, because Intel CPUs have become an international standard, high-level programming languages running on these machines are ultimately translated into assembly language to address the original eight registers.

To do otherwise would have the computational postal delivery worker arriving at an address only to find the house demolished and perhaps even the street replaced with an entirely new one. In other words, on the level of electronics, messengers would never arrive. To write code in assembly, from this point of view, seems like a return to a communication moment practically unimaginable after our fall with Derrida, who pointed out language's fundamental separation between the signifier and what it signifies. In assembly, language seems once again tied to a material referent, albeit arbitrarily. Could we say, to continue our divine code comedy, paradise recovered? If only you don't have to debug it.

This may seem a key moment in critical code studies, the moment when we apply close reading techniques to look at the code of a media archaeologist who said "there is no software" yet wrote thousands of lines of code. Here, a reader might expect a revelation, code that bears the unmistakable signature of an inspired theoretical mind. But let me say at the outset, the assembly of this raytracer is mostly unremarkable. It does not contain some sign of Kittler's genius with code. It does not bear his fingerprints in its functions. It performs the actions of matrices transformations in a rather conventional manner. And yet, just because code is unremarkable does not mean it is unworthy of discussion. Kittler did not have to reinvent matrices transformations, a mathematical operation that has been known for centuries. What is remarkable is that the media theorist wrote—and I use that word to mean collected and combined—these methods in assembly in the conventional way in order to understand the machine at an intimate level, and here I am using *intimate* in a metaphorical sense that I think would also make Kittler squirm a bit due to his time spent meditating in a space that eschews ambiguity, the space of computer code.

At this point, it is useful to return to chapter 1 in which I drew a distinction between two understandings of interpretation. In a humanities sense, *interpretation* refers to the exploration of one or more of the multiple connotations of a symbol. In the computer science sense, *interpretation* refers to a kind of translation that seeks out one-to-one correspondences. One who has entered the world of assembly language programming, in which the code addresses not just a machine but a very particular machine, in which symbols are written for a family or, thanks to backward compatibility, families of processors, this person has entered a world of very strict communication. In assembly, Barbara Marino explains, "you have to understand the hardware to be able to write it" (pers. interview, January 19, 2019). This philosopher is meditating, if you will, on one of the most strict forms of communication in existence.

As an example of Kittler's code, I offer a segment from an assembly file for matrix transformations that is included (literally) in the raytracer software. This file includes various mathematical operations on raytracers, including one that multiplies two matrices. Multiplying matrices is a mathematical operation that has been around since the early nineteenth century.[15] Multiplying two matrices involves multiplying the elements of each row by the elements of each column of the matrix and then summing the product. Most of the code excerpted in the `MTimes` method performs the operations of multiplying two matrices in the conventional manner. A lot of the code of `MTimes` deals with moving data on and off stacks. Counters are used so that the code can perform loops, iterating operations across the matrices.

However, one section of this excerpt of Kittler's code suggests how well the theorist understood the system on which he was programming. To explain this sign, I must first explain a principle in programming. When looking at the code, a program might appear to be executing each line as soon as it reaches it, but that is merely how it appears in the code. When running, the control unit runs through an instruction cycle, including fetching instructions, decoding, reading operands, operating, writing back, and determining the next instructions (or simply fetch, decode, execute). To find where the machine is in that process, we would have to access the state of the machine, which is why Evan Buswell (2019) argues in his dissertation ("The Epistemology of the Credit System") that "state" is the other key dimension to critical code studies. Due to this cycle, the instruction order does not convey the *latency* (how long, or how many cycles, it takes to perform each instruction).[16] As a result, there may be a gap in time between one instruction and another. One way to take advantage of this time is called *pipelining* (Barbara Marino, pers. interview, June 23, 2018).

Pipelining is an architecture that allows more than one instruction to be executed simultaneously. In other words, the controller can start other instruction cycles while waiting for one to complete so that one instruction is completed every clock cycle. In code that employs pipelining, the control unit does not sit idle. Assembly code that has been pipelined therefore can process additional instructions during the latency—that is, while that first instruction is moving through the cycles (fetch, decode, and execute; Antonakos 1999, 556). If the programmer does not write some, the processor adds "no ops," or dummy instructions, which buy time for the system to complete the previous operations.

In his `MTimes` method, Kittler's code optimizes the time the system needs to perform an operation, or latency, so he adds instructions to be processed during this latency:

```
77.   decb    %ch
78.   fmuls    3*FL(%esi)
79.   faddp    %st,%st(1)
80.   jnz     mat1
```

The code at this point is performing a loop. The first instruction, `decb`, decrements the counter, indicating that a loop has been performed. The instruction `jnz mat1` will jump up to `mat1` so long as the counter has not reached zero. (This is the JUMP TO instruction discussed in the previous chapter.) However, the operation of decrementing the counter must make its way through the instruction cycle (fetching instructions, decoding, reading operands, operating, writing back) before `jnz` can perform its comparison—or, put another way, it takes a few steps of the instruction cycle for decrement to complete before the jump instruction can check the branch condition. Because `jnz` relies on `decb` writing back its result, Kittler is optimizing the code by initiating the instruction cycle of two other operations in the meantime (`fmuls` and `faddp`).

Barbara Marino, a professor of electrical engineering at Loyola Marymount University, who is also my spouse (pers. interview, October 1, Marino 2014), has said that Kittler's code here performs the equivalent of emptying the dryer while the washing machine is running.[17] "Most programmers don't think about optimizing a task at the level of the CPU and memory," she explains. To optimize the code in this way shows an uncommon understanding of the timing of the processor. "Here," she adds, "is the sign that Kittler knew what he was doing."

Finding this sign in Kittler's assembly code does not provide the kind of "a-ha" moment that finding `witchingEvent` did in the Transborder Immigrant Tool code or finding "fudge factor" in the Climategate code, misleading as that particular comment was. Instead, it demonstrates through code an understanding of the machine at a very precise level. If reading a writer's notebooks, letters, and drafts offers insights into the person's though process, albeit via speculations that can never be objectively confirmed, reading a person's code offers a sense of the writer's understanding of the processes they are implementing and, in the case of assembly, the machine for which it is being written. So even though this code is conventional to the point of being largely unremarkable, reading the code offers a sense of the understanding of the person who implemented it, even if they did not design it. Again, we need to move away from the idea that critical code studies is a kind of treasure hunt and instead, following the models of cultural, bibliographic, and textual studies, move toward recognizing the treasures in the everyday ordinariness of code being used in context.

In the case of Kittler, reading the code offers a sense of the theorist who developed a form a media archaeology that bore fruit by precise understanding of technology and technological development, down, in this case, to the level of the fraction of a second it takes to perform operations. At the same time, it is also worth noting that the entire raytracer was not written in assembly. That is a Hoelle too dark for Kittler to enter. That is not to call it hypocrisy but instead to show how using "there is no software" as a shorthand for his position is to mistake a headline for a complex critical position.

A Kittlerian Method

Through Kittler's encounter with the code, with these unambiguous systems, he develops a critical intolerance of interpretations built on inaccurate or imprecise understandings of technology. This encounter, I would argue in a kind of programming determinism, also moves him further away from the realm of interpretation as a form of reflection on the connotation of symbols and more deeply into his practice of tracing causal chains between the advent of technologies and the writing of those who experienced them. The other interpretive move this literalism or material accuracy allows is interpretation through analogy, which a few examples can demonstrate.

Kittler once said in a lecture on optics, "Nature is enabled by computers to look into her own eyes" (2011c). In the same lecture, he also said that rather than the philosophical use of the term *reflection*, of which he was not fond, he preferred the technical or optical use. When added together, these claims help show the effects of a media theorist who had created a program to trace rays, reflecting off of surfaces into nature's own eye.

Kittler would have been more comfortable tracing rays in code than interpreting it. And yet by looking at the source code, we can see a theorist's ideas as they evolve. One of the keys to Kittlerian method, this vision of the technological a priori, is to learn the technology, to determine how it built on, transformed, or rendered obsolete previous technology, and then to see where that conceptualization appears elsewhere in society after that technology has proliferated and circulated, through analogies. For example, in a lecture on optical media, when Kittler explains the difference between raytracing and radiosity, he characterizes, through analogy, raytracing as mathematical integration and radiosity as differentiation. He draws similar analogies throughout his scholarly writing. In another lecture he explains that he chose the media of gramophone, film, and typewriter for the title of that book because they can be mapped onto the von Neumann architecture of memory, bus, and CPU. This is a form of interpretation that does not ask what the technological signifies, but rather what other processes or hardware it parallels, interpretation by analogy.

In Kittler's writing, we get a sense of what he feels are legitimate and illegitimate gestures to make when reading technology. For example, in *GFT* he draws connections between Turing's imitation game and gendered labor in the workplace. The interpretive move goes something like this: The imitation game featured a computer trying to pass itself off as a human when communicating via teletype with an interrogator. That imitation game is based on a parlor game in which a man tries to convince an interrogator that he, and not his opponent, is a woman. Kittler takes this moment as foreshadowing the way machines (here Remington typewriters) would take the place (again, think of imitation game parallels) of the women who did the handwriting. Kittler explains, "Computers write by themselves, without secretaries, simply with the command WRITE" (Kittler 1999, 246). Notice that this interpretive gesture involves an analogy between a thought experiment and both social and technological historical fact.

Nonetheless, Kittler is not beyond interpreting an extrafunctional significance in code as he interprets the "simple feedback loop" (Kittler 1999, 258) of the if-then statement.[18] Kittler writes, "Computers themselves have become subjects. IF a preprogrammed condition is missing, data processing continues according to the conventions of numbered commands, but IF somewhere an intermediate result fulfills the condition, THEN the program itself determines successive commands, that is, its future" (258). Note here that Kittler seems on the surface to merely be articulating the nature of control flow in conditional statements, but by discussing it against the backdrop of subjectivity, he has made the technological specification philosophical. By way of some Lacan, Kittler will conclude, "Computers operating on IF-THEN commands, are therefore machine subjects. Electronics, a tube monster since Bletchley Park, replaces discourse, and programmability replaces free will" (259). A deterministic philosophy drawn from a computational example and an instructive lesson for critical code studies—and yet certainly not the only one.

Kittler's meditation on computers did not just inflect the philosophy he drew from digital machines but shaped his other media theory as well. The title for *Gramophone, Film, Typewriter*, as Kittler notes in a lecture (2011b), and presumably the notion of this tripartite structure of the book, was chosen to parallel the three-part structure of the von Neumann computational architecture. This is the same architecture that has informed computer design for much of its development so far, containing the CPU, memory, and the bus that shuttles information back and forth. Kittler argues, in that lecture, that this tripartite structure replaces the long-held ancient Greek notion of "matter and form" with the media theoretical trinity of "processing, addressing, and storing"—or, in other words, "data, commands, and addresses." In so doing, the media determinist has performed for us a subtle illustration of his theory as he looks back upon these technological developments and conceptualizes them as the inside of a computer.

In his assembly code, we can see Kittler tracing the interconnections between this triumvirate, as he issues commands and shuttles manipulated data to and from storage locations in the stack, following the control flow, monitoring latency, the theorist with his stethoscope to the heart of the machine—or perhaps more accurately, the theorist philosopher in his miniature ship taking a fantastic voyage through the body of the machine, only to emerge with a deeper sense of these prevailing conceptual metaphors, as well as with a mind even more rigorously and precisely tuned to specificities of the machine, a kind of mental discipline that we can hear when he spends hours recounting scientific facts with occasional gestures toward brightest Heaven and darkest Hell.

From Kittler, however, we can take a corrective that we can also see in the media theory of N. Katherine Hayles, Matthew Kirschenbaum, Jussi Purikka, and Alexander Galloway. To maintain the current truce in the so-called science wars between scientists and technolcultural critics who see and seek the meaning in the science, we have to get the science right.[19]

Conclusion

Friedrich Kittler may have argued that "there is no software," but an exploration of his software proves not only its relation to his philosophy but the code's expressive potential. Even if we follow his code to the level of the assembly, in which he is assigning value to registers, we can still encounter an expression of understanding that is valuable in reflecting on his theorization of the machine. Meaning does not end at the level of electronic hardware, even if it appears to be devoid of language.

In a thread on the 2014 Critical Code Studies Working Group website (Marino 2014), Evan Buswell takes up this notion, writing, "I suppose if you get a few steps below that, low-level enough that you are talking about physical processes, then indeed, an electron zipping across a PN junction is a language only through metaphor. But then, it might be the same kind of metaphor whereby the following glowing dots on your screen are only a metaphor for the number zero: 0." Following similar lines to Kittler, Buswell follows the code to the level of electrical signals. However, rather than seeing that as the end of language, Buswell sees another form of language. As he goes on to explain, "I'm not sure what to make of this slight retreat from code-as-language ... but I'll be steadfastly taking the side that it is linguistic all the way down, and that in fact that is pretty much the entire point of code. Code as a method to control electro-mechanical systems is secondary; there could be and were previously ways to do this that didn't involve code (many of which would be 100s of times faster than the code method if implemented today)."

I raise this example not to argue that Kittler is somehow wrong about the nature of code, but to argue that the linguistic or symbolic system, and hence meaning, does not disappear at the moment those symbols displayed to the programmer turn into electrical signals. Instead, I would argue, alongside Buswell, that those signals are a material form of communication, no less meaningful by their lack of additional symbolic representation. It is not the representational symbols that qualify code as language, but the system that allows us to use them in meaningful ways. In fact, such a reading is particularly Kittlerian, in as much as it sees the structures of languages all the way up and down the hierarchy. I am arguing that the electronic signals have been placed within a system of language and in this way have been rendered meaningful.

These layers of signification then proliferate on the level of hardware, code, and running software. This fact makes Kittler's work in and on code continuous with his larger project that traces the movement of language, particularly printed language, from the sole domain of the hierarchy, particularly the religious in their monasteries, to the commoners. For Kittler to develop knowledge, perhaps literacy, in the use of code is to transgress the walls of the abbey, to trace the lines of light like Descartes, but in the language of the monks of machines: programmers.

If reading and writing are fundamental to subject formation in the age of letters, so to is the reading and writing of code in the age of digital machines. Fundamental to early programming languages, Kittler reminds us, were expressions that directed the machine to read and write. Notably, when making this remark Kittler performs a bit of code analysis himself, noting that English—unlike, say, Latin—can tolerate "context-free verbal units" that can stand alone, unconjugated (i.e., read and write).

More importantly, as he reflects on the proliferation of redundancy in languages due to backward compatibility, he speculates on the role discourse analysis could play, despite the fact that it "can neither tame nor debug the proliferation of languages" (Kittler 1999, 218). Kittler concludes, "Codes begin to proliferate and approach the opacity of everyday languages that, for millennia, has subjected people to these same languages" (218). The alphabetical man, to borrow a phrase from another media theorist, Marshall McLuhan, is subject to language. With irony, Kittler adds, "The lovely phrase 'source code' names the literal truth," that code, or encoded languages, is at last the technological a priori that frames our digitized thoughts. Nonetheless, Kittler in making his raytracer has demonstrated how these codes can be operationalized for a creative method of analysis that not only accesses the machine's physical memory but also allows him to trace media advances of mathematics and physics to reflect on being itself as a philosopher programmer.

Through this example of Kittler's code, I have tried to demonstrate how programming, working with code, requires a form of thought akin to meditation. To read a person's code, or at least the code they have collected and connected, is to be able to explore their meditations on the machine over time. Furthermore, code itself becomes a means of symbolic thinking and reflection—not merely an illustration of ideas, but an expression of them. Reading them, therefore, is a gesture of communion with the ones who assembled them, incomplete though that communion may be.

7 Generative Code

Taroko Gorge

Author: Nick Montfort
Year: 2009
Languages: Python 2
File: taroko_gorge.py, an updated file available at https://nickm.com/code/taroko_gorge.py

Code

```
1. #!/usr/bin/env Python
2. #
3. # Taroko Gorge
4. #  A one-page Python program to generate an unbounded poem
5. #
6. # Nick Montfort
7. #  8 January 2009, Taroko Gorge National Park, Taiwan and Eva
Air Flight 28
8. #
9. # x() splits a string into a list      c() is just random.
choice()
10. # f() picks a fresh value from a list  p() prints a line and
pauses
11. # cave() -- walking through the tunnels carved in the
mountains
12. # path() -- walking along outdoors, seeing what is above (a)
and below (b)
13. # site() -- stopping at a platform or viewing area
14.
```

```
15. import time,random,sys
16. def x(s): return s.split(',')
17. def c(l): return random.choice(l)
18. a=x('brow,mist,shape,layer,the crag,stone,forest,height')
19. b=x('flow,basin,shape,vein,rippling,stone,cove,rock')
20.
21.     def f(v):
22.         l=globals()[v]
23.         i=c(l[:-1])
24.         l.remove(i)
25.         globals()[v]=l+[i]
26.         return i
27.
28.     def p(s=''):
29.         print s.capitalize()
30.         sys.stdout.flush()
31.         time.sleep(1.2)
32.
33.     def cave():
34.         j=['encompassing',c(x('rough,fine'))]+\
35.         x('sinuous,straight,objective,arched,cool,clear,dim,dr
iven')
36.         t=c([1,2,3,4])
37.         while len(j)>t:
38.             j.remove(c(j))
39.         v=' '+c(x('track,shade,translate,stamp,progress
through,direct,run,enter'))
40.         return v+' the '+' '.join(j)
41.
42.     def path():
43.         v=c(x('command,pace,roam,trail,frame,sweep,exercise,ra
nge'))
44.         u=f('a')
45.         if c([0,1]):
46.             if u[0]=='f':
47.                 u=c([u,u,'monkey'])
48.             h=u+'s '+v
```

```
49.              else:
50.                  h=u+' '+v+'s'
51.                  return h+' the '+f('b')+c(x(',s'))
52.
53.         def site():
54.              return f(c(x('a,b')))+'s '+c(x('linger,dwell,rest,rela
x,hold,dream,hum'))
55.
56.     p()
57.     while True:
58.         p(path()+'.')
59.         m=c([0]*6+[1,2])
60.         for n in range(0,m):
61.              p(site()+'.')
62.         p(path()+'.')
63.         p()
64.         p(cave()+' --')
65.         p()
```

Notes

1: # precedes comments in Python.

3–4: Montfort gives the name (Taroko Gorge), constraint (one-page), and genre ("unbounded poem").

6–7: Although putting his name in the code is somewhat unusual, putting the location where he wrote the code is highly unusual, suggesting not only that he expected a wider readership of this code beyond those merely looking to implement it, but also that he wanted people to consider its location of composition when perusing the code.

9–13: Montfort decodes all his variables and functions here, using one-letter variable names that give his code a minimalist feel.

16–17: Another feature that gives Montfort's code its minimalist feel is that he reassigns the functions of split and random to single-character method function names (x and s, respectively). That also makes this code a bit harder to read.

18–19: These lists only contain eight words each, and two of the words appear on both lists, a simple set of inputs to create unbounded outputs.

34: Although some of his code draws from a longer list, this choice is merely between two adjectives.

46: Finding an f at the start of an "above" word (as in the case of "forest") triggers a sequence that includes the word *monkey*.

47: This monkey feature will become a staple of Taroko Gorge variations.

48–50: For greater variation from a small swap, the program cleverly adds the s to either the subject or the verb.

58–65: Start here. This section presents the main function for producing the stanzas. I recommend beginning to read the code here and then traversing the waterfall upward to find the definitions of the methods and variables.

Functionality

Taroko Gorge produces an endless stream of poetry, following a consistent set of randomized patterns. The basic pattern offers a path (noun + verb + object), followed by zero-to-two sites (noun + verb), another path, and a cave (verb + the + noun + adjective + object). The pattern is roughly ABBA-C, with some additional Bs on occasion. The lines of poetry continue to scroll until the program is stopped.

Code and Poetry

To the relief of many programmers, critical code studies does not read all computer code like poetry, but code that has been written as poetry invites just such exploration and exegesis. Much of the code analyzed so far in this book was not designed explicitly for wider audiences beyond its developers (and maintainers), although most of the examples have turned out to have wider audiences with more varied backgrounds and reading agendas and interests than the authors anticipated. The notion of artful code has been around since Knuth's Turing Award Lecture, at least. The O'Reilly collection *Beautiful Code* (Oram and Wilson 2007) celebrates artful code found in the wild, examples of artful code for coders. However, this computational age has introduced a new figure, the artist-programmer, artists who write code, who write *with* code, who bear a sense that when they are creating code, they are creating aesthetic art objects, either poetic in themselves or in combination with what they produce. Geoff Cox and Alex McLean (2012) offer many examples of this conscious, artful communication in *Speaking Code*. Perhaps a bridgework between code written aesthetically and the aesthetics of code can be found in Angus Croll's (2015) ingenious *If Hemingway Wrote JavaScript*, which offers creative reflections on how literary artists would write source code. Some beautiful code presents its signs with a visual aesthetics; the code looks like other poetry. Other beautiful code appeals to valences of concision or clever devices, such as a particularly novel use of recursion. Of course, beauty is only one aesthetic category and is obviously subjective. What seems to differentiate art-ful code and code art is the intentional development for human readers as a primary audience.

Code artists not only write to wider audiences but are creating code with their own poetic sensibilities. The realm of code and code-like texts (used here loosely to mean literary art objects) includes works that compile and those that do not, such as the hybrid of computer-code-like elements and natural language found in the *mezangelle* of Mez Breeze. It includes programmers hiding concrete poetry in code, as in bpNichol's First Screening written in BASIC and published in 1984 (see Huth 2007).[1] It also includes Zach Blas's queer programming language Transcoder (2017), which mixes queer theory and code-like methods and which has been used by Julie Levin Russo to create a kind of speculative fiction program (Marino 2012). Similarly, Winnie Soon (2017) created Vocable Code, inspired by *Speaking Code* (Cox and McLean 2012) and Arielle Schlessinger's speculative feminist programming language, known as C+= (Soon 2018). It also includes poetic works that look like programs but that are not written in existing programming languages, such as the poetry of Margaret Rhee in *Love, Robot* (2017), a collection that includes poems as encoded algorithms. In the book *Moonbit*, James Dobson and Rena Mosteirin offer "erasure poetry," created by selecting words from the code used in the Apollo 11 moon landing.[2] This category also includes the creative works of Alan Sondheim (2005) and John Cayley and the disruptive projects of Ben Grosser, who sees his programming as a form of critical code studies in executable form.[3] Other code, like that of the Transborder Immigrant Tool, offers poetry through its functioning, the resonance of its processes, following the traditions of conceptual writing, whether following the Latin American, North American, or other variety of this experimental tradition, placing process and premise above what we once called poems but here call "output."

To write code *for* and *as* poetry is very different than writing code to solve a utilitarian problem, although again I have been working in this book to unsettle the notion that code ever exists in a purely utilitarian space. Perhaps Heidegger offers a way out of this binary in his mediation on the root of technology, *techne*, which in ancient Greek names both craft and art. Combine that with the interventions of conceptual artists such as Duchamp, who famously framed a factory-made snow shovel as a work of art, and the distinction between "code for making art" and "code as art" becomes even more porous. If "craft" becomes art just by means of its recontextualization by an artist, then can even very ordinary, mundane code participate in an aesthetics of immanence? If Sol LeWitt could make the instructions to create art into the work of art itself, is not code that makes art also art? I don't mean to return to the threatening prospect of reading all code as poetry. I only wish to question a notion of codework that limits code art to those works that have aesthetic sensibilities in their code.[4] Before we get caught in an endless loop, let us bracket it or, in the parlance of coding, comment it out for now.

In this chapter, I take up a more clear instance of code as poetry as I explore code written and remixed by poets.[5] The object of study is Taroko Gorge, code that generates a work of electronic literature, or rather code that *is* a work of electronic literature, demonstrating how poets can explore the aesthetics of code through their programming practices. I will be reading this code as an aesthetic object and more specifically as a work of poetry.

The story of this code begins with a grand challenge issued in 2008 at Visionary Landscapes, a conference of the Electronic Literature Organization (ELO). The Electronic Literature Organization is a community of scholars and artists focused on the potential for digitally born literary works. At this conference dedicated to innovation and experimentation in the digital literary arts, there were at least four presentations that discussed the program ELIZA, at least one of which cited Janet Murray, author of the influential *Hamlet on the Holodeck* (1998), as she situates the program as one of the first works of electronic literature. ELIZA is the well-known program by Joseph Weizenbaum that, when it follows the DOCTOR script, plays the role of a Rogerian psychotherapist, asking questions of the interactor and following those questions with further questions. In one particular talk, blogging partners Andrew Stern and Nick Montfort offered a challenge, which on its surface seemed fairly simple but at its core stood as a kind of grand challenge to creators of electronic literature gathered for that congress.

By Montfort and Stern's reading, ELIZA's success was not that it deceived people into thinking it was human, achieving what Noah Wardrip-Fruin (2009) would later call "the ELIZA effect." These scholars were interested not so much in ELIZA the running software but ELIZA the artifact of code. In this presentation before a community of avant-garde digital artists, Montfort and Stern proposed that ELIZA's power was its ability to inspire so much creativity in those who would encounter it, whether drawing them in to play with it, inciting their critical readings, or inspiring their own adaptations, of which there are legion, more if you count sophisticated great-great-granddaughters such as Amazon Alexa and Apple's Siri. In their words, ELIZA is "a rather small amount of code that lacked multimedia elements, contained very little pre-written text, and was developed by a single person, Joseph Weizenbaum" (Stern and Montfort 2008). The challenge they placed before the community of electronic artists

was to create code objects such as ELIZA that were simple, yet elegant enough to instigate this flurry of activity, both creative and critical.

ELIZA, according to Montfort and Stern, was a model for future works of electronic
literature because of its key features:

Engaging deeply with language.

Dealing with a fundamental issue, concern, anxiety, or question about computing and
technology.

Being interactive and immediate—impressing the interactor in an instant.

Being understandable after more effort is applied and the program is explored further.

Being general to different computer platforms and easily ported.

Being process-intensive—driven by computation rather than data. (Montfort and Stern
2008)

Critical to their framing of ELIZA was a sense that even though the program did not
rely on computational networks or whiz-bang graphics, its relatively simple (and published) code offered rewards to those who interacted with it, either when processed to
execute or as code to be read, analyzed, and adapted.

At the time, I heard in the keynotes of this speech the outlines for a project, as if
Stern and Montfort were describing their work in progress. As it turns out, Montfort
was offering a kind of manifesto for his own life's work. In this chapter, I look at one
of his works that in partially meeting ELIZA's challenge offers a few insights into the
generative potential of code art.

A year earlier, Montfort had presented another aspect of the ELIZA challenge, as I
am calling it, in a presentation on the BASIC game *Hammurabi*, which he discussed in
a talk with another *Grand Text Auto* collaborator, Michael Mateas (Montfort and Mateas
2007). In the talk, the two creator-theorists[6] again offer a reading of a fairly easy-to-
follow program. *Hammurabi* is a BASIC game, "the first popular simulation game,"
which "was popularized in David H. Like, the German magazine *c't*, Ahl's 1978 *BASIC
Computer Games* and went on to be often ported, rewritten, and adapted by computer
hobbyists" (Montfort and Mateas 2007). Ahl's book offered owners of the newly available home computers code they could enter right into their machines and watch it
execute, just as they had with 10 PRINT. The through-line from *Hammurabi* to ELIZA is
the notion of relatively legible code or scripts that can be easily read and modified. The
title of the talk plays on the fact that the code for the game takes the laws governing
transactions from ancient Babylon (Hammurabi's code) and places it in the hands of

programmers who can be little Hammurabis creating code of their own, which creates simulations of the lands that they virtually rule.

Such tantalizing fun certainly evokes the magic implied by the magicians on the cover of Abelson and Sussman's *The Structure and Interpretation of Computer Programs*. Quoting John Barth's short story "Chimera," those authors note: "It's in the words that the magic is—Abracadabra, Open Sesame, and the rest—but the magic words in one story aren't magical in the next" (1996, 487). This magical mastery is also the "sourcery" that Wendy Chun cautions against when programmers imagine that their words are making things happen through source code (2011). Montfort in his 2007 and 2008 talks is imagining not magic in code, but the magic of a teacher who presents those he encounters with objects that they can then learn from and then reimagine. As he and Stern presented, "We are interested in imagining a system that would introduce a new form, like that of the chatterbot, and that would inspire reworking and reimagining by artists" (Stern and Montfort 2008). As it turned out, less than a year later, Montfort would compose just such a piece.

Generous Poetry Generators

Before exploring code that forms (and is) poetry, let us reflect on pervasive poetic forms, such as the sonnet. The sonnet has been around for centuries. Petrarch wrote sonnets. Shakespeare wrote sonnets. Different forms, of course, but sonnets nonetheless. By now there are probably enough sonnets to wallpaper Westminster Abbey several times over. Haiku is an even older and (deceptively) simpler form. To number haiku would be to sit on James Joyce's immortalized Fontana beach, counting grains of sand. These poetic forms are merely a set of formal constraints and conventions of content, yet when attempted by generations of artistic minds of varying linguistic and cultural backgrounds, those restrictions, those boundaries, prove to be highly generative.

Of course, the quest to create new poetic forms has likewise produced its own vast bestiary. In fact, the challenge to create a new form has been so attractive that poetry collectives like the Ouvoir de Literature Potential (Oulipo) have made the creation of new forms, or Synthouliposm, their primary raison d'être. As Oulipian Raymond Queneau explained, "We call potential literature the search for new forms and structures that may be used by writers in any way they see fit" (quoted in Wolff 2007). Obviously creating a new form is one task, but convincing other writers to use that form is another. Enter onto that pitch digital computers, engines of procedural creation, and the potential for the creation of new poems has increased beyond measure, for a computer program can create a new poetic form and then iterate that form ad infinitum.

One branch of the Oulipo, the Atelier de Littérature Assistée par la Mathématique et les Ordinateurs (ALAMO), took the primarily paper- and print-based approaches of the group into the realm of algorithms and digital computers. This spinoff cadre attempted to implement and extend some of these procedures. As the Oulipans declared, "This is a new era in the history of literature: 'Thus, the time of created creations, which was that of the literary works we know, should cede to the era of *creating creations*, capable of developing from themselves and beyond themselves, in a manner at once predictable and inexhaustibly unforeseen'" (Wolff 2007).

Poetry generators have been around arguably since the first computers. Christopher Strachey, who worked with Alan Turing on the Manchester Mark I, developed a program to generate love letters (Wardrip-Fruin 2005). Although these love letters were not specifically poetry per se, or not framed as poetry, this early linguistic generator did point the way for countless generators to come. A poetry generator works with the sublime potential of combinatorics, an artistic constraint Bill Seaman (2001) has identified, which relishes the infinite potential of new combinations. With the advent of the personal computer and the rapid development of creative networks across the World Wide Web, the number of computer-based poetry generators has multiplied like our lists of sonnets and poetic forms. Over the next few pages, I would like to consider not the poems generated by these programs, but poetry generators as forms of poetry, focusing on one particular case study, Taroko Gorge, which has generated not only poems but a legacy of other generators.

Taroko Gorge first appeared in January 2009 as a one-page Python poetry generator on MIT professor and poet Nick Montfort's web page, later republished in his collection *#!* (which he pronounces "she-bang"; Montfort 2014). The program is an elegant piece of code that builds on Montfort's previous experiments with generators. *Elegance* refers to an aesthetic aspect of its code, its beauty, the way that it reads. Elegance is a kind of x factor, a je ne sais quoi for code, no more an objective measure of the code than elegance is in the grace of a stride or in the fall of a hem. Elegance is in the eye of the person reading or writing the code; computational devices, as far as we know, are largely indifferent to such aesthetics. Perhaps a provisional definition of *elegance* is concision mixed with cleverness without obfuscation.

It was in his Turing Award Lecture that computer science pioneer Donald Knuth (1974) argued for computer programming as an art. In his essay, Knuth argues that programming should be elegant, where elegance is not so much about adornment as a kind of Strunk and White, highly clear prose: simple, straightforward, legible, easy to adapt and reuse. It is this last property that Taroko Gorge demonstrates so well. But its elegance may not be readily apparent.

Montfort's own brand of elegance grows out of his love of concision. One of his prior creations, ppg256 (a 256-character Perl poetry generator), exemplifies this aesthetic perfectly. The number 256 is the number of characters (letters, numbers, and punctuation marks) that constitute the software, written in the language Perl. This generator creates poems from what is essentially one line of code. Here's an example of a poem it generated:

```
the nunelf and one hip gungod hit it.
```

The generator works by drawing from sets of syllables and combining them in a poetic structure. Although this poem may not read like contemporary lyrical poetry, such as the work of Poet Laureate Natasha Trethewey, it does resemble sound or abstract poetry. Nonetheless, the continuous generation of similar lines is a feat for a program that looks like this:

```
perl -le 'sub p{(unpack"(A3)*",pop)[rand 18]}sub
w{p("apebotboyelfgodmannunorcgunhateel"x2)}sub
n{p("theone"x8)._.p(bigdimdunfathiplitredwanwax)._.w.w."\n"}
{print"\n".n."and\n".n.p("cutgothitjammetputransettop"x2)._.p("her
himin it offon outup us "x2);sleep 4;redo} #'
```

A nonprogrammer, or even just a newcomer to this approach, might wonder where the words are that the generator uses to create these poems, for they rely on no external texts or grammars or dictionaries. Even without knowing Perl, you can look at the first string of letters, apebotboyelfgodmannunorcgunhateel, and see the little units (trigrams, three-letter combinations) that would become nunelf and gungod. The program creates lines by drawing out individual trigrams and assembling them into words and phrases. No single poem produced by these generators can truly sum them up. For that, one needs to have the code. At that point, the algorithm becomes the poetry. Nonetheless, ppg256's works did not become a genre that others took up and adapted the way they would Montfort's later piece. Perhaps, notes Jeremy Douglass, that has something to do with the nature of Perl, as a language that is famously "write once, read never" (pers. interview, March 5, 2019). What these generators gain in concision, they lose in clarity, along with some of that simplicity and accessibility Montfort saw in ELIZA and *Hammurabi*.

It is worthwhile at this point to characterize Nick Montfort, who has been an active participant in the Critical Code Studies Working Groups and helped spearhead *10*

PRINT, the first book on the topic (Montfort et al. 2013). Even before critical code studies, Montfort was working away at digital art through code, although primarily in the realm of interactive fiction. However, he does not contribute his code solely as an artist. As one of the coeditors of the Platform Studies series at MIT, Montfort has been fostering critical studies in these areas. More importantly, he has been one of the few code artists to publish and present explications of his own code. He has even published a discussion of his code in the comments of his code, in an essay he wrote with collaborator poet Stephanie Strickland about their piece *Sea and Spar Between*.

As I have written elsewhere, Montfort has a programmer-poet's obsession with concision and elegance. Consider, for example, his collaborative book project (on which I was a coauthor) that focused on the exegesis of a one-line BASIC program for the Commodore 64 (Montfort et al. 2013). His interest in the line of code was not necessarily its output (which appears to be a continuously scrolling random maze formation) but rather the way in which that one line of code could inspire novice programmers to experiment. For his part, Montfort remembered that line of code from his first encounter with it, decades earlier, in the programming manual for the Commodore 64. That encounter, I would argue, instilled in the poet a sense of the way simple, concise, and elegant code could generate not only endless varieties of patterns that aggregate into a pleasing whole but also, like all great art, variations, adaptations, and reappropriations. This one-line program taught him not only the power of simple, pseudorandom pattern generation but also the generative power of simple and clever prose. Like the young poet who first encounters Basho's haiku, Montfort had encountered a kind of program that for him would become a genre that he would further explore and adapt.

To understand how this code becomes an aesthetic object, one has to stop thinking about code as something purely functional (such as the plumbing in your house) and instead as something both functional and aesthetic (like the bright pink and blue pipes used in construction projects in Berlin). Or perhaps a better example would be a beautiful stretch of road that is easy to drive on, well maintained, and lined with lovely elms. Code is written not merely for machines to process but as a form of communication between programmers, especially those who must later maintain and develop the code. Montfort values concision highly in his coding aesthetic. When discussing ppg256, he recounts his informal study of *Perl golfers*, programmers who attempt to reduce their lines of code like Tiger Woods, chipping away at their own stroke counts. Fitting his poetry generator into 256 characters puts him on par with some of the very best in the field. But, as the Perl Golf contest demonstrates, it is also an arena in which programmers can demonstrate the grace of their algorithms and the efficiency of their thought embodied in the code. Code is also an expression of thought. A cleverly designed algorithm has the force of a novel poetic conceit. Though some lines of code can be as functionally alike as two nails, they are not necessarily formally or aesthetically equivalent.

It is also important to consider ppg256 against the backdrop of Montfort's other projects. For over a decade, Montfort has worked to create tools to inspire other authors to engage in the computational production of literature. Not only in his work with ELO, having even served as its president, and in his teaching, but Montfort has also developed a platform for writing interactive fiction called Curveship. As an author-ware platform, it is considerably more powerful and extensive than his microscopic generators. However, none of Montfort's previous attempts to invite other writers to a computational pickup poetry game has been as productive as his work Taroko Gorge. In this poetry generator's relatively short existence, it has spawned more than a dozen variations—each drawing upon Montfort's code and developing it in a unique way.

Taroko Gorge

Taroko Gorge is a poem generator that produces stanzas on the topic of the beautiful Taroko Gorge National Park in Taiwan. Like an electronic-age Emerson, Montfort composed the program mostly in the natural setting of the park, finishing it up on the plane afterward. As he is fond of constraints, Montfort applied some to this generator. For example, the code was not to exceed a page. Montfort explains, "I defined this 'single page' very traditionally, in terms of line printer output: The text was not to exceed 66 80-column lines" (2012). This attention to the form of the code presents a visual aesthetic more akin to concrete poetry. Like his poetry generators, Montfort's code has a minimalist character, harmonizing with the simple natural imagery his generator produces.

Unlike the versions of ppg256, the words in this generator come from a very traditional set of images. Rather than long chains of trigrams, Montfort gives himself room here to create lists of readily recognizable words that can be used interchangeably within their particular position in the lines of the poem. Any given word list, or array,[7] offers options of words from the same part of speech—for example:

- Brow, mist, shape, layer, the crag, stone, forest, height
- Command, pace, roam, trail, frame, sweep, exercise, range
- Flow, basin, shape, vein, rippling, stone, cove, rock

- Track, shade, translate, stamp, progress through, direct, run, enter
- Sinuous straight, objective, arched, cool, clear, dim, driven
- Linger, dwell, rest, relax, hold, dream, hum
- Rough, fine

From that selection, the generator produces verse, such as this:

```
Brow ranges the coves.
Forests dwell.
Forests hum.
Brows trail the cove.


  progress through the encompassing cool—


The crags sweep the flows.
Forests relax.
Heights command the shapes.


  enter the sinuous—


The crag ranges the veins.
Forests exercise the veins.
  track the straight objective arched clear—


Monkeys frame the stones.
Shape commands the cove.
  direct the straight objective driven—
```

Much more sophisticated than ppg256, the lines of poetry generated have a sparse quality apropos of their object. The alternating use of the article *the* gives weight to the objects and actors, who seem both specific and timeless. They are both concrete (rocks, stones) and abstract (shapes, flows), metaphorical (brows, veins) and material (mist, forest). Montfort's simple constructs of path, site, and cave reveal an artist creating little units of phrase as meditative spaces.

Montfort has called Taroko Gorge an "unbounded" nature poem, but it is important to realize that he is not referring to any poem generated by the code but to the code itself as the poem. This takes some readjustment. What makes the poem limitless is that the program, once executed, continues to iterate. Boundlessness thus is a characteristic not of any one set out of output, but of the capacity of the program to develop poetry without limit.

Furthermore, the Python code of Montfort's generator presents a kind of elegance that gets lost in the HTML/JavaScript version. In fact, Montfort has written, "Python is a programming language I prefer for when I'm thinking" (2010). Consider a brief comparison. Here is the code for making a line of Python:

```
56.   p()
57.   while True:
58.        p(path()+'.')
59.        m=c([0]*6+[1,2])
60.        for n in range(0,m):
61.             p(site()+'.')
62.        p(path()+'.')
63.        p()
64.        p(cave()+' --')
65.        p()
```

The variable names are all defined in the comment at the head of this code. The pattern of the poetry is this:

```
Path.
    0, 1, or 2 sites.
path
Cave --
```

```
Path = Noun + verb + object.
Site =    Noun verb
Cave = verb + the + noun + adjective + object
```

The word lists are made up of two primary groups, *a* and *b*, which the HTML/JavaScript reveals to be *above* and *below*. From these simple structures, drawing upon relatively brief lists, the generator produces multitudes.

By contrast, here is the same function in HTML/JavaScript:

```
71.  function do_line() {
72.  var main=document.getElementById('main');
73.  if (t<=25) {
74.  t+=1;
75.  } else {
76.  main.removeChild(document.getElementById('main').firstChild);
77.  }
78.  if (n===0) {
79.  text=' ';
80.  } else if (n==1) {
81.  paths=2+rand_range(2);
82.  text=path();
83.  } else if (n<paths) {
84.  text=site();
85.  } else if (n==paths) {
86.  text=path();
87.  } else if (n==paths+1) {
88.  text=' ';
89.  } else if (n==paths+2) {
90.  text=cave();
91.  } else {
92.  text=' ';
93.  n=0;
94.  }
95.  n+=1;p
96.  text=text.substring(0,1).toUpperCase()+text.substring(1,text.
length);
97.  last=document.createElement('div');
98.  last.appendChild(document.createTextNode(text));
99.  main.appendChild(last);
100. }
```

The HTML/JavaScript does in thirty lines what the Python does in ten. The Python has an elegance that the translated version can't quite match.

As a poet and programmer, Montfort is well aware of the challenges of translation. When he published the code on the site *Media Commons* (2012), Montfort printed a JPG image of the printout, treating the printout of the code like a poet's manuscript.

This same code is published in *#!* (Montfort 2014), leading John Cayley (2015) to argue that it is the code that is the poem because the code can be read by humans, whereas the infinitely generated content cannot, a state that again points more toward the regenerating landscape of the national park that inspired the work: its fruits can be experienced only ever as the blossom of a moment. On the other hand, Aden Evens (2018) suggests that the infinite set of all possible conditions is what makes this piece poetry. Regardless of where one sees the poetry, the procedure or the possibility, both exist, in hibernation or as seeds, in the code.

This code has a type of elegance that echoes Montfort's other work. To read the code is like tracing the waterfalls beneath the Eternal Spring Shrine back to their origin. The reader can begin at the bottom and then, in graceful loops, work their way up into the code and back again. After learning the shorthand for the methods, primarily the methods to split, get a random number, and pick an item from a list, the reader can hike the code by beginning with the last section. The code at the end offers the form of each stanza:

```
58. p(path()+'.')
59. m=c([0]*6+[1,2])
60. for n in range(0,m):
61.     p(site()+'.')
62. p(path()+'.')
63. p()
64. p(cave()+' --')
65. p()
```

The first encounter is with the p method, which affects capitalization and timing. Those effects are applied to path. As readers encounter the path method, they can then go and read the definition of the path. Path offers one list of words but also a selection from list a, sending the reader up to read that line of words. Descending back to the stanza code, the reader encounters site, which sends her back up to the site method. Returning again to the stanza, the reader encounters path again and finally cave, which sends the reader back to that method.

As one might take any number of paths through a natural park, sometimes on a marked path, sometimes off, my portrait of reading through graceful loops offers one encounter with the code out of a near infinite array of approaches. However, I would argue that this Python code of Taroko Gorge offers a clear and concise organization that is refreshing to read, especially in contrast to reading some of the other, more elaborate case studies in this book and the larger software from which they were excerpted. Remember, Montfort is writing this code so that, like a snapshot of the falls, the code can be read on one page. He has made specific choices—namely, assigning variables and methods to single-character names—to give his code an austerity akin to his ppg256 works. However, in this case the code's simplicity and elegance are complemented by the content of the code and the continuous spring of simple yet stirring nature imagery that it engenders.

But because the HTML/JavaScript version can be rendered in a web-browser without downloading Python, that is the version that was adapted by so many and that raised Montfort's poem to the level of ELIZA's challenge, at least in part. Not only is the JavaScript more readily accessible to writers and readers on the internet, but Montfort's JavaScript is easier to read because the methods appear in more verbose, rather than abbreviated, form. For example, in place of the method `c` in Python, the JavaScript uses `rand_range`. Consequently, although there are not prominent Python variations of the generator, there are many JavaScript ones created by programmers of all levels, who could more easily see how the piece functioned. Returning to the discussion of readability of code in chapter 4, this analysis of code offers an example of two versions of the same code, one that is concise and elegant to the writer (the first reader) and one that is more accessible for modification by those who would adapt it.

The Descendants

Although Taroko Gorge would become a subject of many adaptations, the artists who would remake the project mostly changed the data, rather than the rules of the code. On the one hand, such adaptations would seem to follow the model of the sonnet or haiku, in which those who take up the form supply new words to fit into its constraints but for the most part do not change the constraints themselves. To write a sonnet is not to change the rules of a sonnet.

However, because Montfort is a poet of code, one who offers his code itself up as the poetry (Marino 2010b), and because we are viewing this work in the context of ELIZA's grand challenge, the adaptations seem on the surface to miss the mark by engaging with the data and not the rules. Such a reading misses the creative intervention of those who followed. They were not forking and adapting the code. Instead their work reimagines the poem, coopts its form, through a process more akin to remix.

To call these adaptations *remixes* is not to denigrate them but instead to locate them in a rich cultural practice of recycling and reinvention. In *Remix Theory*, Eduardo Navas (2012) theorizes the remix as a "cultural glue" that is "always unoriginal" but at the same time a potential "tool of autonomy" (4). The remix artist takes the existing material and transforms it through the method of cut/copy rather than creating something new from scratch. In like fashion, the remixers of Taroko Gorge did not rewrite the program, but copying the code, changed the data. (Technically, the program itself is the remixer par excellence as it is the one reshuffling all the data.) The remixing of Taroko Gorge has acted as a cultural glue that binds together disparate artists with widely varied aesthetic priorities and poetic interests.

The first of the adaptations, or remixes, was written by another of Montfort's blogging collaborators, Scott Rettberg. Rettberg is a writer of digital literature perhaps best known as the cofounder of the Electronic Literature Organization, whose work is known for a postmodern playfulness and ironic tendencies. Rettberg describes his reworking of Montfort's poem as a "hack," originally sending the link to his remix with a note that he had "made a few improvements" (Rettberg 2019, 47–48). At the time, neither Rettberg nor Montfort expected others to follow suit.

As the first of the adaptations, Scott Rettberg's Tokyo Garage (2009) could have been a one-off work of e-lit, or more specifically a one-off adaptation of a one-off poetry generator. Consider the style of its poetry:

> Scholars hate the dog.
> Undercover cops explode.
> Mystics perspire.
> Drummers subdue the Roppongi drunks.
>   imagine the lithe uptight digital blinking—
>
> Spokesmodels proselytize the nose rings.
> Hallucinations transport the subways.
>   digest the scattered—

Rettberg uses a larger set of words than Montfort, but rather than drawing from nature, they arise from a particularly Japanese style of commercial culture (Godzilla, kabuki dancer, Speed Racer) set in a noisy and sullied streetscene (technicolor nightmare, prostitute, pickpocket, bribe, hassle, grope). In his opening comment in the code of his adaptation, Rettberg writes, "This here is a total remix of the classic and elegant generated nature poem Tokoro [sic] Gorge by Nick Montfort. He wrote the code here. I hacked the words to make it more about urbanity, modernity, and my idea of Tokyo, a city I have never been to." If Montfort's poem is an ode to the simple, boundless natural beauty of a park, Rettberg's poem offers a noisy homage to popular culture with a Japanese pop–inspired aesthetic. Although Rettberg claims to have "hacked the words," it is hard to consider this reworking to be mischief. As John Cayley (2015) reminds us, "most, if not all, of his work is published with actual or implicit license allowing copying, reuse, and modification so long as attribution and the same licensing terms are maintained." Rettberg's self-incrimination is a bit of poetic performance of his own.

His gesture might have been the end of the matter, except something about Rettberg's adaptation caught the attention of future developers, as his adaptation developed some of the conventions of this poetic form or perhaps new poetic genre: remixes of Taroko Gorge. One was that the titles would be a play on Montfort's original title, with many of the listed variations starting with the letters T and G, including Takei, George (2011) and Toy Garbage (2011), as well as other wordplay, such as Yoko Engorged (2011), Fred and George (2012), Alone Engaged (2011), and Gorge (2010).

Gorge by JR Carpenter

The next major adaptation of Taroko Gorge was electronic poet J. R. Carpenter's Gorge, which, following Rettberg, she calls a remix. (*Remix* is an interesting term to use because it originally referred to a reworking of a recording of a song.) Carpenter does not rearrange the code or the content of Taroko Gorge, but instead, like Rettberg, changes the data. By the time she worked on her remix, Carpenter was already an established print and electronic poet, known for her own word play and technical innovation, as well as a media art historian and theorist.

Rather than taking a location, such as the park in Montfort's poem or the urban space in Rettberg's, Carpenter takes for her focus an act, that of gorging oneself. Carpenter writes: "A gorge is a steep-sided canyon, a passage, a gullet. To gorge is to stuff with food, to devour greedily. GORGE is a new poetry generator by J. R. Carpenter. This never-ending tract spews verse approximations, poetic paroxysms on food, consumption, decadence and desire." *Gorge* the noun becomes the verb *to gorge*.

Her variables for above and below give a sense of the piece:

```
var above='appetite, brain, craving, desire, digestive juice,
digestive tract, enzyme, gaze, glaze, gorge, gullet, head,
incisor, intellect, jaw,knowledge, language, maw, mandible, mind,
molar, muscle, mouth, nose, passion, sight, smell, spit, sweat,
spirit, thirst, throat'.split(', ');

var below=', bladder, blood vessel, bowl, bowel, crust, dip,
dressing,film, gut, lip, lower lip, proffered finger, finger
```

```
tip, flared nostril, flushed cheek, meal, membrane, morsel,most
intimate odour, palm, passage, persistent scent, pore, sauce, soft
pocket, slightest sliver, stomach, surface, thick spread, tongue,
taste bud, vein, vinaigrette'.split(', ');
```

Montfort's initial eight words have quadrupled in the `above` variable, and `below` has thirty-four words. In the place of simple nature images are words drawn from the realm of eating (glaze, gullet, molar), but also more broadly sensual appetites (proffered finger, palm, flushed cheek). They are the signs and substance of gorging oneself, and that gorging is hardly limited to food: she also adds *film* and *gaze*, words that together conjure a feminist critique of male visual desire (as in the "male gaze"). Both the above and the below groups feature body parts that perform the consumption. The above list includes maw, jaw, mandible, molar, mouth, and throat, the below list lip, lower lip, and tongue. However, the above and below groups do offer a conceptual divide. The seat of this desire in the above section prioritizes the mind (brain, head, intellect, knowledge), whereas the below section emphasizes the digestive (stomach, bladder, bowel, gut). Another group of words in the below list emphasizes body parts that might register arousal (flared nostril, flushed cheek). These words suggest that gorging is a sensual activity. And another list (most intimate odor and proffered finger) suggest a sexual dimension, although that "most intimate odour" could very well refer to flatulence, a mere effect of gorging. Nonetheless, casting that odor as intimate returns us from the itemizing of mere body parts and physiological effects to the above list, with its *craving* and *desire*.

The moments when the list breaks out of an expected pattern change the meaning of the other words on the list because they suggest another dimension of meaning. In a mere list of foods, "thick spread" sounds like mayonnaise, but in the list with "flushed cheek" it evokes a sensual encounter, making this gorge far more than a shopping list and changing the way its other words (blood vessel, vein, aroma) resonate. That is to say, Carpenter has done far more than swap in new data; she has remixed the poem with a poet's methods of connotation and allusion. To read these observations out of the code is not to "cheat" because, as I mentioned, she has published the code for our consumption so that we might savor the lists even in their potential state, even just as ingredients in this poetic pantry. To read these poems is to peruse their code.

Significantly, Carpenter has published the code in a poetry collection with instructions on how to adapt the generator. The generosity of this move is itself generative. Carpenter's publication of the code and its output is also instructive. She presents the contents of the prior authors' code as variables—that is, the Montfort variables and the

Rettberg variables. Her presentation suggests that the code is the same and that only the data changes—similar to presenting the form of a Petrarchan sonnet separate from the various versions.[8]

Even some of Montfort's original words remain in Carpenter's piece. Note that in Rettberg's adaptation, he had changed Montfort's monkey line to the following:

```
if ((words=='pachinko parlor')&&(rand_range(3)==1)) {
  words='mobile phone '+choose(trans)
```

However, in Carpenter's code, the forest trigger for the output monkeys remains:

```
if ((words=='forest')&&(rand_range(3)==1)) {
words='monkeys '+choose(trans);
```

This section of code produces only the lines relating to monkeys. But because Carpenter does not use *forest*, this particular piece of code remains like a memento tucked away in a trunk someone has purchased at a flea market. It may never be used or noticed by the reader yet is a tie to the original owner.

A closer examination of Carpenter's and Rettberg's code reveals a sense of what they consider the data and what they consider the form. On the one hand, outside of monkeys, Carpenter, like Rettberg, replaces the data for all of the main variables (the arrays: above, below, trans, intrans, texture). On the other hand, neither Carpenter nor Rettberg rename these variables themselves (above, below, path, cave). Taroko Gorge persists in these images. Carpenter also does not include these variable names either in the Montfort variables or the Rettberg variables. So whereas Montfort's poem about a trip to a national park follows paths with caves, both Carpenter's Gorge and Rettberg's Tokyo Garage also include paths and caves. The distinction may be that as the author of the initial algorithm, Montfort was thinking more consciously about his code as the thing being read, whereas Carpenter and Rettberg saw their remixing work as something that happens at the level of the data. Nonetheless, by publishing her code alongside sample output, Carpenter surely invited such a reading. Regardless of what they changed, by adapting the poem generator for their own purposes, Carpenter and Rettberg led the way for many subsequent poets to continue the regeneration of this generator.

After Carpenter's adaptation, the descendants multiply. Among the other variations, consider Talan Memmott's Toy Garbage, Kathi Inman Berens's Tournedo Gorge (2012), and Mark Sample's Takei, George. Other adapters include Eric Snodgrass, Maria

Engberg, Flourish Klink, Andrew Plotkin, Brendan Howell, Adam Sylvain, Leonardo Flores, Alireza Mahzoon, Sonny Rae Tempest, Helen Burgess, Judy Malloy, Bob Bonsall, and Chuck Rybak. All these creators' poetry generators share basic underlying programming; however, with the differences in their themes—such as toy nostalgia, culinary quests, and *Star Trek* culture—the generators can hardly be called versions of Montfort's original. They are unique poems in their own right. Or, to return to the beginning of this chapter, they are generators in the new poetic form of Taroko Gorge generators. Each continues to play on Montfort's original title, mostly keeping to the original verse structure but at times varying, and mostly using his code. What Montfort has created, then, is not so much an infinite poem as a genesis of a chain of poetic action, of engagement with poetic elements mostly as data. His generators are generative, and his poetic meditation on nature leads to electronic reflections on pop culture, human vice, and other nuances of being, which we might sum up as the stuff of poetry.

However, the variations on his code in the earlier Taroko Gorge remixes have not attended to the instructions, a central object of Montfort's aesthetic project, but instead to the data. In the hierarchical world of code art, data can take second-class status for it seems like mere content to be shuffled around. It is the content that the computer does not "care" about. Anastasia Salter (2017) warns against such a hierarchical emphasis on code in an age of the "leaky pipeline," which loses (i.e., leaks) its bright and creative female programmers due to unsupportive or hostile learning and work environments.[9] Because she offers Taroko Gorge and its variants as an access point to coding, as a way in for those without formal training, I would be remiss to reinsert the division by celebrating adaptations of instructions over adaptations of data. In fact, I suspect that binary is, like so many used to enforce a hierarchy, false.

Moreover, in this instance, in which the remixers have changed the values of the variables but not the names of the methods, they have, in a sense, changed content that the computer does care about for it will need to store those strings as values—albeit as ones and zeroes and ultimately, as Kittler has acknowledged, as electrical signals. The method names by contrast will disappear at the level of the assembly code. Thus, they exist in the JavaScript but disappear in assembly. Such distinctions, however, are immaterial because JavaScript is the language that the reader encounters, and these method names, though arbitrary, are symbols in that system. Ultimately, the distinction between adaptations that change the instructions of the code and those that change the data can make value claims only in the context of human aesthetics. The computer cares little about art, as far as we know. At this point, it is useful to return to the example that inspired the challenge: ELIZA.

ELIZA is a conversational system built by Joseph Weizenbaum on the MAD-SLIP (Symetric List Processor) system. SLIP is an application programming interface written in FORTRAN II (Weizenbaum 1963). What we generally call ELIZA is actually a script called DOCTOR that Weizenbaum wrote for that system, a script he published in 1966, and it is possible from reading through the keywords and the templates for the responses—or, to use the language of bots, the grammars—to develop a sense of how the program operated. Although we do not have the ELIZA system itself, between transcripts and accounts of interactions with the program and this script, we can get a sense of how it worked. The code begins with a greeting statement:

```
(HOW DO YOU DO. PLEASE TELL ME YOUR PROBLEM)
START
```

Start begins a communication exchange. If the person says the keyword "sorry," the system recognizes it in the following template:

```
(SORRY ((0) .
```

It reacts by drawing from a series of responses:

```
(PLEASE DON'T APOLIGIZE)
(APOLOGIES ARE NOT NECESSARY) (WHAT FEELINGS DO YOU HAVE WHEN YOU
APOLOGIZE) (I'VE TOLD YOU THAT APOLOGIES ARE NOT REQUIRED)))
```

The system seems to store values in variables represented by numerals. For example, the keyword REMEMBER in the following statement:

```
(REMEMBER 5
```

That triggers the following result templates, which make use of the value stored in 4 and 5:

```
((0 YOU REMEMBER 0) (DO YOU OFTEN THINK OF 4)
(DOES THINKING OF 4 BRING ANYTHING ELSE TO MIND)
(WHAT ELSE DO YOU REMEMBER)
(WHY DO YOU REMEMBER 4 JUST NOW)
```

```
(WHAT IN THE PRESENT SITUATION REMINDS YOU OF 4)
(WHAT IS THE CONNECTION BETWEEN ME AND 4)) (0 DO I REMEMBER 0)
(DID YOU THINK I WOULD FORGET 5) (WHY DO YOU THINK I SHOULD RECALL
5 NOW) (WHAT ABOUT 5) (=WHAT) (YOU MENTIONED 5)) ((0) (NEWKEY)))
```

That said, because we cannot currently access a functioning version of ELIZA, the software implementations of ELIZA are functional equivalents. Because the code of ELIZA is unavailable for reading, those who adapt it are not interacting with its code but often customizing the content (the keywords and responses) of a similar system—for example, one of the many JavaScript versions that circulate on the internet. Like the remixers of Taroko Gorge, they can change the data without changing the instructions since we do not have the original instructions of ELIZA system itself.

Since Weizenbaum's publication of ELIZA, chatbots have proliferated (Marino 2006b). Not only do people remix the original ELIZA, but they build their own systems, varying the character, the persona, the nature of the call and response. ELIZA has inspired automated telephone agents, novel generators, and art other projects, such as Peggy Weil's Mr. Mind in *The Blurring Test*, which challenges the player to prove to the computer they are human. They have built platforms for chatbot authoring, such as Richard Wallace's Artificial Intelligence Markup Language (AIML), which powers his ALICE bot. Furthermore, programmers have been inspired to wrestle with more complex systems for character-based human-computer interaction, leading all the way to the Siris and Alexas of today—and who knows what else by the time you are reading this.

Argot, Ogre Ok!

One of the first Taroko Gorge descendants to meaningfully play with the instructions of Nick's code was Andrew Plotkin's variant, which is a remix of the remixes. Plotkin is primarily an interactive fiction writer, well-known to Montfort and the electronic literature community. By calling attention to their interactions with Montfort's code and foregrounding code on the display level of the generator, Andrew Plotkin's Argot, Ogre, OK! (2011) performs its own critical code studies on Montfort's poem and its variants.

In Plotkin's version, named for an anagram of Taroko Gorge,[10] he mashes together pairs of versions of Taroko Gorge, specifically Rettberg's Tokyo Garage; Carpenter's Gorge; Eric Snodgrass's Yoko Engorged; Mark Sample's Takei, George; Talan Memmott's Toy Garbage; Maria Engberg's Alone Engaged; and Flourish Klink's Fred and George.

Plotkin's presentation comments on the Taroko Gorge lineage by displaying the code that generates the poems, one line at a time, beside boxes (iframes) that show the poems they generate. At the same time, Plotkin varies the stanza structure and mixes the word pools from the various projects two at a time. For example, his code creates a new mashup, "Alone and George," which combines Klink's and Engberg's variations. Plotkin notes that his own code lacks a bit of the sparse simplicity of Montfort's, but he feels he has remained true to the aesthetic of the original.

Plotkin documents his process in an elaborate comment at the beginning of his code. In a piece that displays parts of its own code on the screen, it is interesting to see what Plotkin does not display. First, he is quick to assure the readers that "Yes, this page really does execute the code that's displayed in the left column, and it really does generate the text in the right column." Plotkin is addressing readers of this code, whether they are looking to remix Taroko Gorge further or approaching the piece as readers of literature. Just to highlight the point, this is a writer/remixer of code writing a comment in the code to an audience whom he anticipates interpreting the code. We have reached a moment in which poet programmers are addressing outside audiences, inviting audiences to explore, to interpret, and to engage with their code.

Through his code, Plotkin comments on the remix tradition of Taroko Gorge, as emblematized in his treatment of the monkey feature. First, he offers a quote in his epigraph to his opening comment in his code:

"Does it have a monkey?"

"Yes, the monkey is 'taboo.'"
—Nick Montfort and Flourish Klink, Sept 26, at dinner

If you were not yet convinced of the heteroglossia of code or that it it is more than merely instructions and their documentation, here is a passage that would seem more at home in a story by Dorothy Parker. This passage suggests that the monkey of Montfort's original poem, and its presence or omission in its remixes, had become a point of humor. The taboo Klink mentions is her response to the monkey. In her code:

```
if ((words=='wizard')&&(rand_range(3)==1)) {
    words='taboos '+choose(trans);
```

Klink's trigger word, her *forest*, is the word *wizard*, and the word that she adds as a consequence, her monkey, is *taboos*. By including the exchange between Montfort and Klink, Plotkin is identifying the ways in which Taroko Gorge has become a poetic form with its own consistent features. Plotkin's homage to this part of the poetic form is as follows:

```
if ((words==src.monkeysee)&&(rand_range(3)==1)) {words=src.
monkeydo+' '+choose(src.trans);
```

Each poem object has a designated monkeysee and monkeydo, which correspond to the triggers and consequences respectively, including the following:

Taroko Gorge: forest, monkeys

Tokyo Garage: pachinko parlor, mobile phone

Gorge: forest, monkeys

Toy Garbage: BABY ALIVE, MOTHER MAY I

Yoko Engorged: [one space], null

Takei, George: Sulu's smile, Kirk smolders and Sulu vows to

Alone Engaged: old lover, mobile phone

Taroko Gorge: wizard, taboos

Plotkin has made the monkey into the monkeysee that triggers the monkeydo, now an attribute of his object that comically calls attention to this mischief-maker in the code of Taroko Gorge and its remixes. The monkey feature of the code is also now a sign of the degree to which the programming remixer engaged with the code.

By mixing the remixes, Plotkin's code identifies the similarities in the instruction layers while creating a melange of the data. At the same time, Plotkin's own code seems to take up the challenge of Taroko Gorge, reworking at the layer of instructions with a sense of Montfort's original provocation, with some ironic metamixing of his own. Plotkin is hardly alone in playing with the instructions. Other variants of Taroko Gorge have taken them up, adding their own layers of instructions, as in the case of J. R. Carpenter's Along the Briny Beach (2012), which includes a generated graphical coastline among other features. What's notable about Plotkin's intervention is that it uses code to comment on Montfort's code, even foregrounding the code by bringing it to the presentation layer.

So does Taroko Gorge answer the ELIZA Challenge sufficiently? It is certainly too early to tell. On one level, Taroko Gorge is like ELIZA, many of the descendants of which merely follow the same functional structure as that original chatbot but the authors of which have changed the content of the keywords and triggered responses. On the other hand, the true descendants of Taroko Gorge may look nothing like it.

They could generate endless lists of beer names or tiny protests. They could be used to generate whole novels. It all depends on what one counts as Taroko Gorge. What are its specifications? Is it a generator of infinite variations of the ABBA-C pattern? Or is it one in a long line of text generators, the grandchildren of which, like Siri and Alexa to ELIZA, may be unrecognizable (and abhorrent) to the designer of their grandmother.

For the purposes of this book, Taroko Gorge stands as an example of this new literary moment, one in which poet programmers engage with language in and through their code, generating poetry while producing works of art in code that invite exploration whether through reading, execution, or remixing. Regardless of where it stands in the ELIZA challenge, Taroko Gorge has succeeded in drawing poet-programmers in to play with its code as a possibility space of its own. Critical code studies invites readers and writers to reflect on this code, exploring not just what it does, but what it means.

8 Futures of Critical Code Studies

We have reached a moment in which philosophers process, poets publish, and curators collect code knowing scholars will interpret it as discourse. The time is ripe for critical code studies, and it has played a role in the ripening.

Critical code studies as a set of methods and a community of practice is still very much in its infancy, and I am reluctant to limit it by pronouncing its future. However, I wanted to conclude this first collection of case studies with some reflections on the practice and a few suggestions for future exploits. The goal of this book was to demonstrate some initial approaches to reading code based on case studies drawn from hot-button science debates, provocative art projects, the foundational moments in the development of a programming language, and the critical making of a media philosopher. The readings have attempted to demonstrate a variety of interpretive methods, or moves, as I like to think of them, such as exploring the metaphors raised by the names of constructs in the code, examining misreadings and recontextualizations of code, interrogating the cultural stakes of language formation, and reading code as a complement to philosophical tracts, to name a few. These gestures offer a few but by no means all methods, for there is still so much to interpret—and in fact, the methods may be endless, as every new innovation in programming becomes a new opportunity and challenge for interpretation. The work to develop new reading practices must continue and will continue in parallel with the development of technology. Nonetheless, the development of this field is reliant not only on its methods but also its ability to offer insights to others.

Here, then, are four areas to which critical code studies might be productively directed in the future. They apply not so much to the micropractice of individual interpretive moves in close readings but instead to the macrodevelopment of the field in relation to others. I will focus primarily on the growth and development of CCS in the academy—as opposed to, say, in industry or in amateur communities—because through my work in the Humanities and the Critical Code Studies Lab, I have labored in the service of higher education to foster critical thought and to facilitate interdisciplinary exploration, though institutions tend to inhibit the latter. The four actions are as follows:

1. Contributing to humanities curricula
2. Informing computer science curricula
3. Supporting research in the digital humanities
4. Inspiring new work in code

1. Contributing to Humanities Curricula

Critical code studies was born of the humanities. Many of the original scholars working in this field were working on or had earned their masters and doctorates in literature departments, cutting their teeth not on code but on Shakespeare and Morrison, along with philosophers such as Cixous and Derrida. The practice of critically reading code arose in part from the close-reading practices on which most students are taught, starting in secondary school but beginning even earlier. More of these students should be encouraged to explore code.

Following the liberal arts tradition, most university-level core curricula include a science requirement to complement the humanities, arts, and social sciences, with an eye toward enriching each student's experience. For example, students might take a course in programming or engineering for nonmajors. There are a great many new books directed at such an audience, including Martin Erwig's *Once Upon an Algorithm: How Stories Explain Computing* (2017) and Nick Montfort's *Exploratory Programming for Arts and Humanities* (2016), to name just two. In addition to these programming courses, which are quite valuable for their differentiated instruction, colleges and universities could offer courses that straddle the disciplines, rather than reifying the disciplinary divide.[1] A course based in critical code studies, along with software and platform studies, would offer an opportunity for universities to give students science with a humanistic eye. In other words, rather than thinking of these disciplines in their silos, why not think of the way they inflect, inform, and inspire one another?

In many ways, critical code studies speaks to the so-called crisis of the humanities, if one even exists, not by offering English majors coding skills but instead by flipping the script and acknowledging that our ways of knowing, or heuristics, taught in literature, history, art, and cultural studies courses, to name a few, teach a kind of critical analysis of objects that can enrich scientific inquiry—not by making technology that is better, smaller, faster in some grand progress narrative, but instead by adding new dimensions to that inquiry, most notably questions of meaning and of the implication of coding choices. It asks the programmer to reflect on a wider field of significance of the choices they are making as they code. It frames the task of computer programming—as it already is—a site of dialogue and contest, collaboration and cooperation between design and engineering, as well as philosophy, sociology, linguistics, history, art, and many more fields, each bringing rich traditions and methods of exploration.

2. Informing Computer Science Curricula

In addition to enriching the overall liberal arts education, critical code studies can offer particular benefits to the study of computer science. Since its inception, computer science has been an interdisciplinary pursuit benefitting from scientific minds who are also deeply invested in the arts and philosophy. Alan Turing himself is one example, Ada Lovelace another. Not to mention the reflections of influential computer scientists such as Joseph Weizenbaum (1976), who warned against the dehumanization that can attend the race for greater technology. In harmony with the origins of computer science, critical code studies helps bring philosophical and ethical questions into the computer science classroom at a more concrete level.

From a pragmatic viewpoint, most engineering and science curricula include an ethics component and are required to by standardization organizations such as the Accreditation Board for Engineering Technology (ABET), which currently accredits over 3,500 programs (Oudshoorn et al. 2018). Whether or not computer science programs are also accredited, ethics should be a component of their curricula. As I mentioned earlier, there is a growing awareness of bias in algorithms and a need for algorithmic accountability. Courses or course content in critical code studies could help programs attend to the ethical dimension of their instruction in an applied fashion to complement the existing core requirements in philosophy classes. However, ethics is only one dimension that critical code studies brings to the reading of code. CCS also takes seriously the art of code, its rhetoric, and its expressive qualities. CCS considers the social dimensions that attend what seems to be purely technological. Adding critical code studies to computer science courses can augment the ways instruction in this area already spreads beyond a functionalist or utilitarian approach. Here I am inspired by courses like Kim Knight's "Fashioning Circuits," which brought together "computational craft" with "domestic technologies" and "soft activism," stitching together areas to see what new possibilities arrive. Critical code studies can both lead to reflection on past code craft and inform future creation.

The question, ultimately, is not how to get English majors coding or even what the programming world can learn from the arts and humanities—but what would a university be like without this unnecessary border between two disciplinary clusters that have so much to offer one another?

3. Supporting Research in the Digital Humanities

Although it may seem that we have been promoting methods for critical code studies in contrast to or distinct from other approaches, once these methods are more fully developed, demonstrated, and established, they can serve to support other, larger studies in the digital humanities. In other words, a code studies approach can complement a reading of a digital object that includes attention to hardware, other software, and other systems.

Consider, for example, the supporting role CCS played in the book *Reading Project* (Pressman, Marino, and Douglass 2015), in which two other scholars, Jessica Pressman and Jeremy Douglass, joined me for a collaborative exploration of one work of digital literature. Rather than taking the center of that discussion, the code reading offered insights and answers, as well as new questions, in the larger investigation, contributing to the overall interpretation. Critical code studies is not meant to be an ends in itself or an isolated framework for interpretation but instead a library of methods in an ever-expanding set of methods, to be called upon as needed to support analysis and exegesis.

4. Inspiring New Work in Code

Although critical code studies is not principally designed as a tool for innovation, studies in code can inspire creativity in the realm of programming. Consider, for example, some of the artistic works that have been developed since the start of CCS. Two examples are the Transborder Immigrant Tool, which was being developed during the initial years of CCS, and *Sea and Spar Between*. In both cases, the developers released the code of the works to be read and were well aware of critical code studies. Prior to releasing the code, Electronic Disturbance Theater member micha cárdenas presented with me on a panel where I was describing critical code studies, and Nick Montfort of *Sea and Spar Between* had participated in a Critical Code Studies Working Group, along with leading the writing of one of the first books of CCS, *10 PRINT CHR$(205.5+RND(1)); : GOTO 10* (Montfort et al. 2013). Subsequently, EDT released the code for the Transborder Immigrant Tool at the first conference of critical code studies, and Montfort and his collaborator Stephanie Strickland (2013) published an essay on *Sea and Spar Between* inside the code itself *Digital Humanities Quarterly* in an issue that included my interpretation of TBT.

These are just a few examples of the way that critical code studies, and its attendant awareness that one's code may be read closely by diverse audiences, has made more explicit the knowledge that code is a medium for discourse and has contributed an awareness of more varied audiences to the development of code. The questions scholars ask of code will inform the development processes of the programmers who hear them, as they ask those same questions of their own code.

These four areas of growth are not the only ways critical code studies can contribute in the future, but I offer them as potential lines of flight to those holding this book and wondering where to head next.

How to Interpret Code

At this early stage of this field, I would severely limit its growth if I enumerated the definitive method to interpret code. This book only scratches the surface. However, because many reading this book may look to its models as a basis for their own readings, I want to leave a few of the steps I have found useful in reading code, with the understanding that these are only the most basic. Admittedly, interpretation begins with the choice of the code the scholar wishes to analyze. That choice is the first sign of the scholar's incipient insight to be pursued and illuminated by all subsequent work.

A Preliminary List of Approaches

Even in this nascent field, scholars in critical code studies have already demonstrated some effective methods of interpreting code. Rather than spelling out a definitive list of approaches, I offer the following list of methods as a bit of a brainstorm based on techniques that have been fruitful so far:

- Reading code against output
- Reading code against its social implications
- Reading code against its social historical contexts (immediate and broader)[2]
- Reading code against its genre
- Reading code against its uses in other code
- Reading code against its adaptations

- Reading code against its paratexts
- Reading code against cultural paradigms
- Reading the aesthetics of the code against the aesthetics of the software's interface or output
- Reading functionality against sociohistorical context
- Reading "interpreted code" against content
- Reading code from an ethical vantage
- Reading instructions against data
- Reading code and its evolution over time
- Examining the rhetoric of the code
- Examining the design priorities of the code
- Examining models and other world representations
- Examining the code's impact on identity in terms of race and ethnicity, gender, sexuality, and socioeconomic status
- Examining what the code says about its author and vice versa
- Examining how different audiences read or use the code differently
- Examining the code in comparison to a cultural logic[3]
- Examining the degree of obfuscation or clarity
- Examining the algorithmic integrity or accountability or values-sensitive design[4]
- Examining readings and misreadings of the code
- Examining how the form complements its processes or output
- Examining how the code is informed by secondary purposes[5]
- Examining how the code takes advantage of affordances or limitations of other hardware and software
- Examining analogous systems through the lens of code studies[6]
- Comparing implementations in different languages
- Writing more code to understand the code[7]
- Writing ports to understand the code
- Modifying the code and examining changes
- Creating visualizations of the code
- Searching the code for insight
- Searching the code for originality

- Searching the code for clever repurposing[8]
- Applying the lens of an unlikely discipline to the code
- Flipping traditional valences[9]

And of course, *against* here signifies in tandem with, intertwined with, in dialogue with. These approaches, however, can only yield effective readings when coupled with research into the code and its contexts. What follows are some avenues of research to consider. The first is key.

Determine the Functioning of the Code

Obviously, a primary step is to develop an understanding of the functioning of the code. However, I would not go so far as to call this the first step. Following the specific ins and outs of any code takes careful, patient, and methodical work and a serious investment in understanding the programming language, the programming paradigms, and, sometimes, the hardware on which the code was implemented. For this reason, I have found that a basic understanding of the functioning of the code—for example, based on its primary effects—is enough to embark on the subsequent fact-finding before returning to the detailed step-by-step reading. I suspect someone more versed in programming or the programming language of the code might be able to dive right in, but most people I have spoken with, even experienced programmers, find the prospect of reading someone else's code to be unpleasant, if not daunting. Inevitably, though, the critic must determine the function of the code before they can begin to understand its extrafunctional significance.

Research the Context of Its Creation

Behind any code is the story of its creation, the concept behind its conception, the context of its development, and the constraints faced by its creators. Like any origin story, the context can offer insight into design choices, explain method and variable names, and even give the reason for shortcomings in the code. Following the habits of good science and technology studies and media archaeology, reading code requires uncovering these stories and understanding how they shaped the code.

Research the Creators

Part of looking at the context is understanding the programmer or programmers who worked on the code. *Creator* here may be too strong a word, as much of programming involves building out of new and preexisting code, including libraries or circulated code snippets or even whole programs that are being adapted. Nonetheless, one or more people are responsible for *assembling*—and here I use that word in the noncomputational sense—the code. For that reason, a code reading benefits from discovering as much relevant information about the code's creators as the reader can gather.

When possible, I prefer to interview the code authors, but scholars can also read their writing or watch or listen to their discussions of the code. Here code interpretation is a bit different than traditional literary interpretation, in which scholars often treat the objects of study as artifacts floating in history, removed from further shading by the author. Perhaps that is one of the ways reading code is different than reading literary artifacts. Because literature is created to be interpreted, deferring to "authorial intent" tends to be the death of literary interpretation. However, because most code is an expression of thought in a kind of shorthand, typically not an ends but a set of symbols that emerge from the process of making something else, knowing the thought process that produced the code, in as much as that is available, can be greatly illuminating.

Research Its Evolution
Programmers iterate code, releasing new versions, sometimes refactoring large portions. Often code is revised or extended by programmers who take up the project later in its life. Examining the changes to programs over time is a useful strategy for understanding the life of the code, how it made its current form known to its developers.

Research Any Required Hardware and Software
Most high-level code does not require particular hardware. That is the beauty of a high-level language. When code does require hardware, however, knowledge about that system enriches an understanding of the code. Code also interoperates with other software, such as operating systems. Knowing the interplay between code and those systems is useful because those systems shape what that code can do and, consequently, its significance. Code readers should also attend to any development software used to produce the code, as in the example of NetBeans, which was used in the Transborder Immigrant Tool. These tools are particularly important because they offer the reader a glimpse into the way the developers encountered their code while creating it and because these tools have shaped and even produced some of the code.

Research the Genre of the Program
Programs can be organized into types based on their function, structure, or purpose. A genre-based, or generic, understanding of the code can help the reader understand what aspects of the code are novel and which are conventional or acting as boilerplate.

When examining some of the code in this book, once I developed my understanding of the genre of software, certain design choices that seemed remarkable proved to be conventional, and other aspects that were more unique to an implementation of the software rose to the surface.

Research Its Components and Elements

Code is never simply code. It is made up of many aspects that are worthy of and necessary for exploration. These include but are not limited to the programming paradigm of the architecture, its overall structure, and the programming language or languages. Code can have methods, variables, objects, data, and subroutines. Code has comments that, as Douglass contends, are a meaningful component. At an abstract level, code can have models and procedures. As I mentioned earlier in the book, I add *state* to this list of code attributes, inspired by the work of Evan Buswell (2019), who makes the case for the significance of state (as the other half of code reading) in his dissertation. On a more granular level, code can have white space that is significant or insignificant. Code also has qualities: clarity versus obfuscation, verbosity versus concision, elegance versus sloppiness. More recent explorations have turned to the ethics embedded in the code—for example, the potential for destructive bias in AI code. In these cases, code can write other code, which, as Catherine Griffiths (2018) has argued, can be inaccessible to human readers, but might be more effectively rendered for examination through visualizations.

Read Paratexts

As the case studies demonstrate, the code is often attended by additional writing, either as further documentation, commentary by the developers (as in the case of TBT), communications between developers (as in Climategate), or even sales materials (in the case of FLOW-MATIC). At times, the creators of the code have written related texts that express the ideas of the code in other ways. Sometimes these texts can be very far removed from the code, as in the case of Kittler's philosophical writing, or reimaginings of the code, as in the case of the play produced out of the Transborder Immigrant Tool or the adaptations of Taroko Gorge.

Read the Code with Others

Just as the code in software is worked on by many hands and benefits from many kinds of expertise, the critical reading of code does as well. I could not perform any of the readings by myself; I relied heavily on those with much deeper understandings of programming. But even those experts noticed different aspects of the code from one another. The Critical Code Studies Working Groups are premised on the collective readings of code with the understanding of the multiplicity of intellectual backgrounds and perspectives necessary to unpack the meaning of code. Consider, for example, the collective annotation of the code for *Adventure* that was performed in the 2010 Critical Code Studies Working Group (Jerz 2011) or *10 PRINT* (Montfort et al. 2013), a book in which ten scholars examined just one line of code. Critical code studies benefits not just from many eyes on the same code but from many lenses and many perspectives. The biannual Critical Code Studies Working Group offers one place for collective code reading, and teams are working on tools for the collective annotation of code, such as ANVC Scalar and ACLS Workbench (see, e.g., Pressman, Marino, and Douglass 2015, 145), which will help collectives read code together.

Research the Programming Language

Like any good textual study, the better scholars understand the language and its origins, the better they will understand the code. Those languages, rooted in rich intellectual histories, are informed by paradigms, such as imperative and declarative structure, aesthetics, and temporal contexts. By the time you are reading this book, no doubt there will be many new paradigms to explore. As with any semiotic analysis, the signs have meaning through their relation to the full language.

Research Its Circulation

As with any cultural text, interpretation does not change the object but does change its significance. As we saw in the case of Climategate, the meaning of code changes as new groups encounter and interpret it. That said, because any body of code can be made of many diverse parts, each of its elements may have its own history, as in the case of the matrix operations in Kittler's assembly. Knowing more about these histories can only enrich the reader's understanding of the meaning of the code.

Apply a Critical Lens

The chief characteristic that differentiates critical code studies from other science and technology studies is its emphasis on theoretical approaches or hermeneutics from the humanities. I list this last even though the use of lenses (if not the conscious choice of them) precedes the process of inquiry, not to mention that each of the preceding steps is already mediated by ideology. In the world of media and literary studies, these are generally referred to as *critical theory*, and they are constituted by the widely varied interpretive practices that generally have their roots in philosophy, as well as linguistics, anthropology, and beyond. Critical theory generally challenges, at times by identifying, existing social and communication conventions rather than treating culture and signification as neural arenas. These lenses include interpretive frameworks such as structuralism and formalism, and deconstruction; identity-related approaches such as feminism and critical race studies; globally oriented approaches such as postcolonialism; and many more. Although I list them individually, a scholar rarely uses just one and a strong case has been made for thinking more intersectionally to begin with, especially when focusing on social categories. This is not to say that the lenses cannot come from computer science but rather that they would likely come from the more philosophical texts on computer science instead of the more practical ones. Nor is that to argue that critical code studies intends to colonize computer science with Continental philosophy but to accept that the exploration of code is never a neutral activity, free from an epistemology or a world view, and instead to draw upon the interpretive force of these critical theories, to adopt and adapt them for even greater insights.

Final Words

Ultimately, as with any interpretation, the journey into code is an exploration that says just as much about the code as it does the mind of the person examining it. Unless someone wishes to embark on the task of uncritically documenting military-industrial-academic artifacts on behalf of those who created them to the benefit of their creators' self-regard, I do not recommend treating this examination as an empirical activity rooted in objectivity. Instead, the objective reality of the code is shaped by social constructions and provides an occasion for subjective reflection. Code itself is neither the end nor the beginning of this reflection, but as an expression of thought, as a trace record of labor and development history, as an artistic medium, and as a connection point in human-machine assemblages, code offers an opportunity to reflect on technoculture with symbols that are at once completely unambiguous and at the same time open to interpretation. What you find at the end of the exploration will say just as much about you and your cultural history as it will about the code. Such reckless and indulgent humanism may not lead to smaller, faster, more efficient code, but it may lead to something far more valuable: understanding.

Notes

1   Introduction

1. *Code smells* are indications of weaknesses in code (Sharma, Fragkoulis, and Spinellis 2017).

2. The code and related supporting materials can be found at the website for this book: http://criticalcodestudies.com.

3. Echoes and evocations are always worth noting. Although named for the programmer of the file, in the mind of a reader in 2009 Harry_Read_Me could well evoke then Democratic Speaker of the House Harry Reid, a proponent of legislation to combat climate change. However, though the file was released in 2009, it was written in 1998—nine years before he took that position and a year before he became minority whip. A *read me file* typically names documentation accompanying a piece of software intended to be read before use.

4. In IDL, *ne* is a comparator that means *not equal*, so the *Oooops* flag is triggered if there is not the same number of elements in both arrays.

5. For a full discussion of briffa_sep98_decline1.pro, see chapter 4.

6. The language and approach of this section are staged to parallel Turing's "Computing Machinery and Intelligence."

7. For another analysis of code used in hiring, see Kevin Brock's writing on FizzBuzz, in *Rhetorical Code Studies* (2019).

8. I owe this explanation to Todd Millstein, who considered this solution too clever for its own good (pers. interview, October 5, 2017).

9. This decision is not exactly a coin toss. Jeremy Douglass has told me, however, that the majority of businesses that need teams of programmers working together would prefer the more orderly code (pers. interview, October 17, 2017).

10. In 2017, a ten-page memo that was circulating through Google questioned hiring practices allegedly put in place to counteract the gender imbalance at the company. For more on that controversy, see Conger 2017.

11. That there could be a gender performance or inference in this programming test is also apropos of the Turing test, which, as Carol Wald notes, begins with a gender-imitation game (cited in Hayles 2008, ix).

12. Sherry Turkle theorizes "evocative objects" in her anthology of that title (2007).

13. The r/geek subreddit: http://www.reddit.com/r/geek/comments/juyns/protesting_in_c_xpost _from_rindia/.
    The r/India subreddit: https://www.reddit.com/r/india/comments/jumm3/lokpal_protest_in _it_style/.

14. I classify this code as *pseudocode* because it would not compile, although chapter 5 demonstrates that the meaning of that word has historically included code that compiles, just not written in a low-level language.

15. Although void main() is commonly taught, the message boards debate whether instead she should have used int main(), which would return a value related to the success or failure of the method. As one commenter (losethisurl) notes, void main() is taught "in many entry level programming courses." This danger of being considered a newbie patrols the borders of online discussions of code, acting as a warning to outsiders and newcomers.

16. One commentator jokes that hopefully the bill will pass before the number reaches 2,147,483,647 (redshirt 07, comment on "Protest in India" 2012), which another explains is the "Maximum range in a 32bit Integer" (james1o1o, ibid.).

17. Despite making up 45 percent of enrollment in computer science in India, women in India's tech industry make up only 25–30 percent, half the density of the United States, and are disproportionately limited to junior positions (Thakkar et al. 2018).

18. For a discussion of toxic geek masculinity and its effects on programming culture, see Salter and Blodgett 2017.

19. For example, see the work of Mez Breeze and her *mezangelle*, discussed in chapter 2.

20. Admittedly, we do not know for certain the identity characteristics of the woman holding the protest sign. Even my assumptions about her gender involve my interpretation. Nonetheless, I choose this second example based on perceived identities.

21. See https://women-on-github.herokuapp.com/.

22. Technically, "echo" writes the HTML for parsing by a web browser.

23. See http://fontawesome.io/.

24. See, for example, this question on Stack Overflow: https://stackoverflow.com/questions/ 17308954/where-can-i-find-the-github-id-in-my-account.

25. Just as reading the gender of the woman holding the sign is unstable, so too is accepting the gender of these GitHub contributors based on their inclusion in these rolls. For now, I will accept this project's presentation of the gender of its participants.

26. *Encoded chauvinism*, not limited to realms of gender and nationalism, though it arises in both, describes a tactic of shaming or belittling others by asserting one's own superior knowledge of technology, particularly related to programming and source code.

27. The CCSWGs are built on weekly discussions and code critique threads on which participants post code snippets and invite discussion. For an example from the 2012 working group, see Kevin Driscoll's "Altair Music of a Sort," which he also posted on his website: http://kevindriscoll.org/projects/ccswg2012/fool_on_a_hill.html.

28. Video game studies presents a realm with much potential to be enriched by critical code studies. Take Shane Denson's (2017) work on *Super Mario Bros.* for one small example.

29. The CCS community has taken this contextual comment to heart. Among the responses to Kirschenbaum's call for context is Anne Helmond's (2017) approach to analyzing the code of the *New York Times* website by harvesting links from the Internet Archives Wayback Machine record of the site.

30. I chose this code specifically because it has been previously analyzed by Berry in *The Philosophy of Software* (2011) to demonstrate how readings of code build on each other.

31. When Jessica Pressman, Jeremy Douglass, and I wrote *Reading Project* (2015), analyzing William Poundstone's *Project for Tachistoscope*, we purposefully did not interview Poundstone in order to see what we could make of his software and code as literary readers without access to the author. However, we did use Poundstone's other writing and paratexts to guide our interpretation.

32. Mackenzie (2006, 18) offers the examples of adjacent texts that impact the meaning of the code and software, including licenses, patents, legislation, prices, branding, design, and product marketing.

33. Code studies could be similarly performed on visual programming languages, programming in spreadsheets, or other forms, which all contain some form of symbolic representation and thereby communication.

34. Ricoeur was referring to Marx, Freud, and Nietzsche, but I am expanding this phrase to refer to a wide range of "suspicious" reading practices.

35. Clyde W. Ford, author of *Think Black* (2019a), a memoir of his father, the first Black software engineer at IBM, writes, "'Garbage in, garbage out,' software engineers say. Likewise, racism in, racism out. Biased developers produce biased code" (2019b).

36. For a fascinating discussion of whether programming can be considered a literacy at all, see Vee 2017.

37. "There Is No Software" was first delivered as a lecture at Stanford on March 2, 1991, before appearing in printed form in *Stanford Literature Review*.

2   Critical Code Studies, a Manifesto

Originally published in *Electronic Book Review* (Marino 2006a), this essay has been revised and extended for this manuscript.

1. Richard Hollander suggested it has to do with recursion of the language that gets demonstrated, saying, "Every language has something it's good for" (pers. interview, March 3, 2005).

2. It is worth noting that since the original version of this essay was published in *Electronic Book Review*, Hello, World has become the Hello, World of critical code studies, with versions of its interpretation appearing in Brown 2015, Vee 2017, and Kirschenbaum 2009, for example.

3. Bolter and Grusin's (1999) term *remediation* names the process by which one medium is recreated in another.

4. Even at the MLA presentation during which I first presented this manifesto, Cayley had softened this position.

5. The site even earned the Geek Site of the Day award on February 1, 1996, according to the project website.

6. For an in-depth discussion of programming as literacy, see Vee 2017.

7. ACLS workbench was funded by the American Council of Learned Societies and designed by Lucas Miller in collaboration with Craig Dietrich and Erik Loyer as a fork of ANVC Scalar.

8. Bruno Latour (2005) offers a full articulation of actor-network theory, which offers in place of individual human subjects a model of networks of machines and humans acting together and in concert.

9. Daniel Temkin, who runs the Esoteric Codes blog (https://esoteric.codes/) recommends considering Lobjan, a language "that's both spoken and formal, with unambiguous denotation (and connotation!). It's the closest spoken language to a programming language, and of course nearly all the conversations are people correcting each other" (pers. comm., July 23, 2019). He also recommends contrasting minimalist languages, such as Brainfuck and Ook!. Both are minimalist languages, but he notes that Ook!, which he calls "actively hostile to reading," is visually harder to parse.

3 The Transborder Immigrant Tool

1. Although a reader can keep careful track of curly brackets, it is easier to determine this structure by using an IDE or code editor. With TextWrangler, a simple code editor, I was able to collapse all the code contained in that declaration and found that it contains all the rest of the code in this file.

2. For examples, see https://www.programcreek.com/java-api-examples/index.php?class=org.apache.commons.lang.exception.ExceptionUtils&method=getRootCause.

3. Clearly, the tool's accurate initials indicate TIT, linking the project to the life-sustaining force of the mother's breast. However, according to Amy Sara Carroll, they changed the name "not wanting to facilitate a too easy misogynistic dismissal of the project" (pers. comm., September 17, 2019). I would argue that the project retains this purposeful link to biological, maternal, life-giving sustenance.

4. By *ritual*, I mean a prescribed procedure embedded with communal or personal significance.

5. The Electronic Disturbance Theatre has a long history of disruptive political art projects. TBT was built by the group's second incarnation.

6. TBT can be set to navigate any border or any other geographic space.

7. Virginia Kuhn (pers. comm., August 18, 2011) speculates that the phrase *last mile* may actually derive from internet network providers, rather than border politics.

8. Dominguez was in part responding to a university-wide call for projects that dealt with the theme "transborder" (Marino 2011c).

9. The poems have been translated into Nahuatl, Ayuujk/Mixe, Spanish, Russian, German, Finish, Mandarin Chinese, Farsi, Portuguese, Latvian, Greek, Malayalam, and Arabic.

10. For an example of a hack that exploits this vulnerability, see the 2018 ransomware attack on the British hospital system (Palmer 2018; see further discussion in Brock 2019).

11. The play is a PDF script of sorts that includes passages for a chorus and other characters—though it is difficult to determine, for example, a set order of the script given the layout.

12. Foucault's notion of the *author function* describes the way a socially constructed impression of the author's identity comes to affect the interpretation of the works attributed to him or her. In this case, rather than inferring the intention of the programmers for every element of the program, the notion of the author function describes how our sense of who Najarro and Stalbaum are will affect our reading.

13. I attribute the comments to Najarro, as opposed to Stalbaum, based on my interview with Stalbaum about the code (Marino 2011a).

14. Even the in situ deployments have not been straightforward user tests. One such deployment involved walking with the tool from the United States into Mexico. Another deployment, called "Passages," traced the final steps of Walter Benjamin in Portbou, Spain, before he crossed the border between life and death. Each deployment represents a new artistic intervention as it complicates any simple understanding of the tool only as a survival app for the undocumented trying to cross into the United States.

15. Setting these variables to null is an unnecessary step here because merely declaring them would set their contents to null.

16. As mentioned earlier, this code defines that class, but it does not start the app; that will occur in a different file.

4 Climategate

1. Mitchell is mentioned as "Tim" in Harry_Read_Me.txt. You can see his own account of his timeline on his personal page: https://crudata.uea.ac.uk/~timm/personal/index.html.

2. Although Mitchell receives a lot of attention in the discussions, the Harry_Read_ME.txt file mentions Mark New and that he lost a coefficients file.

3. This mistake may be linked to an oft-quoted email from Phil Jones: "As far as I'm concerned he has the data—sent ages ago. I'll tell him this, but that's all—no code. If I can find it, it is likely to be hundreds of lines of uncommented fortran!" "He" refers to Stephen McIntyre, a retired engineer, who had started a personal inquiry with Ross McKitrick into the climate research.

4. Again, see Vee 2017 for a more thorough discussion of the applicability of literacy to coding.

5   FLOW-MATIC

1. Key team members included F. Delaney, L. Cousins, M. Harper, T. Jones, M. Mulder, R. Rossheim, E. Somers, and D. Sullivan (Sammet 1969, 316).

2. The functioning of the code was documented by Damen Loren Baker, who analyzed it in the Critical Code Studies Working Group, and it is spelled out in the FLOW-MATIC manual (Remington Rand 1958, 31–33).

3. For a discussion of the rise of the managerial class and its effects on language and literature in particular, see Strychaz 1993.

4. In a 2018 Critical Code Studies Working Group, Elizabeth Losh, Judy Malloy, and Jacqueline Wernimont (2018) led an analysis of the code of Margaret Hamilton, who worked on the Apollo lunar spacecraft systems, which led to a search for the uncredited women who worked in programming in the field of space exploration.

5. In a letter to Bob Bemer, Hopper (1957) attributes the FLOW-MATIC name to the sales department of Remington Rand in the employment of which she codeveloped the language.

6. I owe this explanation to programmer Sarah Lehne, who offered many insights to this chapter.

7. From Sammet's *Programming Languages* (1969, 310).

8. Credit for this example goes to Ray Toal, email correspondence, October 5, 2018.

9. See more of this recovered history in Hicks 2017.

10. For more on this topic, see Nathan Ensmenger's insightful *The Computer Boys Take Over* (2012).

11. In the current model of the smartspeaker/assistant, even the phrase "Alexa, turn on the lights" will not automatically activate a corresponding action.

12. Further research is needed in this area. From what I gather, even the Address programming language, developed by Ekaterina Yushchenko for use on Glushkov's Kyiv computer, used the Latin alphabet instead of the Cyrillic one.

13. In 2016, we addressed the postcolonial force of global English in the Critical Code Studies Working Group. Roopika Risam, Adeline Koh, and Amit Ray led a week-long exploration of the topic, focusing on the work of Ramsey Nasser.

14. Unpublished abstract from the "Ethnoprogramming: Decolonizing Computation through Indigenous Languages" panel at HASTAC 2019, Decolonizing Technologies, Reprogramming Education, Unceded Musqueam (xʷməθkʷəy̓əm) Territory, UBC Vancouver, May 16–18, 2019. http://hastac2019.org/hastac2019FinalProgram.pdf.

15. For more on their work and approach, see Lewis et al. 2018.

6 Kittler's Code

1. Peter Berz has noted to me that there were other programmers Kittler consulted (pers. comm., March 31, 2019). Their identities and involvement offer an opportunity for future scholarship.

2. Scholar Moritz Hiller notes, "From the perspective of code, one could go even further and rethink the notion of authorship in regards to 'Kittler's' theoretical writings as well, as both modes of textual production become recognizable as two different but inseparable articulations of a specific (cultural, technical, … ?) knowledge that transcends the realm of the human, or is, at least, not merely human" (pers. comm., July 19, 2019). Hiller (2015, 2019) has worked extensively with Martin Stinglin on the preservation of Kittler's writings and has developed a philological approach to preserving software that he calls *machine philology*.

3. Kittler (1999) offers the formulation *technological a priori* in an elliptical line, in which he notices imagery of film editing in Foucault's writing. Kittler notes that it is "as if contemporary theories, such as discourse analysis, were defined by the technological a priori of their media" (117). This notion will come to epitomize Kittler's approach to analysis. He sees in the theoretical and philosophical formulations the impact of innovation, with new philosophical formulations following new technologies.

4. A Google Scholar search at the time of this writing turns up 292 citations.

5. Susanne Holl notes that the original file for this essay was created in 1991, with the last changes made in 1992 (pers. comm., March 14, 2019).

6. For now, I will bracket a latent sexual metaphor in accessing the machine, overcoming barriers, making intimate contact, et cetera.

7. Boluk made this remark after I presented Kittler's code at the 2014 conference of the Society for Literature Science and the Arts (SLSA) in Atlanta.

8. On the use of umlauts versus the phonetic spelling of Hoelle, Paul Feigelfeld notes "a peculiarity of his: he usually classified all his files according to encoding (*.lat for latin9, later on *.utf), and I assume he considered a *.c file so sacred in its technicality that he avoided umlauts" (pers. comm., April 1, 2019).

9. Perlin developed a technique for generating textures in an algorithmic process known as *Perlin's noise*, for which he won an Academy Award in 1997 (Perlin, n.d.).

10. In a lecture, Kittler (2010b) once said he preferred the use of *reflection* drawn from optics to its use to refer to philosophical musings.

11. Note that 5008 manages globally declared objects.

12. Translated by Feigelfeld from "Der Füllroutine machen im Gegensatz zu Mephisto gerade die angenagten Pentagramme Pein" (pers. comm., March 27, 2019).

13. Peter Berz points out that Kittler could always have reexamined the assembly code with the GNU debugger. As he writes, "Everyone with some practice in programming knows that without these machines to understand machines, better to say: software, on all levels, nothing is done in programming. Debuggers are the textbooks of software archeology" (pers. comm., March 31, 2019).

14. Feigelfeld notes that "his emacs background color was always set to parchment, which he considered to be proven to be the best color for writing" (pers. comm., March 27, 2019).

15. Oliver Knill (2014) traces the operation back as far as 1812, with a publication by Jacques Philippe Marie Binet.

16. The *throughput* is the number of instructions completed per unit of time.

17. This analogy is particularly apt because I am the one in our marriage primarily in charge of laundry.

18. Kittler's signature use of *einfach*, simple or simply, noted in Winthrop-Young and Wutz 1999 (xxxi).

19. For further discussion, see my article on the science wars as I experienced them in the early years of critical code studies (Marino 2016).

7 Generative Code

1. bpNichol includes a concrete poetry allusion to the Biblical story of Noah's Ark by using the REM or comment statements of BASIC, punning into REM ARK (remark) and REM AIN (remain; quoted in Huth 2007):

```
3900   REM   ARK
3905   REM   BOAT
3910   REM   AIN
3915   REM   RAIN RAIN RAIN RAIN RAIN RAIN RAIN RAIN RAIN RAIN RAIN RAIN RAIN
RAIN RAIN RAIN
```

2. Incidentally, this same code was the subject of a 2018 CCSWG discussion led by Judy Malloy, Jacqueline Wernimont, and Elizabeth Losh. See http://wg18.criticalcodestudies.com/index.php?p=/discussion/11/week-1-gender-and-programming-culture-main-thread.

3. See Ben Grosser's Facebook Demetricator (2012), for example, which removes the metrics (likes and followers) from Facebook, or Go Rando (2017), which replaces the emotion responses (smile, cry, shock, anger) with a multiemoji that is quite inscrutable, the code for which includes an ASCII art version of the Rando emoji itself.

4. Burt Kimmelman (2017) has led me down this path in his quite Kittlerian article on the relationship between conceptual art and code art.

5. These remixes have been anthologized in the *Electronic Literature Collection*, volume 3 ("Taroko Gorge Remixes" 2016).

6. Mateas is the other half of the team that made *Façade*.

7. Python differentiates between arrays, lists, and tuples, all of which have many overlapping properties. Technically, these Python variables are being constructed as lists through the "split" method. In this chapter, I use "array" and "list" in a more general meaning since JavaScript, from which most of the remixes were adapted, does not make this same distinction.

8. Reading the data of poetry generators is a chief way to analyze these pieces. For another example, consider Leonardo Flores's reading of Loss Pequeño Glazier's "White-Faced Bromeliads on 20 Hectares" (2013).

9. However, sometimes the leaks are the closed valves of biased hiring practices. Clyde W. Ford writes, "The percentage of blacks and non-Asian minorities in high-tech professions consistently remains under 2%. For minority women, the numbers are even more dismal. Recent studies conclude this is not a 'pipeline' problem—qualified candidates can be found" (2019b).

10. Note the return of anagrams, a format that Montfort is also particularly fond of.

8   Futures of Critical Code Studies

1. In general, algorithms offer a higher-level entry into software to complement code studies, as exemplified in Ed Finn's *What Algorithms Want* (2017).

2. *Context* is not merely the material context that obviously ties to the technology's history. Tara McPherson's essay on Unix offers an example of how to include a broader social context by discussing the notion of redlining and racial segregation concurrent with the development of Unix (reprinted and extended in McPherson 2018).

3. See my essay on software worms and heteronormativity (Marino 2012), for example.

4. For more on values-sensitive design criteria, see Flanagan, Howe, and Nissenbaum 2008. Algorithmic accountability is one of the more recent terms to arise from the algorithms and ethics movement.

5. For example, the FLOW-MATIC code in chapter 5 was used for marketing purposes as a demonstration of the new language's features.

6. In a CCSWG and elsewhere, Samara Hayley Steele (2018) has read live-action role play (LARP) as code.

7. Among examples of this are the "maze walker" in *10 PRINT* (Montfort et al. 2013, 243–260) and Adrian Mackenzie's technique of "code reconstruction" (2018).

8. For example, John Bell's argument in his CCSWG 2018 discussion on "Calvinball and Coding" emphasizes his creative reuse of previously written code.

9. Montfort and Mateas's essay on obfuscated code (2005) offers an example.

Works Cited

Abelson, Harold, and Gerald Jay Sussman. 1996. *Structure and Interpretation of Computer Programs.* 2nd ed. Cambridge, MA: MIT Press.

Allen, Ben. 2017. "Critical Approaches to the Materiality of Source Code: Between Text and Machine." PhD diss., Stanford, 2017, Stanford University Archives (3781 2017A).

Allen, Ben. 2018. "Common Language: Business Programming Languages and the Legibility of Programming." *IEEE Annals of the History of Computing* 40 (2): 17–31.

Antonakos, James L. 1999. *An Introduction to the Intel Family of Microprocessors: A Hands-on Approach Utilizing the 80x86 Microprocessor Family.* Upper Saddle River, NJ: Prentice Hall.

Baker, Damon Loren. 2014. "In Pursuit of Natural Language: FLOW-MATIC." CCS Working Group 2014. http://wg14.criticalcodestudies.com/discussion/comment/176#Comment_176.

Barthes, Roland. 1979. "From Work to Text." In *Textual Strategies: Perspectives in Poststructuralist Criticism*, edited by Josue V. Harari. Ithaca, NY: Cornell University Press. http://courses.wcupa.edu/fletcher/special/barthes.htm.

Bell, John. 2018. "Week 2: Critical and Creative Coding—Calvinball and Coders." CCS Working Group 2018. January 23, 2018. http://wg18.criticalcodestudies.com/index.php?p=/discussion/31/week-2-critical-and-creative-coding-calvinball-and-coders.

Berry, David M. 2011. *The Philosophy of Software: Code and Mediation in the Digital Age.* New York: Palgrave Macmillan.

Beyer, Kurt W. 2009. *Grace Hopper and the Invention of the Information Age.* Cambridge, MA: The MIT Press.

Blas, Zach. 2007. *transCoder | Queer Technologies.* Code. http://users.design.ucla.edu/~zblas/artwork/transcoder_archive/; http://www.zachblas.info/works/queer-technologies/.

Bodanis, David. 2000. *E = mc2: A Biography of the World's Most Famous Equation.* New York: Walker Books.

Bolter, J. David, and Richard Grusin. 1999. *Remediation: Understanding New Media*. Cambridge, MA: MIT Press.

Booker, Christopher. 2009. "Climate Change: This Is the Worst Scientific Scandal of Our Generation." *Telegraph*, November 28, 2009. https://www.telegraph.co.uk/comment/columnists/christopherbooker/6679082/Climate-change-this-is-the-worst-scientific-scandal-of-our-generation.html.

Borovoy, Rick, Brian Silverman, Tim Gorton, Matt Notowidigdo, Brian Knep, Mitchel Resnick, and Jeff Klann. 2001. "Folk Computing." In *CHI '01 Proceedings of the SIGCHI Conference on Human Factors in Computing Systems*, 466–473. New York: ACM Press. https://doi.org/10.1145/365024.365316.

Borovoy, Richard Daniel. 2002. "Folk Computing: Designing Technology to Support Face-to-Face Community Building." Thesis, Massachusetts Institute of Technology. http://dspace.mit.edu/handle/1721.1/8326.

Briffa, Keith R., F. H. Schweingruber, P. D. Jones, T. J. Osborn, I. C. Harris, S. G. Shiyatov, E. A. Vaganov, H. Grudd, and J. Cowie. 1998. "Trees Tell of Past Climates: But Are They Speaking Less Clearly Today? [And Discussion]." *Philosophical Transactions: Biological Sciences* 353 (1365): 65–73.

Briffa, Keith R., F. H. Schweingruber, P. D. Jones, T. J. Osborn, S. G. Shiyatov, and E. A. Vaganov. 1998. "Reduced Sensitivity of Recent Tree-Growth to Temperature at High Northern Latitudes." *Nature* 391 (6668): 678–682. https://doi.org/10.1038/35596.

Briffa, Keith R., Timothy J. Osborn, Fritz H. Schweingruber, Ian C. Harris, Philip D. Jones, Stepan G. Shiyatov, and Eugene A. Vaganov. 2001. "Low-Frequency Temperature Variations from a Northern Tree Ring Density Network." *Journal of Geophysical Research: Atmospheres* 106 (D3): 2929–2941. https://doi.org/10.1029/2000JD900617.

Briffa, Keith R., Thomas M. Melvin, Timothy J. Osborn, Rashit M. Hantemirov, Alexander V. Kirdyanov, Valeriy S. Mazepa, Stepan G. Shiyatov, and Jan Esper. 2013. "Reassessing the Evidence for Tree-Growth and Inferred Temperature Change during the Common Era in Yamalia, Northwest Siberia." *Quaternary Science Reviews* 72 (July): 83–107. https://doi.org/10.1016/j.quascirev.2013.04.008.

Brock, Kevin. 2019. *Rhetorical Code Studies: Discovering Arguments in and around Code*. Ann Arbor: University of Michigan Press.

Brown, James J., Jr. 2015. *Ethical Programs: Hospitality and the Rhetorics of Software*. Ann Arbor: University of Michigan Press.

Buck, David. 2001. "The Early History of POV-Ray." POV-Ray, Documentation, 1.1.5, August 2001. http://www.povray.org/documentation/view/3.6.0/7/.

Buolamwini, Joy. 2016. "How I'm Fighting Bias in Algorithms." TEDxBeaconStreet. November 2016. https://www.ted.com/talks/joy_buolamwini_how_i_m_fighting_bias_in_algorithms?language=en.

Buswell, Evan. 2019. "The Epistemology of the Credit System and the Formation of Programming Languages." PhD diss., University of California, Davis.

Camnitzer, Luis. 2007. *Conceptualism in Latin American Art: Didactics of Liberation*. Austin: University of Texas Press.

Cantwell, Robert. 1993. *Ethnomimesis: Folklife and the Representation of Culture*. Chapel Hill: University of North Carolina Press.

Carpenter, J. R. 2011. *Generation[s]*. Vienna: Trauma Wien.

Cayley, John. 2002. "The Code Is Not the Text (Unless It Is the Text)." *Electronic Book Review*, September 10, 2002. https://electronicbookreview.com/essay/the-code-is-not-the-text-unless-it-is-the-text/.

Cayley, John. 2015. "Poetry and Stuff: A Review of #!" *Electronic Book Review*, January 31, 2015. http://electronicbookreview.com/essay/poetry-and-stuff-a-review-of/.

Chun, Wendy. 1999. "Sexuality in the Age of Fiber Optics." PhD diss., Princeton University. http://search.proquest.com/docview/304546645/?pq-origsite=primo.

Chun, Wendy. 2011. *Programmed Visions: Software and Memory*. Cambridge, MA: MIT Press.

Clark, Paul. 2009. "The Smoking Code, Part 2." *Watts Up with That?* (blog), December 5, 2009. https://wattsupwiththat.com/2009/12/05/the-smoking-code-part-2/.

Claussen, Ute, and Josef Pöpsel. 1993. "Himmel Und Hölle: Dreidimensionale Texturen Und Ihre Implementierung." *c't: Magazin Für Computertechnik*, January: 160–167.

"Closing the Climategate." 2010. *Nature* 468 (7322): 345. https://doi.org/10.1038/468345a.

Coleman, E. Gabriella. 2012. *Coding Freedom: The Ethics and Aesthetics of Hacking*. Princeton, NJ: Princeton University Press.

Conger, Kate. 2017. "Exclusive: Here's the Full 10-Page Anti-Diversity Screed Circulating Internally at Google [Updated]." *Gizmodo*, August 5, 2017. https://gizmodo.com/exclusive-heres-the-full-10-page-anti-diversity-screed-1797564320.

Connor, Richard L. 1984. "COBOL, Your Age Is Showing." *Computerworld*, May 14, 1984.

Conrad, Frederick G., Benjamin B. Bederson, Brian Lewis, Emilia Peytcheva, Michael W. Traugott, Michael J. Hanmer, Paul S. Herrnson, and Richard G. Niemi. 2009. "Electronic Voting Eliminates Hanging Chads but Introduces New Usability Challenges." *International Journal of Human-Computer Studies* 67 (1): 111–124. https://doi.org/10.1016/j.ijhcs.2008.09.010.

Corbett, Jon. "Four Generations." 2015. Video still, single-channel video, 1:30. Collection of the artist. November 10–January 6, 2019, in "Transformer: Native Art in Light and Sound" at the Smithsonian's National Museum of the American Indian, George Gustav Heye Center in New York City.

Cox, Geoff, and Alex McLean. 2012. *Speaking Code: Coding as Aesthetic and Political Expression.* Cambridge, MA: MIT Press.

Cox, Geoff, Alex McLean, and Adrian Ward. 2000. "The Aesthetics of Generative Code." *Generative Art 00.* Milano: Politecnico di Milano. https://gem.puredata.info/pd/pd/Members/zmoelnig/testing/cox2001aesthetics.pdf.

Cramer, Florian. 2005. *Words Made Flesh: Code, Culture, Imagination.* Netzliteratur.net. http://archive.org/details/WordsMadeFlesh.

Croll, Angus. 2015. *If Hemingway Wrote JavaScript.* San Francisco: No Starch Press.

Dan, Viorela, and Øyvind Ihlen. 2011. "Framing Expertise: A Cross-Cultural Analysis of Success in Framing Contests." *Journal of Communication Management* 15 (4): 368–388. https://doi.org/10.1108/13632541111183352.

DeBevec, Paul. 2006. "The Story of Reflection Mapping." Last modified September 2006. http://www.pauldebevec.com/ReflectionMapping/.

Delgado, Richard, and Jean Stefancic. 2001. *Critical Race Theory: An Introduction.* New York: New York University Press.

Delingpole, James. 2009. "Watching the Climategate Scandal Explode Makes Me Feel Like a Proud Parent." *Spectator*, December 9, 2009. https://www.spectator.co.uk/2009/12/watching-the-climategate-scandal-explode-makes-me-feel-like-a-proud-parent/.

Dendrite. 2009. "The CRU Hack: Context." *RealClimate* (blog), November 23, 2009. http://www.realclimate.org/index.php/archives/2009/11/the-cru-hack-context/.

Denson, Shane. 2017. "Visualizing Digital Seriality or: All Your Mods Are Belong to Us!" *Kairos: A Journal of Rhetoric, Technology, and Pedagogy* 22 (1). http://kairos.technorhetoric.net/22.1/topoi/denson/introduction.html.

Dilger, Bradley, and Jeff Rice, eds. 2010. *From A to <A>: Keywords of Markup.* Minneapolis: University of Minnesota Press.

diSessa, Andrea. 2001. *Changing Minds: Computers, Learning, and Literacy.* Cambridge, MA: MIT Press.

Dijkstra, Edsger W. 1982. "EWD 488: How Do We Tell Truths That Might Hurt." In *Selected Writings on Computing: A Personal Perspective*, 129–131. New York: Springer-Verlag. https://www.cs.virginia.edu/~evans/cs655/readings/ewd498.html.

Dobson, James E., and Rena J. Mosteirin. 2019. *Moonbit.* Earth, Milky Way: Punctum.

Douglass, Jeremy. 2010. "Jeremy Douglass | Comments on Comments in Code." In *Critical Code Studies 2010 Conference Proceedings.* Critical Code Studies. July 23, 2010. University of Southern California, Los Angles, CA. Vectors Thoughtmesh. http://thoughtmesh.net/publish/369.php.

Douglass, Jeremy. 2011 "Critical Code Studies Conference—Week Two Discussion." *Electronic Book Review*, April 14, 2011. http://electronicbookreview.com/essay/critical-code-studies-conference-week-two-discussion/.

Du Gay, Paul, Hugh McKay, Keith Negus, Linda Janes, and Stuart Hall. 2013. *Doing Cultural Studies: The Story of the Sony Walkman*. London: SAGE.

Dunbar, Alex. 2009. "Follow the Gps, Ése." *Vice*, November 1, 2009. http://www.vice.com/read/follow-the-gps-225-v16n11.

Dworkin, Craig. 2003. "Introduction." UbuWeb: Anthology of Conceptual Writing. http://www.ubu.com/concept/.

Eilperin, Juliet. 2009. "Hackers Steal Electronic Data from Top Climate Research Center." *Washington Post*, November 21, 2009. http://www.washingtonpost.com/wp-dyn/content/article/2009/11/20/AR2009112004093.html.

Elbow, Peter. 1973. *Writing without Teachers*. New York: Oxford University Press.

Electronic Disturbance Theater 2.0. 2010. *Sustenance: A Play*. Artist and Activist. Printed Matter, Inc.

Electronic Disturbance Theater 2.0. 2014. [({ })] *The Desert Survival Series/La Serie de Sobrevivencia Del Desierto*. Ann Arbor, MI: University of Michigan, Office of Net Assessment.

Elliott, Melissa. 2014. "Language Field Trip: IDL." *PHP Manual Masterpieces* (blog), November 14, 2014. https://phpmanualmasterpieces.tumblr.com/post/66992896812/language-field-trip-idl.

Ensmenger, Nathan. 2012. *The Computer Boys Take Over: Computers, Programmers, and the Politics of Technical Expertise*. Cambridge, MA: MIT Press.

Erwig, Martin. 2017. *Once upon an Algorithm: How Stories Explain Computing*. Cambridge, MA: MIT Press.

Evens, Aden. 2018. "Combination and Copulation: Making Lots of Little Poems." In *The Bloomsbury Handbook of Electronic Literature*, edited by Joseph Tabbi, 217–235. London: Bloomsbury Academic.

Farrell, Joyce. 2008. *Object-Oriented Programming Using C++*. Boston: Cengage Learning.

Feigelfeld, Paul. 2013. "Kittler Is a Liar." Edited by Arndt Niebisch and Martina Süess. Translated by Daniel Bowles. *Metaphora. Journal for Literary Theory and Media. EV 1: Was Waren Aufschreibesysteme?* 1 (December). https://metaphora.univie.ac.at/3-Edited_Volumes/4-Poetiken_der_Infrastruktur/21-Kittler_is_a_Liar_.

Feinstein, Max, Clarissa Lee, Jarah Moesch, Peter Likarish, and Richard Mehlinger. 2011. "Critical Code Studies." HASTAC Scholars Forums. https://www.hastac.org/initiatives/hastac-scholars/scholars-forums/critical-code-studies.

Fernandes, Leela. 2000. "Restructuring the New Middle Class in Liberalizing India." *Comparative Studies of South Asia, Africa and the Middle East* 20 (1): 88–104.

Finn, Ed. 2017. *What Algorithms Want: Imagination in the Age of Computing*. Cambridge, MA: MIT Press.

Fitzpatrick, Peter, and Alan Hunt. 1987. "Introduction." *Journal of Law and Society* 14 (1): 1–3. https://doi.org/10.2307/1410292.

Flanagan, David. 1999. *Java in a Nutshell: A Desktop Quick Reference*. Sebastopol, CA: O'Reilly.

Flanagan, Mary, Daniel C. Howe, and Helen Nissenbaum. 2008. "Embodying Values in Technology: Theory and Practice." In *Information Technology and Moral Philosophy*, edited by Jeroen van den Hoven and John Weckert, 322–353. Cambridge: Cambridge University Press. https://doi.org/10.1017/CBO9780511498725.017.

Flores, Leonardo. 2013. "A Shifting Electronic Text: Close Reading White-Faced Bromeliads on 20 Hectares." *Emerging Language Practices* 2. http://leonardoflores.net/blog/a-shifting-electronic-text-close-reading-white-faced-bromeliads-on-20-hectares/.

Ford, Clyde W. 2019a. *Think Black: A Memoir*. New York: Amistad.

Ford, Clyde W. 2019b. "My Father Was IBM's First Black Software Engineer. The Racism He Fought Persists in the High-Tech World Today." *Los Angeles Times*, September 22, 2019, sec. Opinion. https://www.latimes.com/opinion/story/2019-09-20/ibm-nazi-germany-tech-racism-father.

Foucault, Michel. 1982. *The Archaeology of Knowledge: And the Discourse on Language*. New York: Vintage.

Frabetti, Federica. 2010. "The Legend of Mariner I." In *Critical Code Studies 2010 Conference Proceedings*. Critical Code Studies Conference. University of Southern California, Los Angeles, CA, July 23, 2010. Vectors: Thoughtmesh http://thoughtmesh.net/publish/344.php.

Fry, Alexander Bastidas. 2008. "Interactive Data Language, IDL: Does Anybody Care?" Stack Overflow. https://stackoverflow.com/questions/260851/interactive-data-language-idl-does-anybody-care.

Fuller, Matthew. 2008. *Software Studies: A Lexicon*. Cambridge, MA: MIT Press.

Gardner, Timothy. 2009. "Analysis: Hacked Climate E-mails Awkward, Not Game Changer." Reuters, November 23, 2009. https://www.reuters.com/article/idUSN23263425.

Galloway, Alexander R. 2006. *Protocol: How Control Exists after Decentralization*. Cambridge, MA: MIT Press.

Golumbia, David. 2009. *The Cultural Logic of Computation*. Cambridge, MA: Harvard University Press. http://ebookcentral.proquest.com/lib/socal/detail.action?docID=3300785.

Graham-Cumming, John. 2009a. "About that CRU Hack." *John Graham-Cumming* (blog), November 26, 2009. https://blog.jgc.org/2009/11/about-that-cru-hack.html.

Graham-Cumming, John. 2009b. "The 'Very Artificial Correction' Flap Looks like Much Ado about Nothing to Me." *John Graham-Cumming* (blog), November 30, 2009. http://blog.jgc.org/2009/11/very-artificial-correction-flap-looks.html.

Grandia, Kevin. 2009. "Michael Mann in His Own Words on the Stolen CRU Emails." *DeSmog* (blog), November 25, 2009. https://www.desmogblog.com/michael-mann-his-own-words-stolen -cru-emails.

Greiner, Richard. 2009a. "Climategate: The Smoking Code." *Cube Antics* (blog). Reprinted in *Watts Up with That?* (blog), December 4, 2009. https://wattsupwiththat.com/2009/12/04/climategate -the-smoking-code/.

Greiner, Richard. 2009b. "The Smoking Code, Part 2." *Cube Antics* (blog). Reprinted in *Watts Up with That?* (blog), December 6. https://wattsupwiththat.com/2009/12/05/the-smoking-code-part-2/.

Griffiths, Catherine. 2018. "Visual Tactics toward an Ethical Debugging." *Digital Culture & Society* 4 (1): 217–226. https://doi.org/10.14361/dcs-2018-0113.

Griffiths, Dave, Leif Elggren, Brendan Howell, Jonathan Kemp, Laura Oldfield Ford, Eleanora Oreggia, and Sabrina Small. 2010. *Exquisite_code*. Edited by Edit-Software in Python. London: Mute Publishing Ltd.

Grist Staff. 2007. "A Look at Barack Obama's Environmental Platform and Record." *Grist* (blog), July 31, 2007. https://grist.org/article/obama_factsheet/.

Grosser, Ben. 2012. Facebook Demetricator. Software. http://bengrosser.com/projects/facebook -demetricator/.

Grosser, Ben. 2017. Go Rando. Software. https://bengrosser.com/projects/go-rando/.

Hall, Stuart. 1992. *Culture, Media, Language: Working Papers in Cultural Studies, 1972–79*. London: Psychology Press.

Hamming, Richard R. 2014. *Art of Doing Science and Engineering: Learning to Learn*. Amsterdam: CRC Press.

Harbison, Samuel P., and Guy L. Steele. 1994. *C: A Reference Manual*. 4th ed. Englewood Cliffs, NJ: Prentice Hall.

Harrell, D. Fox. 2013. *Phantasmal Media: An Approach to Imagination, Computation, and Expression*. Cambridge, MA: MIT Press.

Harris, Ian C., and Keith Briffa. 1998. Briffa_sep98_e.Pro. IDL source code. http://di2.nu/foia/ harris-tree/briffa_sep98_e.pro.

Hayles, N. Katherine. 2005. *My Mother Was a Computer: Digital Subjects and Literary Texts*. Chicago: University of Chicago Press.

Hayles, N. Katherine. 2008. *How We Became Posthuman: Virtual Bodies in Cybernetics, Literature, and Informatics*. Chicago: University of Chicago Press.

Hayles, N. Katherine, and Anne Burdick. 2002. *Writing Machines*. Cambridge, MA: MIT Press.

Heffernan, Olive. 2010. "'Climategate' Scientist Speaks Out." *Nature* 463 (7283): 860. https:// doi.org/10.1038/463860a.

Helmond, Anne. 2017. "Historical Website Ecology: Analyzing Past States of the Web Using Archived Source Code." In *Web 25: Histories from the First 25 Years of the World Wide Web*, edited by Niels Brügger, 139–155. New York: Peter Lang Publishing.

Hicks, Marie. 2017. *Programmed Inequality: How Britain Discarded Women Technologists and Lost Its Edge in Computing*. Cambridge, MA: MIT Press.

Hiller, Moritz. 2015. "Signs o' the Times: The Software of Philology and a Philology of Software." *Digital Culture and Society* 1 (1): 151–163. https://digicults.org/files/2016/11/IV.1-Hiller_2015 _Philology-of-Software.pdf.

Hiller, Moritz. 2019. "Maschinenphilogie." Thesis, Humboldt University of Berlin.

Hofstadter, Douglas R. 1979. *Gödel, Escher, Bach: An Eternal Golden Braid*. New York: Basic Books.

Holl, Susanne. 2017. "Friedrich Kittler's Digital Legacy—PART II—Friedrich Kittler and the Digital Humanities: Forerunner, Godfather, Object of Research. An Indexer Model Research." *Digital Humanities Quarterly* 11 (2). http://www.digitalhumanities.org/dhq/vol/11/2/000308/000308 .html.

Hopper, Grace. 1952. "The Education of a Computer." In *Proceedings of the 1952 ACM National Meeting*, 243–249. ACM '52. Pittsburgh: ACM. https://doi.org/10.1145/609784.609818.

Hopper, Grace. 1957. Grace Hopper to Bob Bemer. New York. April 1, 1957. https://archive .computerhistory.org/resources/access/text/2016/06/102724637-05-01-acc.pdf.

Hopper, Grace. 1980. Oral History of Captain Grace Hopper. Interview by Angeline Pantages.

Hudak, Paul, John Peterson, and Joseph H. Fasel. 1999. "A Gentle Introduction to Haskell." https://www.haskell.org/tutorial/haskell-98-tutorial.pdf.

Hunter, Rick. 2009. "The Literacy of Proceduracy: A Conversation with Annette Vee." HASTAC, September 18, 2009. https://www.hastac.org/blogs/rikhunter/2009/09/18/literacy -proceduracy-conversation-annette-vee.

Huth, Geof. 2007. "First Meaning: The Digital Poetry Incunabula of bpNichol." *First Screening: Computer Poems*. http://www.vispo.com/bp/geof.htm.

Jameson, Fredric. 1991. *Postmodernism, or, The Cultural Logic of Late Capitalism*. Durham, NC: Duke University Press.

Jerz, Dennis G. 2007. "Somewhere Nearby Is Colossal Cave: Examining Will Crowther's Original Adventure in Code and in Kentucky." *DHQ: Digital Humanities Quarterly* 1 (2). http:// digitalhumanities.org/dhq/vol/001/2/000009.html#.

Jerz, Dennis G. 2011. "Critical Code Studies Conference—Week Three Discussion." *Electronic Book Review*, May 25, 2011. http://www.electronicbookreview.com/thread/firstperson/colossal.

Johnson, Jessica Marie, and Mark Anthony Neal. 2017. "Introduction: Wild Seed in the Machine." *The Black Scholar* 47 (3): 1–2.

Kalbhor, Lakshay. 2016. "Is a Github Project Worth Mentioning on a Resume?" Quora, September 13, 2016. Accessed December 12, 2017. https://www.quora.com/Is-a-Github-project-worth -mentioning-on-a-resume.

Kimmelman, Burt. 2017. "Code and Substrate: Reconceiving the Actual in Digital Art and Poetry." *Humanities* 6 (3): 48. https://doi.org/10.3390/h6030048.

Kirschenbaum, Matthew. 2009. "Hello Worlds." *Chronicle of Higher Education*, January 23, 2009. http://www.chronicle.com/article/Hello-Worlds/5476.

Kirschenbaum, Matthew. 2011. "<!--Opening Thoughts-->" Comment. HASTAC. https://www .hastac.org/initiatives/hastac-scholars/scholars-forums/critical-code-studies.

Kittler, Friedrich A. 1992. "There Is No Software." *Stanford Literature Review* 9 (1) (Spring): 81–90. Republished in *CTheory*, October 18, 1995. http://www.ctheory.net/articles.aspx?id=74.

Kittler, Friedrich A. 1997. "The World of the Symbolic—A World of the Machine." In *Literature, Media, Information Systems: Essays*, 130–146. Amsterdam: G+B Arts International.

Kittler, Friedrich A. 1999. *Gramophone, Film, Typewriter*. Translated by Geoffrey Winthrop-Young and Michael Wutz. Stanford, CA: Stanford University Press.

Kittler, Friedrich A. 2001. "Computer Graphics: A Semi-Technical Introduction." Translated by Sara Ogger. *Grey Room* 2 (January): 30–45. https://doi.org/10.1162/152638101750172984.

Kittler, Friedrich A. 2008. "Code (or, How You Can Write Something Differently)." In *Software Studies: A Lexicon*, edited by Matthew Fuller, translated by Tom Morrison and Florian Cramer, 40–47. Cambridge, MA: MIT Press.

Kittler, Friedrich. 2010. *Optical Media*. Malden, MA: Polity Press.

Kittler, Friedrich A. "The Relation of Art and Techne." 2007a 1/6. 2005. European Graduate School Video Lectures. EGS, Saas-Fee, Switzerland. https://www.youtube.com/watch?v=ZBMN9R_zypc.

Kittler, Friedrich A. "The Relation of Art and Techne." 2007b 6/6. 2005. European Graduate School Video Lectures. EGS, Saas-Fee, Switzerland. https://www.youtube.com/watch?v=D4rJRX53nQ8.

Kittler, Friedrich A. "Friedrich Kittler. Evolution of Programming Languages. 2010." 2011a. YouTube. 2010. European Graduate School Video Lectures. EGS, Saas-Fee, Switzerland. https://www .youtube.com/watch?v=vtuC6FRGEoQ.

Kittler, Friedrich A. "Friedrich Kittler. Non-Linear Oscillators & Computer Motherboards. 2010 1/2." 2011b. YouTube. 2010. European Graduate School Video Lectures. EGS, Saas-Fee, Switzerland. https://www.youtube.com/watch?v=CxIHwCnVYIE.

Kittler, Friedrich A. "Friedrich Kittler. Principles of Computer Graphics. 2010." 2011c. European Graduate School Video Lectures. https://www.youtube.com/watch?v=ZBMN9R_zypc.

Kittler, Friedrich A. 2014. "Protected Mode." In *The Truth of the Technological World: Essays on the Genealogy of Presence*, edited by Friedrich A. Kittler, 209–218. Stanford, CA: Stanford University Press.

Knight, Kim A. Brilliante. 2011. "Welcome—Fashioning Circuits." *Fashioning Circuits* (blog). September 10, 2011. https://fashioningcircuits.com/?p=13.

Knill, Oliver. 2014. "When Was Matrix Multiplication Invented?" Oliver Knill homepage, July 24, 2014. http://www.math.harvard.edu/~knill/history/matrix/.

Knuth, Donald E. 1973. *The Art of Computer Programming.* 2nd ed. Reading, MA: Addison-Wesley.

Knuth, Donald E. 1974. "Computer Programming as an Art." *Communications of the ACM* 17 (12): 667–673. https://doi.org/10.1145/361604.361612.

Knuth, Donald E. 1984. "Literate Programming." *The Computer Journal* 27 (2): 97–111. https://doi.org/10.1093/comjnl/27.2.97.

Knuth, Donald E., and Luis Trabb Pardo. 1980. "The Early Development of Programming Languages." In *A History of Computing in the Twentieth Century*, edited by N. Metropolis, J. Howlett, and Gian-Carlo Rota, 197–273. San Diego, CA: Academic Press. https://doi.org/10.1016/B978-0-12-491650-0.50019-8.

Kress, Gunther R. and Robert Hodge. 1979. *Language as Ideology.* London: Routledge & Kegan Paul.

Kun, Josh. 2011. "Playing the Fence, Listening to the Line: Sound, Sound Art, and Acoustic Politics at the US-Mexico Border." In *Performance in the Borderlands*, edited by Ramón H. Rivera-Servera and Harvey Young, 17–36. London: Palgrave Macmillan. https://doi.org/10.1057/9780230294554_2.

Laiti, Outi. 2016. "Ethnoprogramming: An Indigenous Approach to Computer Programming: A Case Study in Ohcejohka Area Comprehensive Schools." Master's thesis, University of Lapland. http://urn.fi/URN:NBN:fi:ula-201612021380.

Laprarie, Michael. 2009. "The Heart of ClimateGate." *Wizbang* (blog), November 27, 2009. https://wizbangblog.com/2009/11/27/the-heart-of-climategate/.

Latour, Bruno. 2005. *Reassembling the Social: An Introduction to Actor-Network-Theory.* Oxford: Oxford University Press.

Lee, J. A. N. 2009. "John von Neumann." History of Computing, February 9, 2009. http://ei.cs.vt.edu/~history/VonNeumann.html.

LeMieux, Patrick. 2015. *Everything but the Clouds.* Platform Games. Babycastles, New York. https://vimeo.com/241966869.

Lessig, Lawrence. 2006. *Code: And Other Laws of Cyberspace, Version 2.0.* 2nd rev. ed. edition. New York: Basic Books.

Lewis, Jason Edward, Noelani Arista, Archer Pechawis, and Suzanne Kite. 2018. "Making Kin with the Machines." *Journal of Design and Science*, July 16, 2018. https://doi.org/10.21428/bfafd97b.

Liu, Alan. 2004. *The Laws of Cool: Knowledge Work and the Culture of Information*. Chicago: University of Chicago Press.

Losh, Elizabeth, Judy Malloy, and Jacqueline Wernimont. 2018. "Week 1: Gender and Programming Culture (Main thread)." CCS Working Group 2018. January 2018. http://wg18.criticalcodestudies .com/index.php?p=/discussion/11/week-1-gender-and-programming-culture-main-thread.

Luther, Martin. 1912. *Die Bibel, oder Die ganze Heilige Schrift des Alten und Neuen Testaments*. Stuttgart: Privilegierte württembergische bibelanstalt.

Mackenzie, Adrian. 2003. "The Problem of Computer Code: Leviathan or Common Power." Institute for Cultural Research, Lancaster University, March 2003. https://www.academia.edu/ 2718446/The_problem_of_computer_code_Leviathan_or_common_power.

Mackenzie, Adrian. 2005. "The Performativity of Code Software and Cultures of Circulation." *Theory, Culture & Society* 22 (1): 71–92. https://doi.org/10.1177/0263276405048436.

Mackenzie, Adrian. 2006. *Cutting Code*. Bern, Switzerland: Peter Lang Publishing.

Mackenzie, Adrian. 2018. "Personalization and Probabilities: Impersonal Propensities in Online Grocery Shopping." *Big Data & Society* 5 (1): 2053951718778310. https://doi.org/10.1177/ 2053951718778310.

Malafronte, Allison. 2009. "The History of the Plein Air Movement." *American Artist* 73 (802) (October): 20–24.

Mann, Michael E., Raymond S. Bradley, and Malcolm K. Hughes. 1998. "Global-Scale Temperature Patterns and Climate Forcing over the Past Six Centuries." *Nature* 392 (6678): 779. https:// doi.org/10.1038/33859.

Mann, Michael E., Raymond S. Bradley, and Malcolm K. Hughes. 1999. "Northern Hemisphere Temperatures during the Past Millennium: Inferences, Uncertainties, and Limitations." *Geophysical Research Letters* 26 (6): 759–62. https://doi.org/10.1029/1999GL900070.

Mann, Michael E., Zhihua Zhang, Scott Rutherford, Raymond S. Bradley, Malcolm K. Hughes, Drew Shindell, Caspar Ammann, Greg Faluvegi, and Fenbiao Ni. 2009. "Global Signatures and Dynamical Origins of the Little Ice Age and Medieval Climate Anomaly." *Science* 326 (5957): 1256–1260. https://doi.org/10.1126/science.1177303.

Manovich, Lev. 2002. *The Language of New Media*. Cambridge, MA: MIT Press.

Marcotty, Michael, Jean E. Sammet, and Betty Holberton. 1981. "V-COBOL Session." In *History of Programming Languages*, edited by Richard L. Wexelblat, 199–277. New York: Academic Press. https://doi.org/10.1016/B978-0-12-745040-7.50010-7.

Marino, Mark C. 2005. "Critical Code Studies." Presented by Stephanie August at ISR Graduate Student Research Forum, UC Irvine, June 3, 2005.

Marino, Mark C. 2006a. "Critical Code Studies." *Electronic Book Review*, December 4, 2006. http:// www.electronicbookreview.com/thread/electropoetics/codology.

Marino, Mark C. 2006b. "I, Chatbot: The Gender and Race Performativity of Conversational Agents." PhD thesis, University of California, Riverside.

Marino, Mark C. 2010a. "Critical Code Studies Conference—Week Four Discussion." *Electronic Book Review*, October 3, 2010. http://www.electronicbookreview.com/thread/firstperson/decoded.

Marino, Mark C. 2010b. "The ppg256 Perl Primer." *Emerging Language Practices*, no. 1. http://writing.upenn.edu/epc/ezines/elp-old/issue-1/ppg256.php.

Marino, Mark C. 2011a. "Brett Stalbaum Complete Interview." San Diego, CA. August 12, 2011. http://archive.org/details/BrettStalbaumCompleteInterview.

Marino, Mark C. 2011b. "Micha Cardenas Complete Interview." Los Angeles, CA. August 11, 2011. https://vimeo.com/27601923.

Marino, Mark C. 2011c. "Ricardo Dominguez Interview." USC, November 3, 2011. https://vimeo.com/31568562.

Marino, Mark C. 2012. "Of Sex, Cylons, and Worms: A Critical Code Study of Heteronormativity." *Leonardo Electronic Almanac* 17 (2): 184–201. https://www.leoalmanac.org/vol17-no2-of-sex-cylons-and-worms/.

Marino, Mark C. 2013. "Code as Ritualized Poetry: The Tactics of the Transborder Immigrant Tool" 7 (1). http://www.digitalhumanities.org/dhq/vol/7/1/000157/000157.html.

Marino, Mark C. 2014. "In Pursuit of Natural Language: FLOW-MATIC—WORKBENCH." CCSWG 2014.

Marino, Mark C. 2016. "Why We Must Read the Code: The Science Wars, Episode IV." In *Debates in the Digital Humanities*, edited by Matthew K. Gold and Lauren F. Klein, 139–152. Vol. 2. Minneapolis: University of Minnesota Press. http://dhdebates.gc.cuny.edu/debates/text/64.

Mateas, Michael, and Nick Montfort. 2005. "A Box, Darkly: Obfuscation, Weird Languages, and Code Aesthetics." In *Proceedings of the 6th Digital Arts and Culture Conference*, edited by Alexanderson and Diddle, 144–153. Coppenhagen: IT University of Copenhagen. https://pdfs.semanticscholar.org/5b3c/7bc9d7619df71abd99e8aa476d8a1fa48de2.pdf.

McCarthy, John. 1978. "History of LISP." *ACM SIGPLAN Notices* 13 (8): 217–223. https://doi.org/10.1145/960118.808387.

McPherson, Tara. 2010. "Color Coding: Race and the Origins of Digital Media in Post-War U.S." In *Critical Code Studies 2010 Conference Proceedings*. Critical Code Studies Conference. University of Southern California, Los Angeles, CA, July 23, 2010. Vectors: Thoughtmesh http://thoughtmesh.net/publish/380.php.

McPherson, Tara. 2018. *Feminist in a Software Lab: Difference + Design*. Cambridge, MA: Harvard University Press.

Miller, Joshua Rhett. 2010. "Critics Blast Transborder Immigrant Tool as 'Irresponsible' Use of Technology." Fox News, March 10, 2010. https://www.foxnews.com/story/critics-blast-transborder-immigrant-tool-as-irresponsible-use-of-technology.

Montfort, Nick, and Andrew Stern. 2008. "Provocation by Program: Imagining a Next-Revolution Eliza." *Grand Text Auto* (blog). May 31, 2008. https://grandtextauto.soe.ucsc.edu/2008/05/31/provocation-by-program-imagining-a-next-revolution-eliza/.

Montfort, Nick. 2010. "Once More into the Gorge." *Post Position* (blog), May 25, 2010. https://nickm.com/post/2010/05/once-more-into-the-gorge/.

Montfort, Nick. 2012. "'Taroko Gorge' Printout | The New Everyday." Media Commons. June 6, 2012. http://mediacommons.org/tne/pieces/taroko-gorge-printout.

Montfort, Nick. 2014. *#!* Denver, CO: Counterpath.

Montfort, Nick. 2016. *Exploratory Programming for the Arts and Humanities*. 1 edition. Cambridge, Massachusetts: The MIT Press.

Montfort, Nick, Patsy Baudoin, John Bell, Ian Bogost, Jeremy Douglass, Mark C. Marino, Michael Mateas, Casey Reas, Mark Sample, and Noah Vawter. 2013. *10 PRINT CHR$(205.5+RND(1)); : GOTO 10*. Cambridge, MA: MIT Press.

Montfort, Nick, and Ian Bogost. 2009. *Racing the Beam: The Atari Video Computer System*. 2nd ed. Cambridge, MA: MIT Press.

Montfort, Nick, and Michael Mateas. 2007. "Hammurabi's Code." Paper presented at the Society for Literature, Science, and the Arts (SLSA), Portland, Maine, November 2, 2007.

Montfort, Nick, and Stephanie Strickland. 2013. "Cut to Fit the Tool-Spun Course." *Digital Humanities Quarterly* 7 (1). http://www.digitalhumanities.org/dhq/vol/7/1/000149/000149.html.

Morlan, Kinsee. 2010. "After the Storm." *San Diego Citybeat*, September 8, 2010. http://sdcitybeat.com/culture/seen-local/storm/.

Murray, Janet H. 1998. *Hamlet on the Holodeck: The Future of Narrative in Cyberspace*. Cambridge, MA: MIT Press.

Najarro, Jason, Ricardo Dominguez, Brett Stalbaum, and Micha Cárdenas. 2010. "Transborder Immigrant Tool Project." Poster. http://www.calit2.net/education/ucsd/posters/2007/jnajarro_poster.pdf.

Navas, Eduardo. 2012. *Remix Theory: The Aesthetics of Sampling*. Vienna: Ambra Verlag.

Noble, Safiya Umoja. 2018. *Algorithms of Oppression: How Search Engines Reinforce Racism*. New York: NYU Press.

Oram, Andy, and Greg Wilson. 2007. *Beautiful Code: Leading Programmers Explain How They Think*. Sebastopol, CA: O'Reilly.

Oudshoorn, Michael, Stan Thomas, Allen Parrish, and Rajendra K. Raj. 2018. "The Value of ABET Accreditation to Computing Programs." In *ASEE Annual Conference Proceedings*. Salt Lake City.

Oxburgh, Ron. 2010. "Report of the International Panel Set Up by the University of East Anglia to Examine the Research of the Climatic Research Unit." https://www.uea.ac.uk/documents/3154295/7847337/SAP.pdf/a6f591fc-fc6e-4a70-9648-8b943d84782b.

Palmer, Danny. 2018. "This Is How Much the WannaCry Ransomware Attack Cost the NHS." ZDNet, October 12, 2018. https://www.zdnet.com/article/this-is-how-much-the-wannacry-ransomware -attack-cost-the-nhs/.

PAGES2k Consortium, Julien Emile-Geay, Nicholas P. McKay, Darrell S. Kaufman, Lucien von Gunten, Jianghao Wang, Kevin J. Anchukaitis, et al. 2017. "A Global Multiproxy Database for Temperature Reconstructions of the Common Era." *Scientific Data* 4 (July): 170088. https://doi.org/10.1038/sdata.2017.88.

Parikka, Jussi. 2007. *Digital Contagions: A Media Archaeology of Computer Viruses*. New York: Peter Lang.

Parikka, Jussi, and Paul Feigelfeld. 2015. "Friedrich Kittler: E-Special Introduction." *Theory, Culture & Society* 32 (7–8): 349–358. https://doi.org/10.1177/0263276414567836.

Pathak, Tapasweni, Prabhanshu Attria, and Fatima Rafiqui. 2016. Women-GitHubers. PHP. https://github.com/tapaswenipathak/Women-GitHubers/blob/master/Women-on-Github/ web/index.php.

Pequeño Glazier, Loss. 2006. "Code as Language." *Leonardo Electronic Almanac* 14 (5). http://www .leoalmanac.org/journal/vol_14/lea_v14_n05-06/lglazier.html.

Perens, Bruce. 1999. "The Open Source Definition." In *Open Sources: Voices from the Open Source Revolution*, edited by Chris DiBona, Sam Ockman, and Mark Stone, 171–189. Sebastopol, CA: O'Reilly. http://oreilly.com/catalog/opensources/book/perens.html.

Perlin, Ken. n.d. "Noise and Turbulence." Ken Perlin. Accessed April 1, 2019. https://mrl.nyu .edu/~perlin/doc/oscar.html#noise.

Peters, John Durham. 2009. "Strange Sympathies: Horizons of Media Theory in America and Germany." *Electronic Book Review*, June 4, 2009. http://electronicbookreview.com/essay/strange -sympathies-horizons-of-media-theory-in-america-and-germany/.

Phillips, Kevin. 2004. "Bush Family Values: War, Wealth, Oil." *Los Angeles Times*, February 8, 2004. http://articles.latimes.com/2004/feb/08/opinion/op-phillips8.

Pressman, Jessica. 2014. *Digital Modernism: Making It New in New Media*. New York: Oxford University Press.

Pressman, Jessica, Mark C. Marino, and Jeremy Douglass. 2015. *Reading Project: A Collaborative Analysis of William Poundstone's Project for Tachistoscope {Bottomless Pit}*. Iowa City: University of Iowa Press.

Punday, Daniel. 2015. *Computing as Writing*. Minneapolis: University of Minnesota Press.

Raley, Rita. 2002. "Interferences: [Net.Writing] and the Practice of Codework." *Electronic Book Review*, September 8, 2002. http://electronicbookreview.com/essay/interferences-net-writing-and -the-practice-of-codework/.

Raley, Rita. 2003. "Machine Translation and Global English." *The Yale Journal of Criticism* 16 (2): 291–313. https://doi.org/10.1353/yale.2003.0022.

Raley, Rita. 2006. "Code.Surface ‖ Code.Depth by Rita Raley." *Dichtung Digital*. http://www .dichtung-digital.org/2006/01/Raley/index.htm.

Raley, Rita. 2009. *Tactical Media*. Minneapolis: University of Minnesota Press.

Raymond, Eric S. 2001. *The Cathedral and the Bazaar: Musings on Linux and Open Source by an Accidental Revolutionary*. Rev. and expanded ed. Sebastopol, CA: O'Reilly.

Raymond, Eric S. 2009. "Hiding the Decline: Part 1—The Adventure Begins." *Armed and Dangerous* (blog), November 24, 2009. http://esr.ibiblio.org/?p=1447.

Remington Rand. 1957. "Introducing a New Language for Automatic Programming: UNIVAC FLOW-MATIC." Remington Rand. http://archive.computerhistory.org/resources/text/Remington _Rand/Univac.Flowmatic.1957.102646140.pdf.

Rettberg, Scott. 2019. *Electronic Literature*. Cambridge, UK; Medford, MA: Polity.

Rhee, Margaret. 2017. *Love, Robot*. Brooklyn, NY: The Operating System.

Ricoeur, Paul. 2008. *Freud and Philosophy: An Essay on Interpretation*. Delhi: Motilal Banarsidass Publishers.

Risam, Roopika, Amit Ray, and Adeline Koh. 2014. "Coding in Global Englishes." Critical Code Studies Working Group 2014. Post archived from *Roopika Risam* (blog) at https://web.archive .org/web/20150819084335/http://roopikarisam.com/uncategorized/coding-in-global-englishes/.

Risam, Roopika. 2018. *New Digital Worlds: Postcolonial Digital Humanities in Theory, Praxis, and Pedagogy*. Evanston, IL: Northwestern University Press.

Robert, Kirrily, Yoz Grahame, and Douglas, Jason. 2009. "Forking Encouraged: Folk Programming, Open Source, and Social Software Development." Presented at O'Reilly Open Source Convention: OSCON, July 20–24, 2009, San Jose, CA. https://cdn.oreillystatic.com/en/assets/1/ event/27/Forking%20Encouraged_%20Folk%20Programming%2C%20Open%20Source%2C%20 and%20Social%20Software%20Development%20Presentation.pdf.

Rotman, Brian. 1993. *Signifying Nothing: The Semiotics of Zero*. Reprint. Stanford, CA: Stanford University Press.

Russell, Muir. 2010. *The Independent Climate Change E-Mails Review*. Independent Climate Change Email Review, July 7, 2010. http://www.cce-review.org/pdf/FINAL%20REPORT.pdf.

Salter, Anastasia. 2017. "Code before Content? Brogrammer Culture in Games and Electronic Literature." *Hyperrhiz: New Media Cultures*, no. 17. http://hyperrhiz.io/hyperrhiz17/essays/2-salter -code-before-content.html.

Salter, Anastasia, and Bridget Blodgett. 2017. *Toxic Geek Masculinity in Media: Sexism, Trolling, and Identity Policing*. Cham, Switzerland: Palgrave Macmillan. https://www.palgrave.com/us/book/ 9783319660769.

Salter, Anastasia, and John Murray. 2014. *Flash: Building the Interactive Web*. Cambridge, MA: MIT Press.

Sammet, Jean E. 1969. *Programming Languages: History and Fundamentals*. Englewood Cliffs, NJ: Prentice-Hall.

Sammet, Jean E. 1991. "Some Approaches to, and Illustrations of, Programming Language History." *Annals of the History of Computing* 13 (1): 33–50.

Sample, Mark L. 2013. "Criminal Code: Procedural Logic and Rhetorical Excess in Videogames." *Digital Humanities Quarterly* 7 (1). http://www.digitalhumanities.org/dhq/vol/7/1/000153/000153 .html.

Sandler, Daniel, Kyle Derr, and Dan S. Wallach. 2008. "VoteBox: A Tamper-Evident, Verifiable Electronic Voting System." In *Proceedings of the 17th USENIX Security Symposium*, 349–364. San Jose: USENIX Association. https://www.usenix.org/legacy/events/sec08/tech/sandler.html.

Saussure, Ferdinand de, and Albert Riedlinger. 1983. *Course in General Linguistics*. Chicago: Open Court Publishing.

Schmidt, Gavin A. 2009. "The CRU Hack: Context." *RealClimate* (blog), November 23, 2009. http://www.realclimate.org/index.php/archives/2009/11/the-cru-hack-context/.

Seaman, Bill. 2001. "Oulipo | vs | Recombinant Poetics." *Leonardo* 34 (5): 423–430. https://doi.org/ 10.1162/002409401753521548.

Sharma, T., M. Fragkoulis, and D. Spinellis. 2017. "House of Cards: Code Smells in Open-Source C# Repositories." In *2017 ACM/IEEE International Symposium on Empirical Software Engineering and Measurement (ESEM)*, 424–429. Piscataway, NJ: Institute of Electrical and Electronics Engineers. https://doi.org/10.1109/ESEM.2017.57.

Sheppard, Marc. 2009. "CRU's Source Code: Climategate Uncovered." *American Thinker*, November 25, 2009. https://www.americanthinker.com/articles/2009/11/crus_source_code_climategate _r.html.

Singletary, Mark. 2005. "'Hello, World' Project." Louisiana Tech (website), October 26, 2005. http://www2.latech.edu/~acm/helloworld/.

"Software Development Toolset Unveiled." 1982. *Computerworld*, April 12, 1982.

Sondheim, Alan. 2005. "Part 1: On Code and Codework." *Post-Theory.txt*. http://www.alansondheim .org/post-theory.txt.

Soon, Winnie. 2017. Vocable Code. Software. November 13, 2017. http://siusoon.net/vocable -code/.

Soo, Winnie. 2018. "Vocable Code." *MAI: Feminism & Visual Culture* (blog), November 10, 2018. https://maifeminism.com/vocable-code/.

Sperry Rand Corporation. 1958. FLOW-MATIC Programming system.

Spivak, Gayatri Chakravorty. 1994. "Can the Subaltern Speak?" In *Colonial Discourse and Post-Colonial Theory: A Reader*, edited by Patrick Williams and Laura Chrisman, 66–111. New York: Columbia University Press.

Stancati, Margherita, and Krishna Pokharel. 2011. "Why Was Hazare Such a Media Hit?" *Wall Street Journal*, September 5, 2011. https://blogs.wsj.com/indiarealtime/2011/09/05/why-was -hazare-such-a-media-hit/.

Steele, Samara Hayley. 2018. "Code Critique: Port of Secrets/Snippet of Anti-Code from the Irvine-Based GM-Less Larp Community." CCS Working Group 2018, January 29, 2018. http:// wg18.criticalcodestudies.com/index.php?p=/discussion/43/code-critique-port-of-secrets -snippet-of-anti-code-from-the-irvine-based-gm-less-larp-community.

Stern, Andrew, and Nick Montfort. 2008. "Provocation by Program: Imagining a Next-Revolution Eliza." *Grand Text Auto* (blog), May 31, 2008. https://grandtextauto.soe.ucsc.edu/2008/05/31/ provocation-by-program-imagining-a-next-revolution-eliza/.

Stern, Benjamin A. 2000. "Interactive Data Language." In *Space 2000*, edited by Stewart W. Johnson, Koon Meng Chua, Rodney G. Galloway, and Phillip I. Richter, 1011–1015. Albuquerque, NM: American Society of Civil Engineers. https://doi.org/10.1061/40479(204)125.

Strychacz, Thomas F. 1993. *Modernism, Mass Culture, and Professionalism*. Cambridge: Cambridge University Press.

"Taroko Gorge Remixes." 2016. In *Electronic Literature Collection*. Vol. 3. Cambridge, MA: Electronic Literature Organization. http://collection.eliterature.org/3/collection-taroko.html.

Thakkar, Divy, Nithya Sambasivan, Purva Kulkarni, Pratap Kalenahalli Sudarshan, and Kentaro Toyama. 2018. "The Unexpected Entry and Exodus of Women in Computing and HCI in India." In *Proceedings of the 2018 CHI Conference on Human Factors in Computing Systems*, paper 352. New York: ACM. https://doi.org/10.1145/3173574.3173926.

Thomas, Douglas. 2002. *Hacker Culture*. Minneapolis: University of Minnesota Press.

Thompson, Clive. 2019. "The Secret History of Women in Coding." *New York Times*, February 13, 2019. https://www.nytimes.com/2019/02/13/magazine/women-coding-computer-programming .html.

Toal, Ray, Rachel Rivera, Alexander Schneider, and Eileen Choe. 2017. *Programming Language Explorations*. Boca Raton, FL: CRC Press.

Turing, A. M. 1950. "Computing Machinery and Intelligence." *Mind* 59 (236): 433–460. https://doi.org/10.1093/mind/LIX.236.433.

Turkle, Sherry. 1997. *Life on the Screen: Identity in the Age of the Internet*. New York: Simon & Schuster.

Turkle, Sherry, ed. 2007. *Evocative Objects: Things We Think With*. 4th ed. Cambridge, MA: MIT Press.

Tushnet, Mark. 1991. "Critical Legal Studies: A Political History." *The Yale Law Journal* 100 (5): 1515–1544. http://dx.doi.org/10.2307/796697.

Urrea, Luís Alberto. 2005. *The Devil's Highway: A True Story*. New York: Back Bay Books.

UCSBLitCultureMedia. 2010a. "Dislocative Media: Transborder Immigration Tool as Aesthetic Sustenance [5/11]." April 15, 2010. https://youtu.be/bfdK2rwQ0XA.

UCSBLitCultureMedia. 2010b. "Dislocative Media: Transborder Immigration Tool as Aesthetic Sustenance [7/11]." April 15, 2010. https://youtu.be/qnHwZhZdLqc.

Vee, Annette. 2017. *Coding Literacy: How Computer Programming Is Changing Writing*. Cambridge, MA: MIT Press.

"Votebox: Votebox.Events.ChallengeEvent Class Reference." 2008. Votebox Documentation. August 8, 2008. http://votebox.cs.rice.edu/doxygen/dc/d8d/classvotebox_1_1events_1_1_challenge_event.html.

Walker, John. 1996. "Punch Card Gallery." Fourmilab, August 15, 1996. http://www.fourmilab.ch/documents/univac/cards.html.

Wardrip-Fruin, Noah. 2005. "Christopher Strachey: The First Digital Artist?" *Grand Text Auto* (blog), August 1, 2005. https://grandtextauto.soe.ucsc.edu/2005/08/01/christopher-strachey-first-digital-artist/.

Wardrip-Fruin, Noah. 2009. *Expressive Processing: Digital Fictions, Computer Games, and Software Studies*. Cambridge, MA: MIT Press.

Warren, W. G. 1980. "On Removing the Growth Trend from Dendrochronological Data." *Tree Ring Bulletin* 40:35–44. http://agris.fao.org/agris-search/search.do?recordID=US19820788475.

Watts, Anthony. 2009. "CRU Emails 'May' Be Open to Interpretation, but Commented Code by the Programmer Tells the Real Story." *Watts Up with That?* (blog), November 22, 2009. https://wattsupwiththat.com/2009/11/22/cru-emails-may-be-open-to-interpretation-but-commented-code-by-the-programmer-tells-the-real-story/.

Weizenbaum, Joseph. 1966. "ELIZA—a Computer Program for the Study of Natural Language Communication Between Man and Machine." *Communications of the ACM* 9 (1): 36–45. https://doi.org/10.1145/365153.365168.

Weizenbaum, Joseph. 1976. *Computer Power and Human Reason: From Judgment to Calculation*. San Francisco: WH Freeman.

Weizenbaum, Joseph. 1963. "Symmetric List Processor." *Communications of the ACM* 6 (7): 524–36.

West, Cornell. 1995. "Foreward." In *Critical Race Theory: The Key Writings That Formed the Movement*, edited by Kimberle Crenshaw, Neil Gotanda, Gary Peller, and Kendall Thomas, xi-xii. New York: New Press.

Westfall, Ralph. 2001. "Technical Opinion: Hello, World Considered Harmful." *Communications of the ACM* 44 (10): 129–130. https://doi.org/10.1145/383845.383874.

Wexelblat, Richard L., ed. 1981. *History of Programming Languages*. New York: Academic Press.

Wharton, Mary. 1998. "U2." Video. *Legends*. VH1.

Wheeler, Dave. 2009. "An Expert's Opinion." *Rube Reality* (blog), December 8, 2009. http://rubereality.com/2009/12/08/an-experts-opinion/.

Winthrop-Young, Geoffrey, and Michael Wutz. 1999. "Translator's Introduction." In *Gramophone, Film, Typewriter*, xi–xxxviii. Stanford, CA: Stanford University Press.

Wolff, Mark. 2007. "Reading Potential: The Oulipo and the Meaning of Algorithms." *Digital Humanities Quarterly* 1 (1). http://www.digitalhumanities.org/dhqdev/vol/1/1/000005/000005.html.

Index